What's happening to our girls?

Maggie Hamilton is a writer and publisher, regular media commentator and keen observer of social trends. Her books have also been published in Italy, Holland, Brazil and Saudi Arabia, and include *Coming Home: Rediscovering Our Sacred Selves; Love Your Work, Reclaim Your Life; Magic of the Moment; A Soft Place to Land* and *What Men Don't Talk About.*

www.maggiehamilton.org

Advance praise for

What's happening to our girls?

As Maggie shows in this great book, as fathers and mothers we don't know it all. If we want to find real solutions for our girls, we need to really listen to our daughters.

Stephen Boston, father of three girls

What's Happening to Our Girls? moves parenting into the twenty-first century by highlighting the power of outside forces in shaping the personalities, morality and ultimate wellbeing of our daughters. The idea of teaching girls as early as possible about the importance of appearance in order to mould their later consuming practices is frightening from a psychological perspective. Although directed at raising girls, the message is equally important for those parenting boys. This work is a must-read for both parents and young adults attempting to understand and bridge the generation gap.

Bill O'Hehir, senior psychologist

Having worked with men and boys for 20 years, I was amazed, fascinated and quite horrified to read such a succinct and well-documented account of all the issues facing girls today. The pressures created by society's expectations and the marketing evil that is being unleashed on our girls means that every parent should read this book as a way of understanding what is really going on, and what they can do.

Dr Arne Rubinstein (MBBS, FRACGP),
CEO, Pathways Foundation

MAGGIE HAMILTON

What's happening to our girls?

VIKING
an imprint of
PENGUIN BOOKS

VIKING

Published by the Penguin Group
Penguin Group (Australia)
250 Camberwell Road, Camberwell, Victoria 3124, Australia
(a division of Pearson Australia Group Pty Ltd)
Penguin Group (USA) Inc.
375 Hudson Street, New York, New York 10014, USA
Penguin Group (Canada)
90 Eglinton Avenue East, Suite 700, Toronto, Canada ON M4P 2Y3
(a division of Pearson Penguin Canada Inc.)
Penguin Books Ltd
80 Strand, London WC2R 0RL England
Penguin Ireland
25 St Stephen's Green, Dublin 2, Ireland
(a division of Penguin Books Ltd)
Penguin Books India Pvt Ltd
11 Community Centre, Panchsheel Park, New Delhi – 110 017, India
Penguin Group (NZ)
67 Apollo Drive, Rosedale, North Shore 0632, New Zealand
(a division of Pearson New Zealand Ltd)
Penguin Books (South Africa) (Pty) Ltd
24 Sturdee Avenue, Rosebank, Johannesburg 2196, South Africa

Penguin Books Ltd, Registered Offices: 80 Strand, London, WC2R 0RL, England

First published by Penguin Group (Australia), 2008

3 5 7 9 10 8 6 4

Cover design by Allison Colpoys © Penguin Group (Australia)
Text design by Allison Colpoys © Penguin Group (Australia)
Cover photograph by Gary Heery
Typeset in 12.25pt Perpetua by Sunset Digital Pty Ltd, Brisbane, Queensland
Printed and bound in Australia by McPherson's Printing Group, Maryborough, Victoria

National Library of Australia
Cataloguing-in-Publication data:
Hamilton, Maggie, 1953–
What's happening to our girls? / author, Maggie Hamilton.
1st ed.
Camberwell, Vic. : Penguin Books, 2008.
9780670072323 (pbk.)
Includes bibliography.
Teenagers – social conditions.
Teenage girls – drug use.
Teenage girls – sexual behaviour.
Femininity.
Adolescent psychology.

305.2352

To my beautiful mother Joan
for a lifetime of love and wisdom

Contents

Appreciation

Nothing we achieve is through our efforts alone. This has been a huge project, which would not have been possible were it not for the wonderful support I've received from so many people. My heartfelt thanks to all the girls, who willingly shared the intricacies of their lives. Thanks to my family and friends, whose belief in this project has never faltered.

A special thanks to the experts in child and adolescent health, teachers, child psychologists and counsellors, and law enforcement and medical personnel, whose generous assistance has been invaluable.

Thanks to my wise and talented publisher Julie Gibbs, and to the ever-gracious and perceptive managing editor Ingrid Ohlsson; to my publicist Shelley McCuaig, designer Allison Colpoys, and editor Jocelyn Hungerford, whose ongoing love and commitment mean so much. Thanks to the whole Penguin team – to Dan Ruffino, Sally Bateman, Anne Rogan, Peg McColl and Angela Crocombe for their excellent work on my behalf.

My love and thanks to my husband Derek, whose unwavering belief in all I do sustains me. My profound dedication and thanks to the Great Spirit, who inspires me to look at how life is, and dare to envision how it yet may be.

Introduction

In a few short decades almost every part of girls' lives has been transformed, bringing freedoms previous generations of girls could only dream of. Alongside these dazzling possibilities newer, subtler forces are emerging that threaten the many gains girls have made. Almost every aspect of life is changing and at lightning speed. Our girls are at the forefront of this change. What a girl, now 12, experienced when she was 7 is not what a 7-year-old faces today. That is why it's hard for adults to get a fix on the lives of girls at present.

No previous generation of girls has been where today's girls are heading. Some of the material in this book is shocking, and beyond anything most adults experienced when they were growing up. When we talk about the issues girls currently face, we tend to think of teenage girls. This assumption leaves our younger girls vulnerable.

The book starts with baby girls, because advertisers are now actively targeting babies. They know that at 6 months a baby is able to retain brand logos, and that the trademarked characters on babies' clothing and in their environment will translate into sales from the age of 2 upwards. This early process of turning girls into consumers reduces them to little more than a target market, and has a dramatic and detrimental impact on their aspirations, body image and sense of self.

As our little girls grow, they are spending more time in front of DVDs and TV programs, whose storylines are often thinly disguised product placement. All this takes place at the expense of the warmth and stimulation that comes with human interaction – elements that are crucial for early brain development. This commercialisation of girls compromises their imaginations and their curiosity about the world around them. The opportunity to enjoy carefree childhoods is being lost in the rush to turn them into good little consumers. The sooner our little girls become addicted to shopping, the more money can be generated from them.

The sexualisation of women in the media and popular culture is now also having an impact on small girls. It is influencing the way pre-schoolers talk and behave. As these children grow, so too does their self-consciousness about how they come across. They become anxious about their bodies, clothes and accessories. This preoccupation with looks influences everything, from girls' choice of friends and time spent in shopping malls, to what they wear and play with. Advertisers have done a good job. Girls as young as 5 know their brands and identify with them. Increasingly their friendships are based on who has what.

Alongside the fragmentation of family and community due to relation-ship breakdowns, greater mobility, long working hours and time deprivation, we have seen a rise in the power of the media and new tech-nologies. These forces are exposing girls to concepts way beyond their years. They make it easy for girls to lead lives that parents know nothing about. What was once the domain of adults has become part of the lives of our children. The need to appear 'out there' helps explain why girls are pushing the sexual boundaries so young, why pornography has such appeal to some girls, and why there has been an alarming increase in sexually transmitted diseases amongst our teenagers.

In the past children learned the way forward from adults. But there is no longer a clear link between one generation and the next, because popular culture and new technologies have left adults behind. As a result our girls feel isolated. They believe adults don't care. It is this isolation that prompts girls to cling to their peers, because they are always there for them.

Although we pride ourselves on living in an upfront world, there's a general nervousness about expressing our doubts and quiet despair at some of the things that are happening to girls. While we hesitate, our girls remain vulnerable. It was my desire to know more about them that prompted me to spend two years examining their lives.

To do so I immersed myself in teen popular culture, and in the latest trends in global marketing. My interviews with girls formed the qualitative part of my research. I have used as many of their quotes and thoughts as possible, so we can hear what girls are telling us and respond accordingly. There are over a hundred girls' voices in the book, alongside observations from numerous experts. I spent months surfing the net and observing teen chat rooms and forums. I have included some of the chat room content to show the kinds of discussions that are taking place. None of the online topics covered were initiated by me. I was purely an observer.

I also interviewed consumer and child psychologists, law enforcement and medical personnel, school counsellors, teachers from kindergarten to high school level, and experts in child and adolescent health. Wherever possible I sought to familiarise myself with the leading thinkers and practitioners in the topics covered. Where local case studies and/or statistics were hard to access, which was frequently the case, I have used the most relevant overseas data.

In my one-on-one interviews with girls, most began by giving me the answers they thought I wanted to hear. However, once they relaxed, they began to open up and share their takes on life. I decided not to talk to them about their possible involvement in sex, alcohol, drugs, eating dis-orders or cutting, asking instead what their girlfriends were up to. This approach worked well. The girls were happy to give me a detailed picture of their worlds. One thing that puzzled me during these interviews was how similar the girls' responses were, regardless of their background. It took me some time to realise this was due in part to the overwhelming influence of popular culture, which has become the 'super' parent.

In my quest to understand girls' lives, in no way do I wish to trivial-ise the many hurdles boys have faced, and continue to face. Although I canvassed their challenges in my book *What Men Don't Talk About*, we still need more resources and research on boys to help them through their childhood and teen years. Many of the issues that affect the lives of girls also threaten our boys.

In the book I have attempted to look not only at the detrimental influences tween and teen girls are dealing with, but also at what babies and toddlers are being exposed to, so parents can see how important their early intervention is. Many parents I have spoken with are feeling helpless right now. However, once they understand what girls are up against, they can see what needs to be done, and become motivated to reclaim the ground they have lost in recent years.

Today's girls are more empowered, but we mustn't allow complacency to blind us to the very real challenges they face. With a much more informed understanding of girls' lives, we can continue to provide them with the protection and resources they need to thrive.

Starting out

Our little girls are born into a glittering world of choices. Women can own their own homes and businesses, choose their friends and partners, voice their opinions. Yet while they will have more access to money, careers, travel, education and technology than any other generation, these girls are also facing challenges no other generation of girls has faced. A 7-year-old's world differs from what girls just five or six years older experienced when they were 7. This is why many of the signposts we offer girls no longer apply, and why they wish adults could get where they are at.

Today's girls are facing challenges no other generation of girls has faced.

So what do our girls hope for, worry about, struggle with? Why do they care more about their peers' opinions than their parents'? What makes brand-name clothes, looking sexy and endless trips to the mall so appealing? Why are so many girls drawn to 'out there' behaviour? And why are such issues as depression, cutting, eating disorders and binge-drinking on the rise?

From the moment baby girls are born, many wonderful opportunities beckon. How parents respond to the arrival of their daughters helps baby girls grasp what being a girl is all about. A baby girl's ability to pick up on what is expected of her can't be underestimated. She forms impressions from the way she is spoken to and held, from her toys and clothes, and from her immediate environment. Remarkably, within hours of birth a baby girl is more interested in people's faces than a baby boy is.[1]

Sensitive to their little girl's needs, most parents work hard to nurture her, paying close attention to how she looks, her clothes, the design and colour of her room, her toys and bed linen. Often parents take more care with these choices than they would for a baby boy, because they see little girls as needing more care and protection.[2]

> At 6 months a baby girl is learning how to deal with basic emotions. Already her sensitivity towards how others react to her is being fine-tuned.

Well-off parents may even celebrate the birth of their baby girl with a top-of-the-range pram and designer clothes. The sudden explosion of baby boutiques means there are plenty of cool clothes available, from Rock Your Baby for the 'prematurely hip' to Nappy Head's funky clothing for the 'more discerning and fashion-conscious bambino'. At the top of the tree there's Gucci, Dior, DKNY and others, to ensure a baby girl always looks chic.

By the time a baby girl is 4 months old, her sensitivity to those around her is being honed. Already she can distinguish photos of people she knows from those of strangers.[3] At 6 months she is learning how to deal with basic emotions. By watching the responses she gets from her parents and carers, a baby girl will modify her behaviour accordingly.[4]

'Today, the most intensely targeted demographic is the baby – the future consumer . . . The fresh neurons of young brains are valuable mental real estate to admen.' *Douglas Rushkoff, pop culture expert[5]*

At around 6 months she is also beginning to make simple sounds, and to retain a whole range of images, including corporate logos.[6] Well aware of these critical stages in a baby's development, advertisers work hard at capturing a baby girl's attention. Depending on how much exposure she's had to clever product placement in her first few months, this baby girl may be one of a growing number of children whose first recognisable word is a brand name.[7] As pop culture expert Douglas Rushkoff points out, 'The fresh neurons of young brains are valuable mental real estate to admen.'[8]

'The moment a baby girl can see clearly, she becomes a consumer.'
Susan Gregory Thomas, Buy, Buy Baby[9]

BRANDED BABIES

Amongst the clothes a parent may choose for their little girl, they'll most likely buy her one or two branded T-shirts, bibs or nappies with fun characters on them. When marketing guru James McNeal discovered that drooling babies stare down at their dribble for extended periods, he knew he was on to something. Trademarked characters are now strategically placed on a baby girl's clothing, so that when she dribbles, she gets to know these characters and to see them as a natural part of her world.[10] Without her parents realising it, thanks to the 'drool factor' this baby girl has joined the consumer treadmill, where enough is never enough, and where her self-esteem comes from what she has, not who she is.

This early product placement comes at a time when a little girl doesn't know she is separate from the world around her. She has no idea that her hands and feet are part of her, and that a fun toy is not. So, unless parents want marketers to shape their baby's early impressions, they need to be far more aware of the brands she is exposed to on her clothing, toys, games, food and TV programs.

> **'Chances are, by the time they reach 18 months old, 10 per cent of those object words (things they name) are brands. Around age 2, they're asking for the product by brand name.'** *James McNeal, professor of marketing*[11]

CLEVER BABIES

Because girls now have the chance to achieve far more, many parents feel a responsibility to give their little girl a good start. They may be inspired to give her potential genius a nudge by buying her *Baby Einstein* DVDs, designed for babies 6 months and up. If a baby girl appears to enjoy these programs, there are *Baby Einstein* toys, books, games and puppets to purchase as well. She may also be one of a growing number of babies watching baby TV.

> Just because a baby girl is mesmerised by TV, it doesn't mean she's enjoying or benefiting from it.

But just because a baby girl is mesmerised by TV or DVDs, it doesn't mean she's enjoying or benefiting from them. That's why in 1999 the American Academy of Pediatrics urged parents to avoid TV for under-2s, as it can compromise early brain development.[12] No matter how slick a TV program or DVD is, it can't replace the interactions babies need to develop their social skills and emotions, and to make sense of their world.[13] Without these interactions babies don't get the same chance to learn that, for example, Mum is different to Dad. That she behaves differently, has different likes and dislikes, and different expectations. And that if Mum and Dad are different, then so are other people.

There are additional concerns around babies and TV. Experts in child development know that play is an essential part of childhood. Play allows children to learn to focus on whatever they're doing. It also develops a child's inner voice. When a little girl plays, she is starting to organise her thoughts and experiences as she chatters. TV disrupts these processes.[14]

One of the reasons parents allow babies and toddlers to watch TV is that they believe it helps them learn. While babies soon recognise the colourful trademarked characters on kids' TV and in real life, this isn't the same as discovering more about themselves and their world. Studies show that it takes babies twice as long to grasp a single task shown on TV, as when a parent shows them what to do.[15] When babies and toddlers watch TV they also miss out on the nuances of touch, smell and taste, and how an object or person relates to other people or objects, all of which are essential for their development.

Research also shows that when babies and young toddlers watch even the simplest storyline on TV, they cannot grasp the sequence of events. All they see is a collection of mesmerising visuals. At this age they can only begin to put the pieces together if parents are there with them, helping them to understand what is going on.[16]

As life is pressured, it's not surprising that parents turn to baby TV and DVDs to give themselves a break. This, along with the desire to give their child a good start, helps explain why TV and DVD viewing by babies and toddlers is on the rise. While local figures are hard to come by, one study in the United States revealed that almost one in five children under 1 have a TV in their bedrooms, and 43 per cent of children under 2 now watch TV daily. Around half the programs they watched were not meant for young children.[17]

Little girls don't need to be entertained and stimulated all day, every day. They need time and space to begin to understand themselves and their world. Without quiet moments and real play, it is harder to develop. Studies also suggest that every hour of television a small child watches each day may increase her risk of developing attention problems by almost 10 per cent by the time she is 7.[18] These findings cannot be ignored. Wise parents will free their little ones from the box by choosing a TV-free household, or making TV viewing an occasional activity. Parents who do have TV at home need to closely monitor time spent watching it, as well as its content to ensure their children aren't subjected to a range of influences they are powerless to fight.

With all the pressure on parents to do the right thing, many have lost confidence in their ability to parent. Unless they are providing their child with a whole range of services and products, young parents may feel they are letting her down. Not so, according to early childhood experts, who stress the importance of relaxed one-on-one time with babies. 'Studies show the growth of neural pathways start with the very best beginnings – time to sit and gaze with your baby, lightly massaging their beautiful skin, talking and singing with them,' explains Margot Roberts, early childhood educator and mother of three. 'These beginning activities are not a waste of time, or best done by paid "childcare experts". They are the foundations of good child development activities and are part of the preciousness of good parenting.'[19]

Professionals encourage new parents to value what *they* bring to their time with their little girl. Made-up games which allow a baby to explore her hands and feet, shake a rattle, or enjoy the sensation of the water during bath time are ideal. Squeaking toys above her head, to her left and right and so on, helps her locate sounds. Allowing her to feel different toys on her hands, feet, cheeks and tummy encourages her to learn the nuances of texture. Fun rhymes with elements of play, such as 'This Little Piggy', help engage her and encourage her to anticipate what playful moments together promise. There are dozens of fun and imaginative ways for parents to open up their baby girl's world to her. Simplicity is the key.

Babies worth billions

Often it's hard for new parents to realise just how comforting their presence and interactions are to their baby, because they have become distracted by the sudden explosion in programs and products for babies and toddlers. Marketers encourage parents to believe that unless they are providing their little ones with an endless supply of toys, games and cool clothing, they're depriving them of the basics of life. Early childhood experts disagree. Material goods cannot replace loving, human interaction – it's what enables us all to thrive. Parents who get caught up in the need to shower their baby with new possessions end up passing these values on to their children, who grow up believing they're nothing without brand-name clothes and accessories.

It's not that little girls shouldn't have baby games or toys, but parents need to limit the exposure children have to these products, so they don't compromise their development. This can be difficult, given the massive increase in available products, and the fact that by the age of 2 children can now recognise their favourite brands in shops and let parents know they want them.[1] It's tragic that many small children recognise more items in a shopping centre than in nature. Mountains of toys dull children's imaginations and leave them in constant need of stimulation. Early child-hood development specialists encourage parents to keep things simple by allowing babies to explore the fun of cardboard boxes, cuddly toys, building blocks, pots and pans, and so on.

The products designed for babies and toddlers appeal because their creators take expert advice on what young children will respond to at every stage of their development. Armed with the detailed information such experts provide, companies know exactly which buttons to press with the playful figures and storylines they dream up. Their feedback influences everything, from the choice of colours and textures used in manufacturing fun characters to the way they are merchandised instore.

'Kids spend less time with their parents than with advertising and brands, so the ads have a major influence on the kids' vocabulary and use of brand names.' *Martin Lindstrom, global marketing expert*[2]

Sooner or later most little girls will fall in love with *Sesame Street* or *The Wiggles* or some other form of child entertainment, which come with an attractive range of books and DVDs, branded toys and clothing. While parents are naturally delighted these programs and their related products will keep their little girls entertained for hours on end, it's easy for them to forget this explosion in the many different products for babies and toddlers is relatively recent. Until the huge success of the *Tele-tubbies* TV program and merchandise, marketers to children focused on school-age kids for their sales. After the *Teletubbies*, everything changed. Realising there was big money to be made from preschoolers, or 'tinys' as they are known, manufacturers were quick to get in on the act. Westfield's fastest growing retail area is baby shops.

One of the most depressing moments in the career of a friend who works in marketing was in the lead-up to the launch of a new trademarked children's character. There was massive enthusiasm for the new concept, and the campaign plans were brilliant. She should have been over the moon, because it had the potential to make a lot of money, but instead she felt increasingly disturbed to hear babies and toddlers referred to as 'consumers' throughout the meetings. When we reduce our babies and toddlers to just another target market, we are all diminished.

Within a short space of time some serious money has been generated from babies and young children. In one year alone the Wiggles empire is said to have made around $45 million.[3] There are now Wiggles franchises from Spain to Taiwan, a theme park on the Gold Coast, three in the US, and more on the way. *Bananas in Pyjamas*, now available in seventy countries, is estimated to have an audience of 100 million kids, while *Bob the Builder* has achieved over $2 billion worth of sales worldwide.[4] Baby Einstein, bought by Disney for $20 million in 2001, is now thought to be worth around $200 million. While individual products may be harmless and fun, the number of branded toys and clothes in little girls' lives is cause for concern.

> **'It starts with *Bob the Builder* or *Dorothy the Dinosaur* and it never ends – because if you can get them young, you have them for keeps.'** *Jason Clarke, founder of Minds at Work*[5]

ENTERTAINMENT OR ADVERTISING?

This marketing intensifies as a little girl grows. More and more preschoolers are now watching TV programs whose storylines are thinly disguised product placements. This is ideal for marketers, because the engaging characters in these programs are now available in books and as toys, on shoes and clothing, in games, and on the packaging of lollies and breakfast cereals. Little girls absorb this branding because they have no concept of being sold to.[6] All this is a long way from the

Steiner approach to childhood, for example, where dolls' faces have no features, so little girls can use their imaginations to create their own unique dolls.

Once invited into their lives, these trademarked characters become part of their world. This careful and consistent brand placement will then shape the future purchasing decisions these little girls make. Without realising it, parents often consolidate brands in the minds of their children with their shopping decisions. 'I was in the drinks section of the supermarket, and I heard a mother ask her kids which drinks they wanted. It wasn't about whether they wanted an orange drink or whatever, but about whether they wanted a Bob the Builder or Barbie drink,' Adele, a mother of two girls, told me.

As Jason Clarke of Minds at Work points out, 'As parents we learn to surrender our kids to marketing long before they hit their teens. From the moment they open their eyes they are exposed to colourful, upbeat characters, scientifically designed to dazzle and excite. It starts with *Bob the Builder* or *Dorothy the Dinosaur* and it never ends – because if you can get them young, you have them for keeps.'[7] Parents who want to protect their children should avoid programs and movies that are linked to toys by keeping a selection of DVDs at hand that are not linked to brands.

How many brands little girls can absorb is up for debate. In one landmark study in the United States, children aged 3 to 6 were shown a number of logos, including one for a well-known brand of cigarettes. Even though the advertising for these cigarettes was aimed at adults, just under a third of 3-year-olds correctly matched the logo with a picture of a cigarette. Nine out of ten of the 6-year-olds in the survey made the connection between the product and logo without any difficulty.[8] This study was in 1991. Advertising has come a long way since then.

Our girls now inhabit a mesmerising world of constant entertainment and stimulation, where branded toys, clothes, food and TV programs have become a big part of their day. This happens years before they can read and write, or make their own independent choices. We don't know the full impact of such influences on these small girls, because they haven't grown up yet. We can simply wait and see, or we can reclaim the ground we have lost, by making our own choices about what we want for our little girls and when.

Early childhood educator Margot Roberts reiterates the importance of keeping things simple around children. Instead of buying Baby Mozart, 'baby gyms' and all the other products on offer, she reminds young parents of how comforting it is for tiny children to hear their parents' voices. Reading or singing to babies offers them so much more than TV or a DVD. Lullabies, nursery rhymes, and made-up songs engage them and provide gentle opportunities for learning. 'Encourage repetition, vocabulary, memory, learning, focus and fun,' she suggests. 'Learn finger plays to capture your toddler's attention and have them joining in. It's all about counting, words, co-ordination.' Young parents are busy, but when they allow themselves and their babies more space and less pressure, everyone benefits.

But they're only little

As little girls grow, they continue to absorb powerful impressions of what is expected of them from their toys, clothes, books, accessories, snatches of conversation, billboards and magazines, TV and DVDs. This comes at a tender time in a little girl's life, when her sense of self is beginning to take shape. This is often a time when she insists on wearing pink and falls in love with her Barbie.

Inspired by Lilli, a sexy German cartoon figure, Barbie is still very much a part of little girls' worlds today. Until recently, marketing for Barbie was aimed at girls aged 6 to 8. Now Barbies are purchased for toddlers up. If girls are exposed to Barbie often enough, they can recognise her face and logo when they are babies and toddlers. So, the more little girls see Barbie, the more attached to her they become, which helps explain why Barbies currently sell at the rate of three every second.[1]

Today's little girls can be Barbie girls in a Barbie world, because of the sheer number of Barbie products available. Barbie also has her own virtual world. A little girl can log on to BarbieGirls.com, create and dress her own Barbie avatar (online persona), decorate her Barbie house, play games, earn Barbie money to spend, or watch videos of her favourite

Barbie movies and products. There is something very appealing to a little girl about Barbie pink, having her very own Barbie doll, and Barbie music. But while she is having all this fun, it's a pity Barbie and other unrealistically shaped dolls aren't gently put into perspective, so she doesn't grow up thinking her own body is horrible, unlovable, abnormal.

WHEN PLAY IS MORE THAN JUST PLAY

Sometimes a toy is just a toy, but sometimes its impact on girls is less than ideal. In the sudden explosion of marketing to young girls, good sense seems to be in short supply. One toy that caused an outcry against the Tesco supermarket chain in Britain recently was the Peekaboo Pole-Dancing Kit. Inspired, no doubt, by the growing interest in stripper culture, this toy promised to 'unleash the sex kitten inside'. This game, which came with a chrome pole, instructive DVD, and sexy garter, was a surprising choice for the children's online toy section.[2]

'They're like so young and innocent and they should be doing what little kids should be doing, but it's like parents and the media influencing them so much,' *Missy, 15*

Another toy to hit the market is Digi Makeover, which comes with a digital camera that plugs directly into the TV. With a choice of over fifty hairstyles, as well as make-up and jewellery, it promises young girls 'tons of cool effects for make-up, hair, clothes and accessories', and the opportunity to 'make over your friend in photo booth mode'.[3] When the toy was trialled by a handful of small girls on a recent TV program, the make-overs these little girls chose made them look more like child prostitutes, with their kohl-rimmed eyes and disproportionately large red lips, than little girls at play. Little girls are naturally drawn to a woman's world; however, this is no longer an organic process, but one that is skilfully manipulated and has a price tag attached.

All the teen girls I spoke with were less than impressed at these developments. They don't see this phenomenon as young girls being liberated or having fun. They see it as young girls being exploited for money and robbed of their childhoods. 'They're like so young and innocent and they should be doing what little kids should be doing, but it's like parents and the media influencing them so much,' Missy, 15, told me.

> The toys, programs and clothes we choose for our little girls reveals a great deal about how we see girls and women – how they should look and behave, and what they should aspire to.

Perhaps the most controversial toys for young girls are Bratz dolls, with their fishnet stockings, chokers, skimpy pants, bare midriffs, and exaggerated lips and breasts – and MGA Entertainment isn't complaining. Since the company launched Bratz dolls in 2001, it has sold millions of dolls worldwide. When I asked one kindergarten teacher about her experience with preschoolers and Bratz dolls, she said it had changed the way little girls play. 'They no longer play mother, and care for and play with their doll in that nurturing way,' she told me. 'They become one of the (Bratz) dolls when they play with them.'

Many child health professionals are concerned that through toys and the media, little girls are increasingly being exposed to a superficial, sexualised way of seeing themselves and their world. As these girls are too young to properly judge what they're experiencing, they begin to assume that's what is expected of them.

Another kindergarten teacher pointed out that the way little girls are speaking has also changed, and that they are now using overtly sexual language. This teacher has also noticed that girls are relating to boys in a way that is much more sexually aware. 'They're more aware of boy/girl situations, which never used to be the case. Our toilets have always been communal, but you've got to keep more of an eye on them, because they're more conscious of looking at each other,' she explained. Mothers of small girls said the same thing. Some with children as young as 3 were distressed about the sexual language and behaviour they were seeing.

This trend seems to be growing. 'There is more kissing and things,' one preschool teacher told me. 'I had a little girl of three coming on to a boy last week. She was constantly kissing him and holding hands. She's been doing a bit of that lately. It's all very innocent, because she doesn't know what she's doing, but I wonder where this will lead when she gets to school.' This teacher also noticed more sexualised behaviour with little girls who have older brothers and sisters.

'Puberty issues are happening much younger. Some girls are now fashion-conscious as young as 3 or 4.' *Debra, community liaison officer and mother of two girls*

While there's plenty of talk about the sexualisation of girls, it's not until you get down to the detail that you realise how concerned many parents are. One mother said that her small child had come home from daycare talking of 'sexing' with a friend. Another told me how her pre-schooler had started tongue-kissing since beginning preschool. Most of the time these small children have no idea what they're saying or doing, but such influences do encourage little girls to see themselves as sexual objects, and to view the world through this lens.

While many parents I have spoken to express real concerns about what is happening to their children, often they are reluctant to speak out, as they don't want to appear repressive. This is an ideal scenario for advertisers, because they know how formidable a parents' lobby can be when it opposes something. If they can silence parents by making them seem uncool or out of step, advertisers can do what they like.

The toys, programs and clothes we choose for our little girls reveals a great deal about how we see girls and women – how they should look and behave, and what they should aspire to. It's time to rethink what *we* want for our little girls, and how we can better communicate positive ideas and values to them, because from a very young age girls are hungry to learn about their world. It's not just children's TV programs they're picking up on, but on background TV, conversations and images in magazines. Parents need to monitor these influences closely to ensure the richness of childhood isn't hijacked by a preoccupation with sex and shopping.

Survival of the prettiest

Around the age of 2, little girls begin to recognise themselves in the mirror. As they grow, they soon start to take note of the endless images of glamorous women and girls on TV and billboards, in magazines and catalogues, and at the movies. As there's a wealth of this material, it doesn't take long for them to equate glamour with love and success. So begins what Harvard psychologist Nancy Etcoff refers to as the 'survival of the prettiest'.[1]

This concern about looks makes little girls worried about their appearance, and less able to relax, have fun, be spontaneous. Their resulting anxiety manifests in many ways. 'At the beginning of the year we had a little celebration for the class. All the girls couldn't stop talking about what they were going to wear, and how they would look at the party,' one preschool teacher told me. 'It was all they could talk about. I couldn't believe it. They weren't quite 4.' Another teacher expressed concern about the way fashions were going, because little girls were becoming increasingly preoccupied by how they looked. 'In summer you see them in skimpy tops and backless dresses. This isn't little girls' stuff, it's what 15-year-olds should be wearing,' she complained.

One of the most haunting images of a glamourised little girl is that of JonBenet Ramsey, with her teased hair, false eyelashes and glossed lips, who spent much of her life in green rooms. When she was brutally murdered in her own home, the whole world was devastated. As everyone contemplated her tragically short life, many were left wondering as much about the quality of life she enjoyed during her brief childhood, as about who had killed her.

'I used to do so many types of jazz dance when I was younger, but like now you go and see the concerts and there's like 5-year-olds doing these kind of like sleazy, slutty dances and it's not cool. It just like kind of disgusts you.' *Missy, 15*

While the surreal world of child beauty pageants in the USA — hair extensions, fake teeth and tans, fantastic costumes and swimsuits — may seem a long way from the lives of most small girls, as childhood continues to shrink, girls are getting the message at a much younger age that they must be pretty, pleasing and popular to be loved and accepted. With their growing exposure to TV, DVDs, catalogues and advertising early on, the message is hitting them long before they get to school. 'I just feel everything is happening earlier,' said one kindergarten teacher. 'The way girls dress at kindergarten is a much older style. They want to be fashionable. They are conscious of the way they look.'

While it may amuse some adults to see little girls dressed as miniature versions of themselves, little girls are not adults. They don't have the resources adults have. Many of the parents and teachers I spoke with expressed a growing discomfort with the way things are heading, because they feel young girls are missing out on some of the essentials of childhood, such as being spontaneous and having unselfconscious fun. 'Tanya is at the shops all the time with her mum,' confided one preschool teacher. 'She wears nail polish, bracelets and handbags, and has a skimpy little bikini for summer. I hate what's happening to this little girl. She's only 3, but her mother thinks it's great.' These are not isolated stories.

WHERE'S MY MAKE-UP?

It's not just adult clothes that little girls are wearing. They now have access to their own make-up as well, years before they are even teenagers. While many cosmetic ranges are marketed to girls aged 7 and up, frequently much younger girls have access to cosmetics. On the net they can also join a number of sites where they can make up dolls or photos of themselves with everything from mascara and eyeliner to lipstick and blusher.

Amongst the cosmetic lines for young girls is Hotsie Totsie's make-up for girls aged 7 to 14 in the USA, which offers everything from bubblegum-flavoured lip gloss to scented nail polish. Although it's not yet available locally, it hints at where the market is heading. Billed in trade magazines as 'a definite must-have for the development of your Gen Next business', there are even lip gloss necklaces for girls who want their lip gloss wherever they go. [2]

The hype around this merchandise hints at how irresistible these products can be. 'The in-house favorite is the sugar shack display. It's a great merchandiser for the sweeter side of fun-loving girls. The display resembles a counter top version of your local candy store loaded with candy-inspired components. It just takes one look to be hooked on the flavor-swirled lollipop or saltwater taffy lip gloss topped off with five-layer multi-colored lipsticks.' [3]

'Learn early about appearance and it turns you into a good little consumer.' *Jean Kilbourne, writer and filmmaker* [4]

DO I LET MY DAUGHTER HAVE MAKE-UP?

The make-up decision is a hard one for most parents, who don't want to hold their daughters back. Perhaps it would help parents of little girls who want their own make-up if they knew that when a woman is sexually aroused the increase in her blood flow reddens her lips and cheeks, and makes her more sexually attractive. The reddish tones of lipsticks simulate this arousal.[5] When women are turned on, their pupils dilate, making their eyes more prominent. Eye make-up is designed to create the same effect.

> **'I don't agree with little girls wearing bras and make-up. When I was little I just wore what I had. Girls are growing up way too young.'** *Sara, 17*

Like it or not, make-up does make young girls look more like grown women. Not only are some men and boys likely to regard little girls wearing cosmetics differently, there's the vital question of whether a young girl can handle the attention she receives. Often there's a reluctance to speak out about where things are heading, as we don't want to appear out of touch, but when I talked with teen girls about little girls wearing make-up, they had no such reservations. They feel childhood is under threat, and that little girls are being placed in situations they're not ready to handle. 'Once young girls start wearing make-up, they're becoming self-conscious. They're losing their confidence. When you're a kid you should just go out and do stuff without thinking. They should have some time where they don't have people looking at them,' said Sandi, 14.

> **'It's not good to sexualise little girls. It's not good for a girl of 7 to have that put on them. She's still a kid. From an early age it affects what we become, like desensitised to sex and stuff.'** *Whitney, 18*

Alana, 18, felt the same way. 'Little girls are missing out on the essence of childhood. They're not outside and playing, they're wearing mascara and things. It's all on TV now. Everything's "out there" and normal.' Kiera, 17, was also vehemently opposed to this trend. 'It's silly to wear make-up at 8, you're a kid. Give up! I didn't start wearing make-up until I was like in high school,' she insisted.

Consumer psychologist Dr Amantha Imber, who is well versed in how advertising campaigns are put together, urges parents to intervene early to prevent their daughters becoming sexualised too soon. 'Communicate to your children that the images they see in magazines and on TV are not normal, and not what they should aspire to be. Explain that these celebrities/models are paid a lot of money to pose in particular ways, and that the images are an advertiser's version of what they think is cool, and are absolutely not the norm.' Parents should not feel apologetic about protecting a little girl's childhood. Again, the question of whether to have TV, and/or how it is to be used in the home, is a critical decision for parents to make. By not addicting their little girls to consumerism and shopping, and by taking things more slowly, parents give girls the chance to grow up at a more leisurely pace, and to have many wonderful possibilities to look forward to.

Shrinking self-esteem and imagination

The more little girls focus on appearance, the more insecure they become, because they aren't old enough to have a strong sense of themselves. These days, body issues affect the lives of very young girls, some of whom are only just starting school. In one study of girls aged 5 to 8, over a quarter of 5-year-old-girls wished they were thinner. This figure rose to 71 per cent for girls aged 7. Most of these young girls believed they had to be slim to be popular. Just under half wanted to be thinner than they were, and were prepared to diet if they put on weight.[1]

What are we doing to our girls to have them worrying about their looks before they're fully able to read or write? As today's little girls grow, their anxieties about their bodies are intensifying. The expansion of the fast and junk food industries doesn't help. Millions of dollars are spent annually to keep kids consuming this food. It's been estimated that just under 20 per cent of all fast food restaurant ads offer a toy premium,[2] while food and drink manufacturers pay huge amounts of money to link their products with blockbuster movies.

In one study of girls aged 5 to 8, over a quarter of the 5-year-old-girls wished they were thinner.[3]

In recent years the interest in real, fresh food has declined as a result of the intense marketing of packaged and processed foods to children. Fast-food outlets also keep adjusting the salts and spices used in their meals to ensure kids keep coming back for more. A highly sophisticated industry combining science and high technology has grown up around the manufacture of fast foods. This industry micro-engineers the taste and texture of foods to ensure they are irresistible. 'The impact of this media-saturated world on childhood is that kids are becoming disconnected from aspects of life, including food,' warned Associate Professor Elizabeth Handsley, of media watchdog Young Media Australia. 'The way food is now marketed to kids disconnects them from what food is about and for.'

There are so many ways parents can engage girls with food. Making time for family meals and involving children in meal-making now and then adds important textures to their lives. These gestures are important because good food nourishes the whole person, and is a very special part of life. If girls have the urge to shop, why not teach them to shop for fresh food – how to choose a ripe melon or avocado, and how to know which fruits and vegetables are available when? Why not share the delight of fresh white peaches, shelled peas or a handful of cherries, and encourage girls to try their hand at growing a few vegetables or herbs in the garden or on the balcony? These simple activities help connect our girls to the world they are to inherit far more meaningfully than fast food.

DECLINE IN IMAGINATION

It's not just packaged food that is problematic, the huge increase in packaged entertainment for little girls is also taking its toll. Educators are seeing a dulling of imagination and curiosity in young children. If they can't get the point of a toy or game quickly, many lose interest. This lack of imagination is causing marketers some concern, because they have to work harder to engage young girls. 'Kids were once creative directors in neighbourhood fantasies,' says global marketing guru Martin Lindstrom. 'No more. These days, kids rarely leave their bedrooms.'[4] If their imaginations are not engaged, boredom sets in and nothing seems special any more.

'Kids are so used to having all these whizz-bang toys, they have forgotten how to entertain themselves,' *Bob Becker, Vice-president of Marketing and Sales, 'My Very Own House'*[5]

This lack of imagination is even spreading to traditionally creative toys; for example, Lego has reduced the number of blocks in its standard boxes, and increased the size of individual blocks. A large part of Lego's appeal used to be that children could make anything they wanted with the blocks. This allowed successive generations of kids to give full reign to their imaginations. Now most children simply want to make the figures that appear on the box. Their greatest concern is that they will be able to reproduce the figures as shown. When Lego partnered with Lucasfilm, they took the extra step of providing kids with a ready-made story.[6] This approach also affects the imagination. With so many packaged stories to hand, there's little need for children to dream up their own stories. They simply re-enact the stories they've been fed.

The kindergarten teachers I spoke with have also noticed changes in the ways preschool girls play. 'I don't think there's as much imagination any more when they play. That's kind of gone. It's more play they've seen somewhere else. Some girls still do play like they did, making things up,' one teacher told me. This reduction in imagination affects a girl's ability to solve problems and to be aware of the alternatives available to her.

'A sort of sedentary, screen-based existence has crept up on children. They used to be free-range and now they're practically battery children, living indoors, experiencing through the medium of a screen.' *Baroness Susan Greenfield, neuroscientist*[7]

No longer are little girls playing for extended periods on their own. They're immersed instead in their computers, in TV programs and DVDs, and in trying to acquire the many products marketed to them. Robbed of their creative expression, their life experience narrows, as do their aspirations. Professor Gary Cross, who has written a compelling history of toys, goes further, suggesting our children's bedrooms are little more than shrines to fast-food giveaways and movie tie-ins.[8]

A lot of these challenges are made more acute because parents are so stretched. Parenting is hard, but if parents don't engage their daughters, who will? 'A sort of sedentary, screen-based existence has crept up on children,' warns distinguished neuroscientist Baroness Susan Greenfield. 'They used to be free-range and now they're practically battery children, living indoors, experiencing through the medium of a screen.'[9]

'There is an emotional abuse of kids. Instead of input they buy them something.' *Mae, kindergarten teacher*

As they grow, girls need to engage with their community, and to mix with a variety of people from different generations. They also need time to play on their own, to be out in the fresh air, to experience nature first-hand. There are many creative activities parents can give their children – early childhood development expert Margot Roberts suggests, for example, that parents set up a room, or part of a room, as a mini-kindergarten. 'Nothing beats stimulating imagination like a dress-up box. It can lead to hours of fun. Get some lovely old gear from grandparents, or go to your local op shop. Shoes, hats and bags will get your little one going. Make up stories. Pretend to be a doctor, the list is endless. Cardboard boxes can be trains, garages and cubby houses. Don't forget a table for craft and pretend office work (think old birthday cards, paper streamers, stamps and envelopes). Create a quiet corner for books and puzzles.'

Instead of buying more toys, she encourages parents to pack two-thirds of existing toys away, then rotate the toys and playthings. 'Have a special pack-away song as a signal that things go back to their homes at the end of the day. Join a toy library to get big items that you can return after the novelty has worn off,' she suggests. These kinds of experiences are easy for even the busiest parent to organise, and toy libraries can be readily found on the internet. They stimulate the imagination and help girls thrive.

Welcome to the tweens

Until recently, when girls left childhood behind they became teenagers, then marketers invented tweens – the 8- to 12-year-olds in between. Advertisers love tweens because they're worth billions. As these girls are unsure of themselves, they are more susceptible to suggestion than most. For tween girls peer acceptance is crucial. More than anything they want to belong. They will go to great lengths to ensure they're not embarrassed or singled out.[1] By the time they are tweens, girls are leading busy lives, so much so that in one survey just under half the tweens said they had too much on.[2]

> **'What I like is fashion. I have this kind of T-shirt, but it's got like a collar and it's got a sleeve like that, and then it's got like a flower badge, and then I wear like a little skirt, and I wear black slipper shoes.'** *Nina, 7*

Teenage life can't come quickly enough for most tweens. By now they're more than ready to leave their little-girl self behind. 'Girls my age want to go out with guys. They think about what they like to wear and shopping,' Vanessa, 9, told me. Their ready access to the internet, magazines and sitcoms means they use more mature language, and have a greater sense of the wider world, than previous generations. Tweens are also very visual and tend to find pictures more appealing than words.[3]

LIVING TO SHOP

If there's one thing tweens love, it's to shop. 'I love shopping, like, heaps! Shopping is like basically my life,' said Rebecca, 6. After several years' exposure to slick advertising campaigns in magazines, at the movies and on TV, young girls are well informed about fashion, food and music. Tweens know what they like. They're attracted to possessions which offer glamour and beauty. That's why they love glitter, pretty colours and sparkly tops.

It's during these years that celebrity worship begins in earnest. Mary-Kate and Ashley Olsen, Christina Aguilera, Natalie Portman, Paris Hilton and Beyoncé are an integral part of tween life. Tween girls read about their icons constantly, taking careful note of what they're wearing and working on, and how their personal lives are faring. They get all this and more in tween magazines, which are basically junior versions of women's magazines.

'I love shopping. You can get new clothes and stuff you like. Stuff from Supré, like skinny jeans and tank tops and things. About once every two weeks we go to the shops. We spend a couple of hours there. We wander in and out of the shops.' *Melissa, 10*

Tweens also love their fast food. One poll by market research company Roy Morgan shows that eight out of ten tweens had eaten fast foods in the previous month, and just under a third did so every week. They also ate chocolate every day, watched eighteen hours of TV per week, and spent seven hours playing DVDs and watching videos every week.

The Simpsons was their favourite TV show.[4] For an increasing number of tweens, their spare time is basically a blend of packaged entertainment and consumption. Already their focus is on clothes, accessories, make-up and jewellery.

'I do feel the need to protect little girls from themselves. They're missing out on their childhood and not caring about anything. I just think that they're not getting their childhood at all.' *Peta, 16*

Many professionals who understand the dynamics of marketing to young children are less than impressed. 'I am concerned by the huge media onslaught and advertising pressure that faces today's children. Everywhere they turn, they are hit by advertising on TV, radio, magazines, supermarket shelves, buses and internet sites. There is no place children can go that isn't targeted by advertising,' confessed a former national research manager for a leading kids and teens marketing consultancy. 'I was responsible for researching the 7- to 17-year-old age group – running qualitative focus groups for the big brands around the country. In this role I was in charge of tracking the consumer trends of the youth market, paving the way for the consumer globalisation that has hit here during the past eight years.'

When this professional looks back, she is shocked by how effective her work was. 'I could never have predicted the impact my research would have. The work I did for a major chocolate brand helped win the $1 million promotions account to release their product here. It is now one of the most successful sweet brands in the country. Why did I leave? Even at the time, I was concerned about the damage this was causing to children's peer- and self-identity, as well as the consumer pressure this was causing parents. In 2000, I left and moved into teaching – a move I have never regretted. Today, when I walk down supermarket aisles and see the branding for kids' products, I feel repulsed at how the advertising companies promote the sexualisation and bankability of kids. I also feel sad that it is so-called "responsible" adults who are manipulating young children as a source of income. Where did the days of innocence and accountability go?'

With the amount of advertising directed at tweens, it is difficult for even the most vigilant parents to hold the line. By this age, shopping is part of a girl's way of life. 'What I always do is I go to the jewellery section first and I like buying the necklaces and bracelets and lockets,' Chantelle, 7, told me. 'And when I go to the clothes section, I get a pink top with stripes. I get jeans with the owl, and for summer I get these jeans shorts, and I wear an "I Love Roxy" T-shirt, because I love Roxy.' This compulsion to consume is constantly fed by smart marketers, who know they're on to a good thing. One of the future growth areas for tween spending is thought to be their room décor. Parents need to question whether they are enhancing their daughters' lives, or feeding what may well become an addiction.

CONSUMER KIDS

Having made purchases from the age of 4 or 5, girls are seasoned spenders by the time they reach 7 or 8.[5] At this stage girls are starting to make decisions on their own, and to spend parent-free time at shopping centres, which makes them easier for advertisers to target. Tweens are now adding an estimated $4 billion to the economy, and influencing a further $30 billion worth of family spending. This spending doesn't happen in a vacuum. Whole divisions of leading advertising agencies are devoted to reaching these valuable young consumers.

'Tweens have become a very powerful market with a lot of influence on purchases in the marketplace.' *Chris Wilson, Simmons Market Research*[6]

Most parents don't realise how much their tween girls are marketed to on TV, in magazines, and at shopping centres and fast food outlets, or how easy it is to collect their information, then feed it back to them in personalised ads. These girls are easy targets for marketers armed with detailed psychological profiles of their age group. 'Seeding' products is one of the many clever ways to get tweens on board. Once the coolest kids at school are wearing a company's latest branded clothes, or using their new product, it takes very little persuasion for their peers to follow.

While adults are slow to pick up on what is happening, teenage girls know how quickly things are changing for these young girls. 'When I was a kid, I used to wear big baggy T-shirts and jeans, like from K-Mart and stuff,' said Alana, 18, looking back. 'Now if you wore that you'd be isolated and laughed at. I see this with my sister. She's into all the brands. I don't like it. I don't know how it changed so quickly.' Every girl I spoke with voiced the same concerns.

'Fashion has taken a hold. My 8-year-old refuses to wear her teen sister's hand-me-downs, but will accept clothes from friends, because they're closer to what's in fashion,' confessed Adele, a mother of two girls. Tweens don't see how they're being manipulated, because they so want to be 'grown-up'. When I spoke with Vanessa, 9, she said the great thing about being her age was that she could wear more mature clothes. 'You can wear clothes that you couldn't wear as kids. Now they're adult-ish. You're more in fashion,' she told me.

There's a lot of information for girls to sift through to find out what's cool. All this takes time and effort, and does little for their development as people. In a marketing-driven environment the question is never 'Do I need this or that?', but 'What shall I buy next?'. MIT professor Sherry Turkle, an expert on the impact of new technologies, is concerned about what she calls 'the culture of overstimulation'. 'I think we know very little about the effects of the inundation of kids today with the fast cuts, the fifty commercials, the continual, changing, stimulating media environment.'[7]

'Going online is often thought of as an educational experience for kids, but increasingly it's a shopping experience.' *Kathryn Montgomery, Center for Media Education*[8]

Now companies can reach tweens directly, they're using every which way to capture and keep their attention. Computer 'advergames' are a very effective way to promote products to tweens, as girls will often spend half an hour or more playing them, as opposed to a few seconds viewing magazine and TV ads. Here and elsewhere girls are given regular sneak peeks at new products. Some marketers go further, creating fake tween websites to get to their target market. Others enter chat rooms posing as peers to introduce girls to their products.[9] This latter ploy is very attractive to tweens, as they love new things.[10]

Tweens pay close, uncritical attention to advertising, because they have no sense of being pitched to. For them ads are more like hints to help them be cool. While smaller children may *want* certain products, by the time they hit their tweens, girls feel they *need* specific items, because they want to be accepted by their peers. That's why tweens study magazines and catalogues in detail. They want to be sure they're on the right track.

'The tween market segment is one of the least expensive con-sumer segments to target from a cost-per-thousand perspective.' *David L. Siegel, author,* The Great Tween Buying Machine: Capturing Your Share of the Multibillion Dollar Tween Market.[11]

GOING VIRTUAL

As tweens grow, the pressure to purchase intensifies. One of the latest developments is the creation of virtual tween worlds such as Zwinktopia, Weeworld, Club Penguin, DressUp Games, Cartoondollemporium. com, and Webkinz.com, to name but a few. The hot favourite is Stardoll. com, which attracts around 6 million girls every month. Here girls can choose from over 400 celebrity dolls to clothe, style and make up for free. These dolls include all the usual suspects, from Hilary Duff and Beyoncé to Christina Aguilera. If girls want their own customised 'Me' doll, however, they have to pay, via mobile phone, credit card, or PayPal. Girls can also vote for whose doll is to be the cover girl on Stardoll's virtual fashion magazine. This is a big deal for the winning girl, because her online popularity skyrockets.

The opportunity to have a virtual self and attract lots of online friends is extremely attractive to young girls anxious about how they look and fit in. There are a number of dress-up doll sites. If girls visit DressUp Games they can make-over a huge range of themed dolls, including gothic, Lolita, punk, and emo dolls. Links take them directly to Diesel, Vera Wang, Gap and other sites where they can shop online. Parents need to be aware of the sites their girls visit, and to discourage those that are thinly disguised opportunities to shop.

'Tweens have more market potential than any other demographic group simply because they have all their purchases ahead of them.'
James McNeal, marketing expert [12]

Virtual worlds are taking us in a direction none of us could have contemplated even two or three years ago. It's too early to know the full impact. What is concerning is how this entertainment and pre-occupation with clothes and accessories disconnects girls from everyday life. Some girls are so cut off from nature, for example, that they are literally terrified of it. In *Last Child in the Woods*, Richard Louv looks at the contained lives too many of our children lead, as well as the groups, urban planners and educators who are working to combat this growing alienation from nature. Girls don't have to spend time in the wilds to form a connection with the natural world, but they do need access to nature. Without this important connection our girls are unlikely to appreciate or take care of the earth. What they don't understand, they fear, and what they fear, they may destroy.

Time outside has many benefits, and it's up to parents to lead the way. One doctor recently expressed his concern about how many children he's now seeing with broken bones. Although he hasn't done any formal research, he suspects children's bones aren't as strong as they once would have been, because they're not getting the strengthening that weight-bearing exercise gives them if they play, walk and run around outside.

Pester power

Nothing is left to chance when marketing to tweens. Even the way kids pester parents has been put under the microscope and used to generate more sales. Now girls are armed with the perfect script to persuade time-poor parents to purchase the items they crave. As children's marketing guru Cheryl Idell explains, 'You have to put copy into the ad that gives kids all the reasons they should want this (product), in language they can express to parents.'[1] Some companies go further and advise girls on how to fund their next purchase. One tween website I came across actively encouraged girls to create their own wishlist, email it to a friend or relative, or print it out and bring it into the shop with their mothers. When I visited this site more recently, I was pleased to see it had been toned down.[2]

> 'The Fred Bare thing – that's a bit of an obsession at the moment . . . We'll be walking down the street and she'll say, "That's Fred Bare, that's Fiorucci, that's a Louis Vuitton bag." '
> *Michelle, mother of Aimee, 6*[3]

Abercrombie & Fitch, described as 'ground zero for tween fashion',[4] was one of the first fashion labels to cotton on to the potential of the tween market. One of its smartest moves was to pick a cool group of tweens to appear in its catalogue. The genius of this campaign was that it instantly created the exact image the company wanted tweens to aspire to. Abercrombie & Fitch emphasised the value of the catalogue by charging for it.[5] This 'must-have' item has now morphed into a magalogue, with a beguiling mix of advertising and editorial.

'There's a huge ethical problem advertising to kids under 12, because when children of that age are studied psychologically and neurologically, you can see they think ads are for information and entertainment. They don't view them with a critical eye.'
Dr Amantha Imber, consumer psychologist

Parents need to be more vigilant about what's happening to their girls as personalised marketing gets more sophisticated. Campaigns now allow consumers to interact with ads. Girls can upload a picture of themselves, then select a few features so they can appear in an ad, then send it to friends, or post it on their websites. Our girls can also receive ads with personalised music, voiceovers, copy, video, animation and graphics.[6] Having consumers do their work for them is a perfect scenario for advertisers.

PARENTS ENCOURAGING GIRLS TO SHOP
Tween spending isn't just down to advertising, however. Girls are also influenced by their parents' consumption and values. Most young girls have grown up immersed in a 'shop till you drop' culture. Even before they could read, these girls were drawn to the kiddie catalogues that fell out of the weekend newspapers, and to the endless ads they viewed while watching their favourite TV programs. 'I get the little magazines — I used

to get the small magazines, but now I get the big magazines and it's got all this kind of stuff and I'm like so interested in it, and I've got it in a big pile and I keep on reading about it,' said Nina, 7. If parents want to minimise the consumer grip on their girls, keeping catalogues out of the house is a good start.

Being aware of family shopping patterns is also important. By the time they are 8 or 9, girls have spent literally hundreds of hours shopping with their parents, trawling the malls, and in front of the computer and TV. According to some experts, Generation X mothers may have unwittingly added to girls' consumer addiction by involving their young daughters in purchasing decisions. By so doing, these mothers are training their girls to shop, and again, marketers are well aware of this.

It's important parents become more conscious of their attitudes to shopping. Being more imaginative about how and where they shop can make all the difference. Trips to local craft and food markets provide a much richer experience than visiting shopping centres. Girls will value recycling more if they are exposed to the fun of vintage clothes, flea markets and garage sales. These experiences are also about community. They stimulate the imagination, because they are havens for the unusual and intriguing.

'They're certainly into experiencing make-up, workshopping outfits and things much earlier, like in their tweens.' *Annette, mother of Bridget, 13*

For many girls shopping is an addiction. While it's hard for parents to be across everything that's happening, experts emphasise how essential it is for them to be aware of the items they allow into their homes. 'It's so easy to lose control – especially when you've allowed these different mediums into your life,' confessed Adele, mother of two girls.

If parents want to keep control, what happens on home computers and the internet needs special attention. This is the time for parents to begin to explain how tricky some experiences on the net can be. Training girls not to reveal their passwords or their home or personal details is also a must. Installing web filters and limiting access to certain computer programs is also essential – www.netsmartz.com is an excellent resource for parents.

> Brands are very important to tweens. They now use them to help define who they are and what they aspire to.

BRANDED GIRLS

All this marketing is paying dividends for advertisers. Tween girls know their brands down to the last detail. Brands are very important to tweens as they increasingly define who they are and what they aspire to. The seductive thing about branding is that it focuses girls on buying, not on whether they actually need another pair of shoes or a new handbag.

Brands are about much more than the item itself. Tween girls don't just want a Diesel top or Billabong pants for the cut and colour. They want them because of the kudos they will deliver. Talk to a tween about what statement one brand makes as opposed to another, and you'll be amazed at how much they have to say. This is a strong reason for media awareness training for tweens at home and school, so girls can see the ways they are constantly manipulated into buying products.

> 'Today's junior school children seem to inhabit a seamlessly branded world where celebrities, toys, TV shows and electronics are almost indistinguishable from each other.' Dr Agnes Nairn, researcher[7]

The clothes tweens wear, what they eat and drink, and the kinds of music they listen to help them get noticed, be popular, belong. It is this level of devotion to brands that has enabled tween icons Mary-Kate and Ashley Olsen to amass a personal fortune of nearly $400 million from their books, music, fashion, perfume, cosmetics and other products.

This attraction to brands is such that tweens are now choosing their friends based on what they wear and what music they are into. Girls will fight hard with parents to acquire certain items, because they don't want to end up out on a limb. Brand power is big business – that's why it's so unrelenting. Companies who manufacture tween products know they're on to a good thing, and are not about to let this lucrative market slip through their fingers.

'There's very much that pack mentality,' observed Carla, who has a tween daughter aged 10. 'When I was a teenager you didn't dare stand out from the crowd. Now that's happening at 8 and 9, instead of 15 and 16.' One headmistress I spoke with told me how over the previous week one 12-year-old girl from a modest home had saved up $80 to buy a pair of shoes for a casual celebration at school. Another 10-year-old girl had arrived at the school's 'Italian day' in a plunging halter-neck top and make-up. Anyone who didn't know this girl would have assumed she was at least 15. When girls get everything they want, they grow up to assume life is about instant gratification – instant purchases, instant relationships, instant fun, instant sex – until nothing delights them, or is special any more.

The ad campaigns are so well-crafted girls think they're making their own choices. When girls aren't allowed to buy everything they think they need, they feel thwarted. 'Sometimes parents don't let you have fashionable clothes, because although they might have got teased, they don't care now,' Vanessa, 9, told me. She added, 'It's very hard.'

Tweens are choosing their friends based on what they wear and what music they are into. That's why these girls will fight hard with parents to acquire certain items.

Having worked hard to capture girls, marketers are careful to maintain their grip. 'Every year there's a very definite, different style, and my 8-year-old, Emma, is very conscious of it,' Adele, a mother of two girls, told me. 'There's also a narrowing between the kinds of clothes Emma will wear, and what teens are wearing. She's more vulnerable to fashion than my 13-year-old was [at her age]. She cares more about what people think and how she looks.'

Again, when speaking with tweens, it's surprising how fashion-conscious they are. 'I have these really nice new shorts that I like – they're summer clothes,' Brooke, 7, explained. 'I've got like black little shorts, and then I've got like this pink top, that can be like a dress or a top. It goes like this, like it's really long, and it totally covers you like with jeans. Except I mostly wear the shorts with that top.'

As consumer psychologist Dr Amantha Imber points out, the over-whelming presence of brands has only happened in recent years. 'Now brands and the media are having a huge influence on tweens – on their expectations, on body issues, on what's cool. It's almost like their wants and needs are developing faster than their biology, their neurology,' she reflected.[8] All the mothers I spoke with agreed. 'There's a lot more pressure on kids to conform and a lot less individuality,' one of them told me, adding, 'They're like homogenised little Paris Hiltons.'

This need to consume affects girls' lives on many levels. Recently my friend Kayt moved her 9-year-old daughter Tess to another school, as Kayt was unable to afford the brand-name clothes the girls in Tess's class were wearing. The school wasn't in a wealthy suburb, but as Tess was subjected to ongoing bullying about her clothes, Kayt had to act before Tess was completely demoralised. While it was a hard decision for Kayt and Tess, it proved to be the right one. When parents cave in to 'pester power', ultimately only the marketers win.

Brand power is on the rise. It affects girls younger and causes a lot of unhappiness, because it encourages girls to think that looks, possessions and popularity are what counts. This comes at a time when parents have lost confidence in being able to make good decisions for their children, and in knowing where to draw the line. Several teachers have complained to me about the number of parents who ask them to teach their children boundaries. As one educator, who is also a mother, advised, 'Don't be afraid to parent your children. They need parents, not friends.' When parents do reclaim their role as gatekeepers, they take the pressure to consume off *themselves* and their girls. A whole new world beckons when parents move beyond the need to shop endlessly. There's time for picnics, trips to farmers' markets, parks, museums, the beach, the local library, old cemeteries and still-to-be-explored parts of their town or city. They also strengthen relationships within the family and give girls a wider perspective from which to view themselves and others.

Young girls maturing earlier

Growing up is a complex process, and more so for today's young girls, as they are now dealing with issues their parents never faced. As tweens struggle to get a greater sense of themselves, they often vacillate between the activities they enjoyed as small girls, and the desire to be teenagers. This makes life confusing and exhilarating. What tweens do love is the fact they're no longer little girls, and that younger girls look up to them.

However, not all aspects of growing up are so appealing. Many young girls are developing breasts and pubic hair from the age of 8, due to a range of factors including food additives, pollution and underactive thyroid glands. This can make their lives difficult, as they are still young, and have a fragile sense of self. Most girls of 8 or 9 don't want to be different from their friends, and don't welcome undue attention from boys. Mothers do their girls a big favour by respecting this vulnerability, and by talking about the concerns and embarrassing experiences they had while their own bodies were developing.

Expressed sensitively, a mother's openness, warmth and honesty helps encourage her daughter to ask questions, and to feel more comfortable about the often overwhelming changes she is dealing with.

Some girls cope well with these changes, pressing on regardless. Others respond by hanging out with older kids, which can be tricky, as they lack the maturity to handle the activities older girls are into. One detective, concerned at the problems girls are now facing at a much earlier age, told me he had dealt with a number of rape cases involving girls as young as 11 who had 'boyfriends' 16 and above. No girl should have to navigate this time without good support and nurture.

How girls approach puberty can have a huge impact on their ongoing self-esteem. It is such a pity we have few fun and supportive rites of passage for girls. I was disturbed to discover recently that when some young girls get pubic hair, they are now heading to beauty salons to have Brazilian waxes. That a parent would give a young girl money for a Brazilian seems ludicrous, but when I asked one beauty practitioner, she told me this was quite common, adding, 'It's much more hygienic.' Most young girls struggle with their emerging sexuality, feeling excited one day and terrified the next. How a Brazilian wax helps girls become women is hard to see – not that beauty salons are complaining.

As girls are physically maturing younger and becoming more articulate, it's easy for parents and teachers to forget that emotionally they're still very young. The increasing influence of peers and popular culture on their behaviour and attitudes heightens their vulnerability. It's a difficult balance for these teen wannabes, because while they don't want to be seen as kids, they still have a lot of growing up to do. How tween girls present themselves and how they are feeling inside are often markedly different.[1] As paediatric endocrinologist Jill Hamilton points out, 'Parents need to realise that even if their body has matured, a 9-year-old is still a 9-year-old emotionally and behaviourally, and to treat them as such.'[2]

Regardless of how grown-up girls may think they are, experts stress how important it is to provide clear boundaries for tweens in a positive and respectful way. After disputes they advise parents to get girls to repeat what the agreed boundaries are, so everyone is clear. Boundaries not only protect girls, they teach them how to learn to regulate their own behaviour. They also give girls a safe structure from which to operate. Over time as girls start to push out from this structure, they still have something solid to fall back on should they push out too far.

IN A HURRY TO GROW UP

Tween girls are hungry to know anything and everything. They have been raised with access to more information in a day than previous generations had in a decade. However, information isn't the same thing as insight, as consumer psychologist Dr Amantha Imber is quick to point out. 'The internet has a huge impact on how tweens grow up. They've got access to a whole range of information long before they're able to integrate it, or know how to use it in a way that's constructive.'

How parents react to the stresses facing their girls is critical. While their daughter may seem street-smart, she still needs to be able to talk things through with her parents, so she can gain a more balanced perspective. Sadly this doesn't always happen. Often tweens feel silenced, because they don't know how to raise subjects their parents regard as grown-up, and so the opportunity for important discussion is lost.

Again, it's good for parents to talk about their own vulnerabilities and embarrassing moments when they were young. Girls feel reassured when parents can respect and empathise with what they are dealing with. Weaving casual anecdotes into light-hearted family conversation is ideal, as no-one feels lectured to. When parents relate their own stories, it's also reassuring to girls to know they're not alone. Even though their own issues may seem overwhelming, girls get the message they will survive, and that they may even be able to laugh about them further down the track. Relating real-life situations helps balance the influence popular culture and peers have, giving girls a more comfortable and informed space to fall back on.

'The biggest trend we've seen recently is teenlike pre-teen behaviour. The 12- to 14-year-olds of yesterday are the 10- to 12-year-olds of today.' *Bruce Friend, senior vice-president of Nickelodeon/MTV*[3]

I'M NOT A CHILD

As they grow tweens become increasingly sensitive about being seen as children. This sensitivity can surface in unexpected ways. In one British study of girls and boys aged 7 to 11, researchers were surprised at the responses girls had to their Barbie dolls. Many talked openly about shaving their Barbie's hair, pulling off her head, burning or breaking her. Some even admitted to microwaving their Barbie. When asked why, the girls said she was babyish.[4] They regarded mutilating their Barbie as cool. By contrast the boys in the survey still felt affectionate towards their Action Man, even though they'd outgrown him.[5]

'I don't like Barbies. Barbies are pretty much for little girls. I went to see Pink – I collect T-shirts and dolls of them – the same dolls as her. They look the same as her. I went to the Gwen Stefani concert, and I got this doll. She's got this outfit, and it says G for Gwen on her belt, and she's got a little skirt.' *Chantelle, 7*

Destroying their Barbies seems an extreme way for tweens to move on from their little-girl selves. Girls are clearly keen to put their Barbies aside. As there are few acceptable ways girls can express their anger and frustration, it doesn't leave them much room to move. I suspect we need to look more closely at what might be concerning girls at this time. Do they worry they won't measure up in this culture where sex, beauty and popularity count so much?

Certainly advertising plays on tween sensitivities. Anxiety can be a great motivator to get girls to buy, especially when products promise a girl she's going to feel cool, be popular, or make her friends jealous.

No matter how clever the spin, shopping can't make the pain, hurt and confusion of life go away. It does, however, distract young girls from finding real solutions to their fragile sense of self. When these anxieties aren't addressed, as we'll see, girls tend to turn this hostility inwards and end up hurting themselves.

> **'I still have Barbie dolls, but I don't usually play with them. I just keep them up like sitting down, because it looks nice in my bedroom. I used to play with them at like 6, but I'm 7. I just think I'm a little too old.'** *Brooke, 7*

Once parents are aware of the burning need young girls have to grow up, they can start to find more positive ways to help their tweens feel more mature by giving them small responsibilities, and praising them when they do these things well. Choosing activities with more responsibility, such as helping out at home, or with a local market or charity, ties them more closely to family and community, and is a more productive way to feel responsible than spending hours trawling the mall.

Too sexy too soon

As tween girls watch Britney, Lindsay and Paris and all the other celebrities struggle with alcohol, drugs and relationships, it doesn't take much of a leap for them to assume this is what being a girl is all about. Soon sexy, out-of-control behaviour seems the way to be noticed, and may in part explain why girls are getting involved in risky situations so young.

Again, while adults are still trying to come to terms with what's happening to young girls, teen girls are genuinely concerned for these younger girls. 'It's noticeable the girls wearing make-up and stuff are getting younger – wanting to grow up,' Whitney, 18, reflected. 'When I was like 11, I didn't notice girls doing this. I think they should try and enjoy childhood, and enjoy what they have. It's all the media influencing them.' Sandi, 14, agreed. 'You see some girls wearing like trashy pants, and some girls wearing like massive eye shadow and bright red lipstick as if they were going to a ball, and I think it's really sad, because you had freedom back then to wear what you wanted. You had freedom, because there wasn't anything you had to be.'

It's not just make-up and sexy clothing that is cause for concern, so too is girls' access to inappropriate information and behaviour. Parents speak to me about this frequently. Many now have filters on their computers – it's a good idea for grandparents who are carers to make these provisions also. One grandmother I spoke with was disconcerted to find her 7-year-old grand-daughter surfing porn sites. This woman wasn't even aware her grand-daughter knew how to surf the net. It transpired that her grand-daughter had been given the site address by kids at school. The more pervasive our sexualised culture becomes, the more it influences how girls see themselves. One young girl, also 7, liked a boy in her class so much she said she'd like to have sex with him. This young girl had no idea what she was really saying, except that she'd come to believe that having sex was how you showed someone you liked them. These are not isolated incidents. Teachers and school counsellors are all too familiar with them.

> Teen girls are genuinely concerned for younger girls, because they know exactly what is going on.

This behaviour and language doesn't appear out of nowhere. Our young girls absorb anything and everything around them. Parents need to be aware of how much peripheral information they pick up on. 'I'm concerned about how easily available movies that are for mature audiences are to this age,' another mother confessed. 'There doesn't seem to be any concern by parents as to what they're viewing. There's a lot of sexually explicit and violent material that they just don't need to see.' Where girls are exposed to unsuitable material, parents need to explain why this is not a good idea in ways that a young girl can understand. Educators stress how powerful good discussions in the home can be. Again, the more informally parents can introduce subjects, the better – 'Wasn't it sad that X did Y?', or 'That was really interesting but that's not what happens in real life.'

With all these new influences on girls, childhood is disappearing and fast. Marketers refer to this trend as 'kids growing older younger' (KGOY). Put simply, our young girls are being exposed to adult concepts they're not ready for. But that's only half the problem. Parents are also at sea. They are unsure about how to talk about adult subjects to their children in a way that is helpful. Often they end up lecturing girls, instead of talking them through the emotional implications of certain behaviour – how it may be harmful, feel uncomfortable or be inappropriate if they were to do something that isn't a good idea. When parents get this right they help girls begin to form their own boundaries, and develop their unique sense of self.

Our girls need good information to process what they're being exposed to, because the whole face of childhood has changed. Parents who gloss over difficult subjects aren't doing their girls any favours. They can't judge what their girls are experiencing against their tween experiences, because it just doesn't equate, as I discovered when interviewing Dr Joe Tucci of the Australian Childhood Foundation. 'We're now seeing 6-, 7- and 8-year-olds involved in coercive, manipulative sexual behaviours, because there's a confusion around what sexuality means,' he told me. There is nothing amusing or cool about a child who is acting out adult sexual behaviour, because there's no easy way forward. It can also be extremely damaging to those they abuse. 'This can be very traumatic to the child they're doing this to,' Dr Tucci explained.[1]

'Girls my age want to go out with boys. They think about what they'd like to wear and about shopping,' *Vanessa, 9*

SELLING SEX

Girls are being pressured to appear and act sexy, not to encourage or empower them, but because they're easy to sell to. Companies know how much tweens want to be teenagers, and use this to sell the products

teen girls enjoy – make-up, music, and fashions. That's why tween products have seen considerable growth in recent years. However, with the
teen products come teen aspirations. Mothers complain to me constantly
about how hard it is to buy a good range of age-appropriate clothes.

Some retailers have been a little too quick, however, to respond to
the tween clothing trend. British Home Store found itself in the hot
seat for its Little Miss Naughty g-strings for girls under 10, as did ASDA
for stocking black lacy underwear for 9-year-old girls.[2] After its initial
protest that Funtastic bralettes were 'helping girls to be modest', Target
had the good sense to pull the range. Abercrombie & Fitch caused an
uproar with its g-strings for girls aged 10 and up with 'Eye Candy' and
'Wink, Wink' printed on them. Company suggestions that these were
'cute and fun and sweet', and helped girls hide their panty lines, failed to
impress. While parents may feel hopeless about these trends, they have
a great deal of power. No company wants bad publicity, especially where
children are concerned. It's important parents don't keep their concerns
to themselves. If they don't fight for their girls, who will?

**'Teach a 7-year-old that sex is about accessorising and you've
secured a lifetime of lingerie buying.'** *Jean Kilbourne, writer
and filmmaker[3]*

Parents and child advocates are concerned that young girls are
being encouraged to see themselves as sexy before they're old enough to
understand what this means, but while they remain silent, marketers are
making a fortune. That's why the tween g-string market is alive and well,
and why girls can buy branded g-strings featuring fun figures from *Hello
Kitty* to *The Simpsons*. International market-tracking firm NPD Fashion-
world says the sales of tween g-strings have quadrupled since 2000.[4]
Growing up in such a sex-saturated culture isn't something previous
generations of girls have had to deal with. Our young girls are largely

on their own in handling these issues, because support networks haven't caught up yet.

While some argue these trends are liberating, it's hard to see how, after talking with professionals who deal daily with growing number of girls battling depression, sexually transmitted diseases and eating disorders. 'As our kids rush headlong into a premature adolescence, childhood itself is an endangered species,' reflects writer and cultural commentator Hal Niedzviecki.[5] Alana, 18, feels the same way. 'I have a younger sister. She's growing up way too fast. She's wearing clothes that I'm only just wearing. It looks ridiculous her wearing high heels, and trying to walk in them and things.' Like it or not, these trends influence how girls see themselves, and how they think they should look and behave. If sexy is in, then having sex is no big deal. 'Now kids are having group sex. Some girls start at 11 and 12, then a few more start at the beginning of high school, and it just continues,' one psychologist and school counsellor told me.

'Now, as our kids rush headlong into a premature adolescence, childhood itself is an endangered species.' *Hal Niedzviecki, writer and cultural commentator[6]*

Girls do need to experience their world. The difficulty for parents is where to draw the line. When they see their tweens wearing low-rider jeans and make-up, or insisting on g-strings, many feel despairing because they assume their girls are rebelling. Not so, according to child therapist Ron Taffel. He says this is their way of signalling they are part of a 'very intense, powerful second family of peer group and pop culture that is shaping kids' wants, needs and feelings.'[7] This is an important insight. As belonging is crucial to tweens, parents and educators can better support and guide girls by offering them more profound ways to belong in the family and community.

While some regard attempts to curb the sexualisation of young girls as disempowering, how young girls choose to dress and act doesn't take place in a vacuum. Tweens wear sexy clothing because companies encourage them to believe this will help them take their place in the world. Until there are more positive, yet equally appealing ways for tween girls to express themselves, our young girls will continue to be prey to those whose interest in them begins and ends with the bottom line.

'They (today's children) are pushed by market forces to act and dress like mini-adults and exposed via the electronic media to material which would have been considered unsuitable for children even in the very recent past.' *Extract from a letter by child experts, authors and academics to* The Telegraph[8]

That said, our discomfort at the sexualisation of young girls cannot and must not be ignored, because this is not in the interest of our young girls. If parents are serious about protecting them, they need to rethink what kinds of clothes they'd like their girls to be wearing. New research by De Montfort University found that those who download child pornography from the internet share the same psychological characteristics as paedophiles who actively abuse children.[9] As the addiction to pornography grows, and we are in the middle of what some experts describe as an epidemic of child sexual abuse, how many of these people are out walking the streets? And when they see tween girls dressed as teens, wearing the clothes marketed to them as *the* way to look cool and be accepted, what do they see – young girls trying hard to grow up, or 'eye candy'?

Tween dreams

So what do tween girls want? Like most of us, they want to be acknowledged, to be loved, to belong. The media-saturated world in which they live shapes their ideas about how they will achieve this. Given their constant exposure to the lives of celebrities, it's no surprise that many girls want to be famous. When Paul Kurnit of KidShopBiz asked tweens who they would most like to be, 45 per cent said they would like to be a public figure or celebrity. [1] Amongst the girls I spoke with, Melanie, 10, summed up how many girls her age feel. 'I'd like to be a famous person, an actor, because they get lots of stuff, and they can do stuff with it,' she told me.

In Martin Lindstrom's BRANDchild study of tweens, which took place across eight countries, the number of tweens who wanted to be famous was over 50 per cent. [2] While these figures give us some sense of what tweens are thinking, it's worth noting this study is now several years old. With the more recent impact of reality TV and increased marketing to tweens, the numbers hungry for fame may now be considerably higher. When British researcher Dr Agnes Nairn and her colleagues studied girls and boys aged 7 to 11, the most lively discussions weren't around toys and games, but sports celebrities, pop stars and TV shows. [3]

With the massive amounts of time and money put into marketing to tweens, increasingly tween girls are focusing on externals. Even amongst kids who don't want to be famous, there's an endless fascination with those who are. As consumer psychologist Dr Amantha Imber points out, being a celebrity used to seem unattainable, but now with reality TV there's the expectation that you can become a celebrity overnight just by auditioning for *Big Brother*, regardless of your talent. The more 'human' celebrities appear, the more celebrity status seems attainable. Tweens don't just know about celebrities and why they're well known. They're updated almost daily on what they are up to. All this takes precious time away from girls getting to know themselves and the real world.

Fame isn't the only thing on the tween agenda, they want to be rich as well.[4] In one survey of 11- and 12-year-olds, a staggering 80 per cent said they wanted to be rich.[5] This was the same for the young girls I spoke with. 'I'd like to have money, to know I have a good life,' Vanessa, 9, explained. Tweens want a disposable income, because they know they are going to need plenty of money to buy all the things they want.

While tweens may have more choice, in many ways their life experience is narrowing, and fast. More and more girls are concerned about how they look, what they are wearing, what friends think, and what the rich and famous are doing. This leaves little room for an internal life – to have the freedom to lose themselves in their own thoughts, dreams and passions, or to be intrigued by things that are out of the ordinary or unexpected, which are crucial to imagination.

Having the time and space to think outside the square liberates girls from seeing life merely as it is, and allows them to imagine how else it might be for themselves, for others, for the planet. Parents have a vital role in reclaiming this space for girls by the kind of environment they create in the home – by encouraging hobbies, time for quiet and family fun, for engaging girls with extended family or friends, and making them feel integral to everything that happens within the home.

A FRAGILE STATE OF MIND

Tween girls need this input and sense of belonging, because in spite of everything they now have and aspire to, experts are worried about the level of insecurity and unhappiness they experience. Their lack of motivation is also cause for concern.[6] 'Although this may be the most affluent generation to walk the planet, it also has the dubious distinction of being the most insecure and depressed,' says global marketing guru Martin Lindstrom.[7] William Damon, the director of the Stanford University Center on Adolescence, warns parents not to take their girls at face value. While they may have a 'superficial sophistication', they are still vulnerable.[8]

When I asked tweens what girls their age were anxious about, appearance and acceptance were top of the list. 'It's all about whether anyone likes you, and whether anyone will talk to you,' Melanie, 10, told me. 'They worry about looks. Worry about how their hair looks, their face looks, their eyebrows, and how thin or fat they are.' Vanessa, 9, explained. Vanessa also admitted she worries about 'weight and guys 'n' stuff. Weight cos kids tease you, and people look at you with a mean look, and you're jealous of some girls cos they look better.' These anxieties are so unnecessary and destructive for girls. Parents are much better equipped to turn this situation around when they know what is happening for girls, by encouraging them to feel good about themselves.

'Although this may be the most affluent generation to walk the planet, it also has the dubious distinction of being the most insecure and depressed.' *Martin Lindstrom, global marketing guru*[9]

During the tween years girls begin to question their parents' views, and weigh them up against what friends think. Tweens need to debate issues, and parents and teachers have an important role in creating opportunities for debate. It helps parents to know that tweens tend to see life as black or white, because they aren't fully aware of situations or their likely outcomes. After a long day at work, spending time with your tween talking about what seems like a minor issue can be stretching, but it is essential, because their anxieties are real and can be intense. When issues are talked about openly and in a relaxed fashion, tweens have a much better idea of why something is or is not a good idea.

Helplines for children are reporting an increasing number of children who are depressed. Some are as young as 5.[10] Over a hundred child health experts, authors and academics were so concerned at the growth of childhood depression and problems with children's behaviour and development that they wrote to *The Telegraph*, stating, 'It's now clear that the mental health of an unacceptable number of children is being unnecessarily compromised, and that this is almost certainly a key factor in the rise of substance abuse, violence and self-harm amongst our young people.' They stressed that children need real food and play, a direct experience of life, and regular interaction with the main adults in their lives if they are to develop as rounded individuals.[11]

'Our society rightly takes great pains to protect children from physical harm, but seems to have lost sight of their emotional and social needs.' *Extract from a letter from child experts, authors and academics to* The Telegraph[12]

Neuroscientist Baroness Susan Greenfield went further, pointing out that in cognitive tests 11-year-olds were now scoring on average two to three years lower than children the same age just fifteen years ago. She believes that without the crucial elements needed to develop the brain – human interaction, nourishing food and play, and being directly engaged in life – children's ability to make sense of their world and express themselves creatively will continue to diminish.[13] One of the key messages in this letter takes us back to the question of overstimulation. Just because adults have to process a vast amount of information, it doesn't mean we should expect our children to.

So, where is all this leading? There is no doubt that the pressure on young girls is mounting. Again, teen girls are well aware of this. 'I know like generations below me are going to get ten times more pressure than us,' Carly, 16, told me. One of the main areas tweens seem anxious about is failure. When a group of 11- to 12-year-olds were asked what they were most worried about, at the top of the list was getting poor marks at school.[14] Global marketing guru Martin Lindstrom sees tweens caught between growing personal anxieties and living in a fearful society.[15] This is a lot for any young girl to handle. It is these fears and anxieties marketers exploit to boost sales.

Today's tweens do live in anxious times. As one parent of tweens pointed out, 'Probably the largest difference is that they've got no freedom. My parents had a comparatively easy time. After school they didn't see us. They gave us something to eat and we came home at dark. Everyone I know of my generation says the same thing. You always came home at dark for dinner. Weekends you were off and running again the whole day. These days the child has to be within four feet of you. I think it's the freedom that's gone, which is sad.'

This anxiety may also be due in part to the greater expectations now placed on girls. 'Kids do have more pressure now,' one mother with a tween daughter reflected. 'Success is everything. They're organised within an inch of their lives. Sometimes they don't have time to play. Perhaps TV becomes their time to relax, especially as we don't want them out playing, because the world's not as safe a space. There's less free time, which creates its own pressures.'

I HATE MY BODY

As tween girls grow, so too do their concerns about their bodies. In one US study of girls' attitudes to their bodies, 81 per cent of ten-year-old girls were worried about being fat. Just over half the girls aged 9 and 10 said they felt better about themselves when they were on a diet.[16] These girls have formed these views without knowing that dieting can delay puberty, cause their bones to deteriorate and hinder their growth. Or that if they're on a very strict diet, it can stop them producing oestrogen, which can cause additional health problems further down the line.

All many young girls can think about is how to get and stay slim, so they can be loved and popular. 'It's sad if girls are fat, because they're teased when they're big,' Melanie, 10, told me. 'People think they're different because they're bigger. Tall skinny people do most of the teasing about girls being fat. They do it in a way that the teacher doesn't know.'

'Younger and younger kids are feeling they need to be aware of their bodies. Everyone's so image-conscious. The kids are all trying to create an image with their hair and make-up. It's so sad that they think they have to fit into someone else's image.' *Rose, psychologist and school counsellor*

Some time back Temple University set up MyPopStudio.com to provide girls with creative ways to look at the media. On this innovative site girls can create their own pop star, edit a reality program, or become a celebrity and see how it feels. When the team looked at how the site was being used, they were dismayed to find that regardless of their appearance to begin with, girls were choosing makeovers that enabled them to be blonde, white and thin.[17]

'More attention is drawn to how we look. Young girls are learning this and basing their entire self-worth on their bodies and beauty.' *Vernisha Shepard, psychotherapist*[18]

Girls' ongoing anxieties around their bodies are cause for real concern. One in ten girls who suffer from anorexia say their eating issues began at around age 10 or younger.[19] Surrounded by manufactured definitions of what beautiful women look like, tween girls plaster their bedroom walls with these images and work hard to look like them, because they want to be loved and to belong. One professional I spoke with talked about how powerful attitudes in the home were. She stressed the importance of mothers being happy and confident in themselves, and as women, so they could pass these attributes on to their girls.

ON THEIR OWN

By the time girls reach their tweens, both parents are likely to be working. While this gives tween girls more freedom, many end up spending a significant amount of time on their own. These girls have more money to spend, and now shop for a whole range of items, including groceries, as they're also starting to do some cooking and other work around the house. This increased responsibility can't, however, replace a girl's need for human warmth and connection.[20] As parents are frequently not around, girls turn to their peers for support. This gives young girls a lot of power over each other's lives. Patricia Adler, who has studied peer groups, notes that the more independent girls are from adults, the more popular they are with girlfriends.[21] If we are genuine about nurturing future generations, we need to find better ways to support parents in their parenting, and in filling the hours after school with meaningful programs for girls and boys.

'The steady diet of information, available twenty-four hours a day, seven days a week, through a whole variety of channels, is playing a major role in shaping this new generation.' Martin Lindstrom, marketing guru[22]

Educators are concerned that peer group pressure is now taking hold of girls' lives earlier than ever, and that the cliques which create the pressure are tough and unduly influential. Too often the right to belong to a group is based on girls conforming to a narrow set of rules that dictate who they are, how they dress and what they like – qualities which again are largely defined by the media.

When tweens are interviewed, however, they don't see the influence their friends have over them, even though most admit that they find out what's cool from friends or school.[23] The media is also a huge part of their lives. In one Kaiser Family Foundation study, over a third of tweens aged 10 to 12 said their friends get a lot of their information about drugs, sex and violence from TV, movies and other forms of media.[24] This is very concerning, especially as most of their TV viewing is in adult timeslots.[25] And as single-parent and dual-income families become more common, more and more girls are home alone. Often they eat their meals by themselves in front of TV.

As most parents need to work, it's almost impossible for them to cover the hours immediately after school. Two critical questions we need to examine are: have we fallen into the trap of working to consume, and how much does the culture of consumption permeate the home, fragmenting family life and forcing girls to turn to peers for the nurture and company families used to provide?

TOO MUCH STIMULATION

So, where are the media and new technology taking girls? One of the key areas experts are worried about is the over-stimulation of children. Adults are used to processing vast amounts of information from the media, but it doesn't mean children can handle it. Being constantly busy allows girls no time for reflection, to be comfortable with their own company, or to learn the value of chilling out for a couple of hours. When girls do not learn these important life skills, it can compromise their personal development, because they feel driven to be around others at all costs. Again, the way parents lead their lives helps set the pace.

As our girls are more anxious, we need to balance their concerns about themselves and the planet by helping them develop rich personal lives, which enables them to explore their own creativity. By helping them cultivate these inner resources, we can encourage them to be excited about the future, by reassuring them they will come up with ideas and ways of doing things their parents and teachers can only dream of. The more parents can support girls in this positive way, the more they equip them to deal with the complex world they are about to inherit.

Consumer psychologist Dr Amantha Imber reminds parents that one of the best ways to help tweens navigate the media is to help girls recognise when they're being sold to. 'Educate your children from as early an age as possible as to what advertisements are – that is, that they are purely there to try to sell you something, and do so by presenting the product in a biased and overly favourable light.' There are all kinds of fun approaches parents might take, such as showing children how to count how many ads there are on a page, and work out how much it would cost to buy all the things on offer, then guessing how many products there are in a whole magazine, and how much it would cost to buy everything. Thankfully, media literacy is now being taught in schools, enabling children to see what advertisers, magazine editors, producers of video clips and other forms of media are up to. However, parents also need to be active in family discussions about spending, the impact of consumerism, and the exploitation of poorer nations for cheap goods.

LEARNING THAT LIFE ISN'T JUST ABOUT 'ME'

Many tweens' experiences are centred around themselves and their friends. However, if they are to mature, they need to balance this with more varied experiences. Helping them get involved in neighbourhood activities, where they can mix with different kinds of people and generations, is one way forward. This might mean anything from helping a neighbour or local charity, joining in tree-planting in a local park, or setting up and running a garage sale. Just down my inner-city street, two tween girls hold a regular stall where the proceeds go to charity. Neighbours love this idea. These kinds of activities give girls a wider sense of community and belonging. It helps them find their unique expression and be validated for it.

Shared rituals are another powerful way to give tweens a more profound sense of belonging. This can be anything from having a special family breakfast on Sunday mornings, a mid-week pizza made together, or weekend visits to local markets. These activities feed the spirit. While girls may not appreciate how much family rituals offer at the time, they do teach girls about the textures of life and how to enrich the moment, so they have more resources to fall back on in difficult times.

There's a lot going on for tween girls. Sometimes it's hard to appreciate just how much, as everyone is so stretched. It is said that every year of a young person's life is the equivalent to five adult years.[26] We need to be sensitive to everything our young girls experience and balance out these pressures in any way we can. The tween years are a crucial time in a girl's life. Experts tell us that it is during these years that the habits of a lifetime are formed.[27] This is the perfect time for parents to help girls forge habits that will serve them well.

Teens have it all

Becoming a teenager is still a big deal for girls. As they don't want to be seen as young girls, their need to look sexy, shop and have more 'adult' fun intensifies. 'We have a lot more attitude, we're very materialistic,' Joy, 16, informed me. 'We're now thinking about guys and all the hot movie stars, and getting rompier and wanting heaps more independence, wanting to be as old as possible.' For Carly, 16, it was music, parties, clothes, make-up, and who she was going to hang out with that mattered. Or as Abbie, 17, put it, 'We know what it's like to be an adult. We want the lifestyle of an adult.'

TREADING NEW GROUND

Being a teen today is very different to what it was like for parents when they were teenagers. If parents are to help their girls through these important years, it's essential they realise this. Today's teens are at the forefront of the massive changes taking place in society, from the rapidly changing youth culture to the advances in technology and communications. As the 'traditional' path to adulthood is all but erased, our teen girls are forced to find new ways forward. Navigating this new territory with few markers is tough, especially with the stresses of teen life to cope with. 'Like we're trying to juggle the responsibility of taking drugs, having sex and drinking and stuff, along with the teenage responsibility of school and friends,' Kiera, 17, told me. 'We're all trying to juggle too much. It's a little bit overwhelming.' When parents can empathise with girls and understand more of their world, they build important bridges that will serve them well in the years ahead.

Some of the pressure girls face comes from their constant need to acquire. Teenage girls love new clothes, shoes, make-up and jewellery, trips to the movies, magazines and iPods. But the more choice there is, the more they want, and the more effort they have to make to get it. For most of the girls I talked with, finding a job that makes a lot of money was essential, as there's an endless list of things they want. Many of their parents were also anxious about their girls' ability to support themselves as adults, because their expectations are so high.

GIRLS WITH ATTITUDE

What is impressive about teen girls is their attitude. These girls want to experience life for themselves, they don't want it handed to them on a plate. 'I think we have to work things out for ourselves. You can't just expect us to trust what you tell us, because it's very much *our* lives and *our* discovery, so we've got to make our own mistakes and learn from our own mistakes,' Peta, 16, pointed out.

'We'll do what we want to do, because that's how you learn.'
Evie, 15

'I think you are compared to older generations a bit too much,' Sandi, 14, told me. 'Parents say "when I was young", but we have moved on, times have changed. We have high technology.' This determination can be difficult for parents to contend with, because while their girls might want to do their own thing, they still have a lot to learn. 'Attitude is a really big thing,' admitted Jean, a mother of two teen daughters. 'The younger one, who is just 13, always wants the last word. She's at you and at you. It makes life very hard sometimes.' While it's good that girls can be assertive and passionate, the way it is expressed can be unproductive. Parents need to find creative ways to harness this energy, so it doesn't end up as an endless, exhausting battle of wills. Girls need to be taught gently how to work through issues positively with family and friends, so they can be savvy but fair in their relationships.

More often than not, what girls are seeking is the opportunity to be stretched. So why not take this need and funnel it into projects that will give girls a greater sense of worth and belonging? Community and charity projects are ideal, especially when girls are able to use and develop their skills. One teen girl I know got a lot out of helping a local charity with its database, and by contributing ideas on how to make people more aware of its services. There are so many ways to engage teen girls more meaningfully. The earlier we do so the better. These kinds of activities are important because they allow girls to make a unique contribution, to experience a genuine sense of community, and to be recognised for their effort.

BATTLING THE STRESS AND EXHAUSTION

It's not that our girls have lots of spare time on their hands — most don't. The question is whether their busyness is feeding them and helping them thrive. Part of the challenge for today's teens is the overwhelming amount of information and experience they're dealing with. The more time I spent with teen girls, the more I appreciated just how complex their lives are. At first glance they appeared confident and ready to take on the world. But when I talked with them in more depth, I was struck by how young and vulnerable they were. Many admitted to battling stress and exhaustion. There always seemed to be more to do than there were hours in the day. Even in semester breaks they have an overwhelming number of assignments. 'My sister would come home from school and go out straight away, but with me, I'm tired and I just want to go to bed,' said Evie, 15. 'I talk to my friends and they're all the same. And it's disappointing – I'm tired and not up to much.'

It was concerning to hear how tired most girls were. 'You do get really tired,' Missy, 15, admitted, 'but like you try and get over it. Like you get to school, and like the first period you're kind of tired. It depends on the class, like in science and maths I'm always tired, but then you kind of get awake by lunchtime. But then by the time you go to bed, like 9.30pm, you're like really, really tired.'

As I talked with girls they said they felt they were under constant pressure. 'You tend to be pretty tired, especially towards the end of term,' Peta, 16, confessed. 'The first week you feel tired, because you're getting back into it, then it's all right. Then towards the last couple of weeks of term you just completely slow down and just have to sleep, and even during the holidays you end up sleeping, because you're just so tired.' Again this reflects on our manic lives as adults. If we don't teach girls the value and joy of chilling out, it may take years for them to learn and may compromise their health on the way.

SLEEP DEPRIVATION

Experts agree that teens are not getting enough sleep. 'We're seeing that, on average, teens are getting about seven-and-a-half hours a night's sleep on school nights,' says professor of psychiatry, Mary Carskadon. 'And actually a quarter of the kids are getting six-and-a-half hours or less sleep on school nights. So when you put that in the context of what they need to be optimally alert, which is nine-and-a-quarter hours of sleep, it's clear that they're building huge, huge sleep debts, night after night after night.[1]

'Generally I have enough sleep,' Chelsea, 18, told me, but as she talked it appeared this might not be the case. 'I don't need a lot of sleep.

I might get drowsy mid-afternoon, but then I'm okay after an hour. My body clock wakes me up early if I've had a late night. I don't know how it works, but I don't want to miss out. I want to be where the action is.' Not all tiredness is down to assignments and their busy social schedules. As we'll see, girls also lose huge amounts of time surfing the net.

'We don't have an awful lot of spare time. I just love doing other stuff. Every now and then I'd like to have the chance to sit down and read a book or listen to some music or whatever.' *Peta, 16*

Sleep deprivation can make it hard for girls to concentrate at school as it affects short-term memory, and may even cause them to put on weight.[2] Teens need more sleep than children and adults. When teen girls are short on sleep, the effects tend to be more dramatic than for adults, making them vulnerable to depression and attention deficit disorders. There is now some suggestion that many children thought to be suffering from ADD or learning difficulties are simply sleep-deprived.[3] Lack of sleep can make it harder for girls to cope, and trigger disruptive behaviour and unexpected outbursts.[4] Sleep loss can also contribute to early-onset diabetes.[5] It's important that parents communicate this to girls, and insist on better sleep regimes.

NEEDING TO ESCAPE

As I talked with girls, it became clear that with all these pressures they felt a strong need to escape. 'I like seeing movies, like it's a place where it's not reality, it's somewhere else,' said Sandi, 14. 'You don't care about anything. It doesn't matter what the movie is.' There was a clear link with some girls between the need to chill out and the decision to take drugs and drink alcohol.

When the girls spoke about the stress and exhaustion, I was surprised at how many wished they were little girls again. 'You just want to go back to that little girl who didn't care, who just got up and played all the time, and that's all she had to worry about,' said Andrea, 18. Alana, also 18, agreed. 'I'd love to be magically little again. I like the innocence of childhood. They don't think about anything. They don't have to think about how you look, like now. I don't play any more. When did that die out? I want to go back before that and relive it all.'

It was so poignant to hear these girls recall treasured childhood memories. 'Me and my friends all loved the Disney movies, and you sort of wish that you could just do all the things again,' said Missy. 'Like being little again, because like even though I am only 15, it was such fun being like 9, and like playing with Barbies all the time and like dressing up and everything.'

As adults we can work with this ache to be young and carefree again by helping teen girls find ways to lose themselves in activities that allow them to recapture the innocence and spontaneity of childhood. Many girls I spoke with loved looking after children and babies — playing games with them, or just running around and having fun. The girls enjoyed these activities, because they felt they had something to give children. It made them feel responsible and nurturing. It fed their imaginations, their need to be acknowledged, to belong. There are many ways girls can express this need through art, singing, dancing, picnics in the park and so on. When parents and teachers provide a creative environment for girls, girls are inspired to find their own ways to express themselves.

'I wish I could go back and be 8, yeah. Everyone loved you and you loved everyone, and the problems you had, looking back, were nothing. And like I didn't worry about the "right" kind of shoes, because I didn't know the right kind of shoes. Looking back it was such a great time.' *Sandi, 14*

Teen life is a time of contrasts. One minute girls want to chill out, the next they want to go at a million miles an hour, so parents need to take this into account. While teen girls dislike pressure and wish they had more time to relax, they also love momentum, lots of activities and new experiences. They happily spend hours socialising, shopping and on the net. Some take on part-time work to supplement the household income. Many work to have more money to spend. They certainly feel there's no time to waste.

Living up to expectations

Today's girls know they're much better off than previous generations, because their mothers and teachers constantly remind them. They appreciate these gains. 'I think we've come a long way from not having any rights,' Whitney, 18, admitted. 'There's a lot of women who are doing great things. I look forward to being part of that.'

> 'I think there's more pressure to do well as a woman, because maybe your grandparents or your mother didn't have the same opportunities as you do. They want you to have more opportunities than they did and they want you to take advantage of them.'
> Peta, 16

While for some girls this wealth of choices is exhilarating, for a surprising number of girls the many expectations surrounding these choices were almost paralysing. When asked about their lives, girls would often give a well-rehearsed response, because they know what adults, especially adult women, expect of them. Scratch the surface, however, and considerable anxiety and frustration emerge. 'I don't think that a lot of people of my parents' generation understand the pressure we are under,' confessed Missy, 15. Alana, 18, agreed. 'It's good to think we've come a long way, but sometimes it's negative, because it's like, "Look what you have and you're not making the most of it."'

A few girls found this pressure so great, they talked of being ready to crack. 'Kids are too pressured because they're trying to do too much,' Kiera, 17, admitted. 'It's putting yourself out there in every aspect, so you can get the most out of life.' Peta, 16, felt the same way. 'I don't go out very much during the school terms at all, because there's just too much stuff – not just homework, the amount of pressure put on you at school to do well – and you just get stressed out,' she told me. 'You're like, "I've just got to stay here, I've got to do study, I've got to do this, I've got to do that."'

As girls are now able to achieve so much more, parents and teachers are naturally eager to encourage them to go as far as they can. It's important girls get this support, so they can dare to dream and achieve their dreams. However, the expectations we now have of girls can also make life more pressured, especially at school. 'Personally, like I do my work because I'm scared of what will happen if I don't do it,' Evie, 15, told me.

It was saddening to hear these kinds of comments over and over. While this is not what most parents or teachers want, that's how it often feels. 'Sometimes I'd be in class for the first five minutes, then I'd leave,' admitted Chelsea, 18, 'because they'd be lecturing us. It's like "I don't want to hear this any more, because you're stressing me out."' Many girls were aware their success was part of a wider agenda. As Lily, 13, was quick to point out, 'Teachers want you to do really well, and parents have to go on about their kids doing well, because it makes them feel good. But not everyone can be good at everything.'

Part of the pressure on girls is the need to know where they are heading at a much younger age. Many girls I spoke with were resentful of this. 'I worry a lot about school, and where you're going to start taking yourself,' admitted Carly, 16. 'Teachers, career advisers, and parents in a heaps working-hard home all put on the pressure.' While most parents are simply trying to do the right thing, some are overly ambitious. One article I came across revealed that some parents were paying tens of thousands of dollars a year in coaching fees for sports such as tennis, in the hope their kids might become professional players.[1]

'Professionals working with girls say the pressure to be beautiful, successful and popular is acute and damaging.' *Mary Macleod, chief executive, National Family and Parenting Institute*[2]

FINDING A CAREER

While career counselling is an excellent resource, some girls found it limiting. Georgia, 20, told me her school insisted on career counselling from age 14. She got almost nothing out of her sessions at this age, because she'd no idea what she wanted to do. Feeling the pressure to come up with something, she made it up. She also found these counselling sessions sparked unhelpful competition amongst the girls in her year. Those who wanted to be professionals were seen as successful, while those with humbler ambitions were regarded as losers.

The ways schools deliver career counselling must be handled with care, so as not to overwhelm girls and leave them terrified of failing before they've even begun. As adults we mustn't underestimate the fear factor in girls. This came through strongly in my interviews. 'I'm a bit worried, before I grow up I have to like make these decisions,' Missy, 15, told me. 'I have to try to figure out what I want to do for the rest of my life. Like I have no idea, so that's kind of a bit scary. It's daunting, you kind of have to make your own way.'

'I think that idea that what you are in high school is what you're going to be in life sends the wrong message to girls,' Georgia, 20, reflected.

'It's like if you're seen as a loser in high school, you'll be a loser for life, and it's just not the case. I've found it to be the opposite. The girls who were ultra-high achievers dropped out of uni very quickly, and I feel bad for them. A lot of people who were given no recognition in high school quickly found where they were meant be when they left, in almost every case.' Carly, 16, summed up how many girls felt. 'Now you know you've done well if you are a doctor and marry a doctor, and you have a big house and car, and a couple of kids and a nanny.'

'There are lots more opportunities,' admitted Annette, mother of a 13-year-old daughter, adding, 'but I guess we are in a stage of so many choices that you could feel stressed and overloaded. Girls need skills to deal with that.' Barbara, a school counsellor and psychologist, agrees. 'All the choices girls now have are overwhelming. There is so much choice. I see them struggling because they don't know what to do. We put on them that they have to finish school, but for half the girls school is not for them. It's so wrong and so sad. Not everyone wants or need to go to university. Let's give girls more jobs and choices that are right for them.' This is something parents and teachers need to take on board if they want girls to find their niche.

'My parents are like high achievers. They look at my marks and say, "Look, you've achieved this mark, imagine what you could have done if you'd really studied."' *Chelsea, 18*

PRESSURE FROM PARENTS

Sometimes there is real pressure from parents who want their girls to succeed, especially those at fee-paying schools. The girls I spoke with were acutely aware of the investment their parents had made in their educations, and of the expectation there will be a good return on this investment. Pressure also comes from teachers, who are keen for girls to make the best of their many choices. 'I remember when I went to look at my school I was scared, because they gave this speech about expect-ations,' said Sandi, 14. 'They still do it. They will say things all through the year, which you're like, "What if I can't live up to that?"'

'It's put on you that you have to work – and it's not as if you're work-ing towards something – every night you do work, then it starts again the next morning, so it's never like you're working towards something, it's just constant work.' *Evie, 15*

For many of the girls I spoke with, the constant message that 'You can have it all' was intimidating, and was reflected in their body language. In spite of their apparent confidence and ability to express themselves, teen girls still have to grow up, and in vulnerable moments will acknow-ledge this. 'I feel like I'm not ready,' said Carly, 16. 'Even though lots of adults would say, "It's time for her to grow up", I still feel like I'm a child. I haven't really changed much. It gets a bit overwhelming at times. It's like, "How can you expect so much?" I think one day we'll all eventually crack, then say screw it.' Sara, 17, was also tired of the pressure. 'It's a bit hard for adults to change. You can tell them over and over again. I'm an individual. I need to make my own decisions. By pushing me to study it made me not want to. I don't want to be told what to do.'

Being told you can be anything you want to be isn't necessarily that helpful when you've no idea what that's likely to be. For most people the road to success isn't that straightforward. It may take girls a number of years in the workforce before they discover what they're passionate about, but no-one seems to be telling them this. As one girl pointed out, 'I look at my mum and her age group. They've already made that decision, so they're kind of like in their little comfort zone, as they've already done all that.' Abbie, 17, felt that pressure to succeed was tied to her teachers' political agendas. 'A couple of my teachers are avid feminists, so there's pressure there. More of a pressure than the boys around you to prove you can do it.'

When contemplating their adult lives, it seems there's very little chance for girls to relax and pursue something they are curious about, let alone learn how to deal with failure. Many girls I spoke with clearly believed that one wrong choice could ruin their lives. 'You get a bit nervous about it all and not knowing. Like you make a mistake and you get into a career that you find you actually can't do or you don't like it, or you can't achieve it. It is stressful,' explained Missy, 15. If we want to help our girls succeed, perhaps we all need to be in less of a hurry, so our girls have more time to explore the possibilities that present themselves. Invariably the best staff I have hired over the years have been those who have taken the road less travelled.

WHEN POPULAR CULTURE DOESN'T HELP

The pressure on girls is also apparent in teen magazines, where there's endless editorial on what it means to be a successful woman – how to have a better body, better skin, better grades. In one magazine, teen readers could discover where they rated in the friendship stakes. The criteria included how many texts they received, and whether or not they had organised a party.[3] Other features included a two-page spread on 'Hairstyles Guys Love Most', graded out of ten.[4]

The cult of celebrity and reality TV also puts pressure on girls by promoting a 'winner takes all' mentality. The joy and excitement of learning new things becomes lost in a preoccupation with where girls are in the pecking order in every part of their lives. When you listen closely to what girls are saying, you see how they are constantly rating themselves and others in almost every aspect of their lives. 'Academically, like I don't struggle, but I don't excel,' Sandi, 14, told me wistfully as she started to tell me what school was like for her. It's a big ask for any teenager to be perfect and popular, wear the right clothes, look cool and achieve excellent grades. There's little opportunity here to build solid self-esteem. Is it any wonder so many are feeling depressed?

If girls are going to make the best of 'it all', they need a good map that lays out the possibilities and challenges life is likely to bring. Equally important is the chance to *enjoy* the journey. This is hard to achieve when the emphasis is almost exclusively on the goal. A number of girls wished there was more attention on life skills at school to help them progress and to handle tricky situations. 'Maybe they should focus more on making us more interactive with people, and teaching us like skills like that, instead of teaching us algorithms that we're never gonna use,' reflected Peta, 16. 'Yeah, so I think if they were to start on more the emotional side that'd be good. It's very academic. You're growing at the same time, but you're not being taught that kind of thing.'

> **'They could give us a bit more freedom, and not tie us down so much with as many assignments. When they think they are helping, they're stressing us out to the max. If you ask someone what they've been up to in the holidays, they would say that they'd been doing lots of assignments and studying for tests coming up. It's heaps of pressure in the schoolwork. I've had enough.'**
> *Carly, 16*

WORLDS THAT JUST DON'T MEET

There's an extremely fine, but important, line between encouraging girls and pushing them too hard. What teen girls aspire to and what their parents want for them has always created tension. It's a natural part of growing up. What is new for this generation of girls, however, is the immense power marketers and pop culture have on almost every aspect of their lives. As we'll see, the values and goals marketers promote are often contrary to everything parents and teachers want for girls. Until parents are aware of the full impact of these many pressures, it's hard for them to give their girls the support they need.

'Adults don't understand enough about teen life and what's going on. They need to have a deeper understanding, and to talk to girls. See the differences and appreciate them. It's better to take a positive attitude to changes.' *Alana, 18*

Teen girls are acutely aware their world is different from when their parents were teenagers – something most parents don't seem to get, according to girls. This makes girls extremely sceptical about how much parents can help. 'We need more awareness (of our issues), and perhaps people younger, like closer in age to us, telling us about it too, because you get like someone older saying something to you, and you think they don't understand at all 'cos it's so different,' Missy, 15, told me. Ashlee, also 15, agreed. 'Everybody's getting jobs, getting their licences, getting boy/girlfriends, getting into drugs, if that's their thing – developing their own life. We can't really compare lives anymore.' These comments were echoed repeatedly. 'I love it when they try to relate,' said Sandi, 14, with a wry smile, 'because no matter how hard they try they won't. They can relate to a certain level and no more, so just relax.'

'I reckon we have like heaps more pressure than our parents – in basically anything like getting a job, making money, doing well at school.' *Carly, 16*

It was also interesting to see how hard it was for teens to grasp how things were for their parents as teens, because their world is so different. 'It's hard for us to understand about what happened in the past,' said Alana, 18. 'I don't know what's changed, because I wasn't around.' Teen girls are very aware they will be inheriting a planet with its fair share of issues. That's partly why want to be listened to. 'We don't want to be seen as young,' Ashlee, 15, pointed out. 'We want to be seen as adults, not as kids any more. We want our opinions to be heard. I think sometimes adults should look to teens, because they're going to be the adults of tomorrow.'

These girls have a point. There's no doubt adults have more life experience, but our girls do have technical know-how. Instead of fighting for control, we need to find ways to include girls more by helping them to discover solutions to problems that are presently beyond us. By focusing girls on their strengths, we help them participate in constructing the kind of future we all hope for. This is already happening in community projects to combat the effects of climate change, for example. By acknowledging girls' strengths and mobilising them for the wider good, girls get the kudos and sense of belonging they so crave.

MOTHERS TREADING LIGHTLY

Mothers also have a central role to play in helping girls find their way. Sometimes, without meaning to, mothers can push too hard in an effort to encourage their daughters grasp the opportunities denied to previous generations of women. The best way to support their girls is to help them discover what *they* want to do. For most girls this won't necessarily be one or two fixed goals, but several aspirations, which will evolve over time. This means supporting girls through a number of transitions, and helping them realise there's bound to be a few failures on the way.

> Underneath their attitude are little girls trying desperately hard to grow up.

While girls do still need guidance, the girls I spoke with felt parents frequently overdid it. It's also important for parents to know that while teen girls don't want to fail them, their relationships with peers are central. If pushed too hard these girls may well side with their peers. Though more mature than younger girls, teenage girls are exquisitely sensitive about their friends and family, and about who they are and where they're heading. They are naturally drawn to their peers, because they want to belong, and because their friends understand them — they're battling the same issues, and often they're more available than parents. 'If I say "everyone else is allowed out", and you turn around and say "you're not everyone else", I have to kind of relate to everyone else,' said Sandi, 14. 'I *need* to be the same. I *have* to have the same options.' Girls don't want to be left out. They also have a different perspective on what is and is not fair. Good parents will take the time to listen as well as explain.

TEENS DO CARE ABOUT WHAT PARENTS THINK

While girls may seem super-cool, parents must never take them at face value. Underneath all their attitude are little girls trying desperately hard to grow up. Girls want their parents to be proud of them, and are frustrated when they're not. 'Adults don't get it,' Whitney, 18, explained. 'Compared to kids my age, they are much more conservative, so we disappoint them because we don't live up to their standards with good manners and stuff. But it was never going to be the same, because of the years we were brought up, compared to the Fifties and Sixties.' It's a difficult balancing act for girls and their parents, but once parents can appreciate where their girls are coming from, it will help them approach their daughters' hopes and concerns with greater understanding.

As our girls now inhabit a complex landscape of choices and expectations, more than anything they need active encouragement from their parents to develop their unique sense of self, beyond the shallow representations of girls seen in the media. Once girls start to understand who they are and what qualities they need to thrive, it is much easier for them to make career and other choices that are right for them.

Material girls

When Madonna's single 'Material Girl' was released, it celebrated the affluence women had long struggled for. Now, over twenty-five years later, there's a new generation of material girls who have more money and possessions than at any other time in history.[1] Teen girls think a lot about money and what it can buy. With after-school jobs and allowances, these girls now have significant spending power, and when they run out of money it's no big deal as they know how to hassle their parents to make up the shortfall. Traditionally, teenage boys had more money to spend, but now teenage girls appear to have overtaken them.[2] That's why advertisers go to such lengths to capture their attention.

> Teen girls tend to visit shopping centres more than any other age group.

As girls love to shop, shopping centres are their number one destination. Most girls I spoke with visited their local centre once a week, and often spent several hours there. This isn't unusual. Teen girls tend to visit shopping centres more than any other age group, and spend the most time once they are there.[3] The way girls described the centre made it sound like a fantasy world full of all the things they'd ever wanted. 'When I look at the shops I think "I'm going to get that one day", although I know I'm never going to get it, I'm never going to afford it, because it's like $100 for a pair of jeans. But I like thinking I'm going to get them,' Sandi, 14, told me. As girls wander around the centre, they lose themselves in shopping, see a movie, or enjoy food and casual conversation with girlfriends.

The shopping centre seems to be one of the few places where the pressure is off for girls. 'It's kind of relaxing to go shopping, to have a walk around and see what's new,' admitted Peta, 16. Even though these teens can't afford most items, it doesn't matter, because they can look at all the things they aspire to. 'I like looking at clothes that I think I'm going to buy,' Evie, 15, explained. 'It's almost something you can look forward to, because when I'm going shopping, I say "I am going to wear that one day and look really good in it," or whatever.'

'Lonely, confused, desperate for social acceptance and popularity, teens are as vulnerable as toddlers, but with ready access to disposable cash. They are an ad man's dream.' *Jason Clarke, Minds at Work*[4]

As the shopping centre is a complete experience in itself, many girls don't want to be anywhere else. 'I personally love going. You can be walking around talking and still shopping at the same time, and seeing the stuff we like,' Joy, 16, told me. 'It's got everything – your movies, a huge food court and everything. We spend a lot of time there. We'd spend two or three hours there a week – a large part of my spare time. It's a pretty big thing.' While it's good there's somewhere for girls to relax and have fun, it's depressing to think shopping centres have become such an integral part of a girl's week. If she takes in a movie, she can easily spend four to five hours there at a time.

> 'I like to go shopping. I just like going out and like window-shopping. You don't have to think about anything, you just wander around. I love accessories and cute girl stuff, and trying them on with my friends. And then I go and eat with my friends. Sometimes I spend whole days out there.' *Ashlee, 15*

HOOKING GIRLS IN

When you look at what girls buy, clothes top the list, followed by shoes, CDs or recorded music, food, soft drinks, lollies and magazines.[5] Teen magazines help girls along with endless suggestions of what to purchase, from sunglasses to shampoo. The editorial in magazines is loaded. Girls are encouraged to 'dress to impress', 'raise the stakes', 'get out there and kick butt'. There's page after page of hype.

'You know what the hottest things are, because it's everywhere,' Joy, 16, told me. 'But then it changes so quickly, that sometimes you don't bother catching on to it, because you know it's going to change so quickly – especially if it's heaps expensive. Then you don't bother, because you know in a couple of months it's not going to matter anyway.'

Millions are invested annually on marketing campaigns for companies to build a rapport with teen girls, because this helps capture the brand loyalty of a whole new generation. Magazines are central to helping advertisers build this loyalty. One of the first things that hits you when you pick up teen magazines is the number of ads and advertorials, carefully crafted to look like helpful hints from a girlfriend. 'Relationship marketing' is the name of the game, because a personal relationship with potential customers can reap huge rewards. That's why every other ad offers giveaways, or invites teen girls to SMS or email their comments and ideas.

FEEDING THE BOTTOM LINE

That said, marketing to teen girls isn't easy, as there's so much for girls to choose from. It is worth a fortune, however, for those who get it right. Almost every aspect of a girl's life is up for scrutiny, if not for sale. Companies are now using a whole range of experts from animators to child psychologists to secure their share of this lucrative market. Some parents even allow cultural anthropologists access to their daughters' bedrooms. Here they take careful note of the posters girls put on their walls, what make-up they use, and what they have on their shelves and drawers. Others pay kids to spy on their peers and report back on what's cool and what's not.

> 'I spend my spare time working. Everyone my age is trying to get a job. You want a job to have money to go out. We just want to be able to go out and like be able to shop.' *Evie, 15*

Chat rooms and viral marketing are all part of this multi-million-dollar game. Mobile phone marketing is now on the rise. Increasingly retailers are contacting girls directly, offering them everything from coupons to the chance to enter competitions in magazines, on TV shows and through their mobile phones. Vulnerable teens are no match for this level of expertise, or the brilliantly executed campaigns directed at them. Keen to expand its teen market, Virgin Mobile placed ads in teen magazines with a tear-out phone. Girls could then use these cut-out phones to pressure parents into buying them a mobile phone. The genius of this campaign was that when girls got their parents' approval, there was no question of which phone to purchase.

> 'There's a lot of like cool kind of ads, for like cool brands that you cut out and stick up on the wall, like it's really good.' *Joy, 16*

Girls are continually recruited in the most seductive ways to promote brands to their peers. A recent 'Clean and Clear' ad opened with the slogan, 'Wanna Be the Next Beauty Reporters?' The winning girls got the chance to hang out on the streets and talk to girls about 'real skin issues', interview experts and specialists, and 'star' in the 'Clean and Clear' campaign.[6] One Vera Wang ad I came across looked more like a talent contest, with its search for a 'modern-day princess' who got to wear the Vera Wang crown. In this ad girls were also encouraged to access downloadable freebies on Vera Wang's website, from computer wallpaper 'fit for a princess' and a royal MySpace template, to instant message icons.[7]

'They have ads of how you should dress and what you should look like and this and that, and then they say, "But respect people for what they choose to be like." Okay, so which do we do first?'
Kelsey, 16[8]

No-one wants to lock teen girls away, or deny them access to a wealth of experiences, but the chance for teen girls to be themselves is constantly eroded by the enormous pressure our consumer culture places on them. Every time girls turn on the TV or pick up a magazine, they are exposed to carefully packaged examples of how they should look, think and behave. Now everything, from what they wear to what they drink, makes a statement about who they are. And as what is cool changes constantly, teen girls need to be continually on the case, so they don't get left behind. 'I have like heaps of clothes,' said Chelsea, 18, 'but when I look at them, I don't have a lot in fashion, because everything keeps changing. So I need new clothes.'

If we are to turn this addiction to shopping around, girls need to understand what this continual consumption is doing to them and the planet. They also need to understand how special they are, and how much they personally have to contribute, and be actively encouraged to do so at home, at school and in the community.

> 'Fashions change really quickly. Like I'm wearing ski leg jeans, and before it I wouldn't have thought of wearing ski leg jeans until it came out in all the stores, and it was in all the magazines, and everyone was going "Whoah". I can't wear flares any more, it's just not cool. You kind of get sucked in, and you don't realise that you're going to get sucked in with it, and you go, "Okay, I kind of have five pairs of ski leg jeans", as that happens to be the in thing.' *Kiera, 17*

PLAYING THE GAME

Teen girls are very sensitive about how they come across. The girls I spoke with talked about how important it was to have the right look and attitude, watch the same TV shows, and listen to the same music as those in their group. One 16-year-old said that to do anything else was to risk 'social suicide'. It's an uncomfortable world where today you're on top, and tomorrow you're not. To have to project the right image constantly is exhausting, but some teen girls don't see that they have any alternative. In this hothouse environment there is little room for self-expression or discovery, because conformity enables girls to belong.

> 'Girls are down on themselves and their looks. They think "I'm not pretty, I'm fat, I can't not wear make-up because people will see who I really am." They change their personality to fit in with the cool group, because they're admired by everyone.' *Lilly, 13*

It's not just with their peers that girls feel under pressure to have the right look, and do and say the right thing. When they're around adults, teen girls try hard to appear confident, because they are well aware that's what parents and teachers expect. They know they are meant to get out in the world and make things happen, and worry constantly they might fall short of expectations.

BUYING HAPPINESS

Psychologists are concerned about the growing pressure on teens to acquire, because it encourages them to assume they are nothing without possessions. Popularity and happiness can't be bought, but that's what's continually suggested. The need to consume is not only addictive, it diverts girls from their internal lives and robs them of the opportunity to work through their problems.[9] We can't always be the centre of attention or successful, and even when we are, life will still challenge us, but that's not the message girls are getting. Again, the kinds of values promoted in the home also influence how girls see themselves. If parents want girls to behave differently, they need to lead by example.

When we see how confident many girls are, it's easy to forget they are still finding their way. That's why they tend to view teen magazines as texts on how to live, rather than entertainment. Marketers know that girls pay close attention to ads in magazines. That's why teen magazines are full of ads offering premiums, giveaways and other incentives. According to Mintel, a world leader in consumer trends, eight out of ten teens now read magazines.[10] These teens are likely to purchase more in a whole range of areas, including convenience and grocery shops.[11] Basically, the more teens read magazines, the more spending becomes a habit. Teens are doubly attractive to advertisers, because they now influence household buying decisions, especially larger items, such as computers and DVD players. The faster technology changes, the more parents rely on teenagers to research products online. All this focus on spending makes for lifestyles of continual consumption. To turn this around, parents need to show girls there are more meaningful and enjoyable ways to live, by engaging them in the wealth of activities that don't involve shopping.

'It's all about what clothes you wear, what mobile phone you have, what music you're listening to on your iPod, it's everything like that.' *Joy, 16*

It's not that teen girls shouldn't be allowed to spend, but we need to consider how much they are constantly manipulated into doing so. The psychologists hired to work on big-budget campaigns are well versed in the fragilities and aspirations of girls, and help ensure their messages hits home. Like all magazines, teen magazines are there to sell products. I recently met the editor of one high-profile teen magazine, who introduced herself as the person whose job it was to encourage her readers 'to buy useless crap'.

What concerns health professionals is that teen girls are growing up with the assumption that life's challenges can be solved by buying the right products.[12] '"You are not enough" becomes "You are not cool/thin/beautiful enough",' points out Jason Clarke, from think tank Minds at Work. '"You don't have enough" becomes "You don't have enough friends/clothes/technology", and "Everyone is having a much better time than you" refers to the amount of sex/fun/parties you should be having, but never will unless you buy our product.'[13]

SCHOOLS SELLING OUT

It's not just magazines and TV that market to teen girls. Advertising and company sponsorships are now part of school life. This is a perfect arrangement for manufacturers. If they introduce their product to a girl aged 9 or 10, and maintain that exposure, by the age 14 or 15 she is likely to be a loyal brand user.[14] Brand loyalty is worth its weight in gold, because loyal customers are willing to pay higher prices, sample more products, resist competitors' products, and recommend products to their friends.[15] As funding for schools is in short supply, corporate sponsorship has become an attractive, if not vital, option for schools, and a whole range of products now gain a foothold in teen life. While it's hard to get hold of a full list of 'sponsors' in our schools, they include mining companies and car manufacturers. Amway offers high school students work experience and gives lectures in subjects from agriculture to business studies.[16] One international oil company offers 'education and community contributions and sponsorships' as long as they are 'relevant to the company's marketing and retail activities'.[17]

As marketing expert Lindsay Fadner points out to companies eager to reach teens, 'Schools aren't cluttered with advertising, so an advertiser's message is more likely to stand out. What better way to target "future consumers" than in this familiar and trustworthy environment?'[18] However, with these partnerships there's no free ride. One 'free' educational books campaign I came across offered books in exchange for tokens found on the tops of cereal boxes and cereal bar packs.[19]

Sadly, many products that do end up in schools have questionable benefits to pupils. For some years soft drinks have been available in schools, even though they displace the amount of milk and water girls drink. Again, local figures are hard to come by, but in one ten-year study of girls aged 9 to 19 in the US, the consumption of soft drinks by these girls increased threefold as the study progressed.[20] The more soft drinks girls have, the more vulnerable they are to obesity and tooth decay.[21]

In the United States M&Ms have been incorporated into some maths lessons. Now there are even M&M maths teaching modules. In one exercise pupils were asked to construct a 'candygraph' that 'melts in your mouth not on your graph'. Pupils were encouraged to 'Count and sort M&Ms by color. Record the data on a chart, nibbling as you go.' If you're a manufacturer it doesn't get much better than this.[22] One educational consultancy which promotes marketing to schools actively encourages clients to seize this opportunity, because it comes 'at a time when other marketing disciplines are under close scrutiny'.[23] So, while teen girls are struggling to discover who they are and what to do with their lives, marketers are busy dreaming up yet another irresistible campaign to tease what money girls have out of their pockets. If we want this to stop, we need to ensure our schools are properly funded.

GIRLS SELLING THEMSELVES

As almost every part of girls' lives encourages spending, they can hardly be blamed for focusing on their next handbag or pair of shoes. This ache for possessions is having unexpected consequences. Some teen girls are now having sex to fund their expensive tastes. These girls aren't runaways or drug users, they're middle- and upper-class schoolgirls still living at home. Soliciting is easy for girls who have access to the net or a mobile phone.

'The kids I interviewed regularly spoke of luxury brands Gucci and Chloé and Burberry as if they were talking about family and friends.'[24] *Alissa Quart, author*

According to Toyko's Professor Fukutomi, the girls attracted to 'compensated dating' (paid time spent with men that often culminates in sex) tend to be impulsive and lonely, and lack self-restraint.[25] Add to this a sex-saturated culture that places great importance on looks and possessions, and the willingness of some men to prey on young girls, and it's hardly a surprise this is taking place throughout Japan, Taiwan and Korea. In his research Professor Fukutomi found the girls involved in compensated dating were highly influenced by the media and peers. They were also well aware of how much they were worth.[26] The 'innocent' schoolgirl is high currency in Japan. Assignations are set up via the net or mobile phone, and girls screen prospective clients on video-display mobile. They have sex where it's convenient. Legislation has been passed in Japan to deal with this problem, but it hasn't gone away.[27]

Teen soliciting isn't only happening in Japan. When the University of Pennsylvania's Professor Richard Estes conducted a three-year study into juvenile prostitution in the United States, Canada and Mexico, he was shocked to discover it wasn't limited to homeless or impoverished kids. He came across young people from comfortable backgrounds who were charging adult clients for sex while their parents were out, so they could buy designer clothes and jewellery. The trend is growing so rapidly in the States that the FBI are now targeting over a dozen cities where this problem is most apparent.[28] As far as the girls involved are concerned, sex is a purely commercial transaction.[29] They deliberately choose well-dressed guys, because they know they will pay good money. Once they're done, these girls return home and behave as if nothing has happened. Not even best friends are let in on the secret.

'I know a girl who had anal sex for a Louis Vuitton bag.' *Dell, 18*

There's nothing liberating about a girl selling her body for branded products. When we allow girls to think they're nothing unless they're wearing this season's clothes and cool accessories, we stop them developing their unique sense of self. If we are to reverse this damaging trend, teen girls need to be more media-savvy. They also need to be aware that cheap clothes are made possible by exploiting underprivileged workers at home and overseas. If our girls are made more aware of the need for fair trade practices, then perhaps they will be less vulnerable to the need to consume continually.

Addiction to shopping begins long before the teenage years. How often a family shops, and the degree to which shopping is a leisure activity, influences a teenage girl's attitude to consumption. Naturally girls want to experiment with clothes as part of their wider identity. Teaching girls the joy of vintage clothes and accessories, for example, helps break the influence of marketers and promotes recycling. Inspiring girls to rework vintage items helps get their creative juices going, and allows their self-expression to come to the fore. Having a 'one-in-one-out' policy also promotes recycling and consumption awareness. If every time they buy a dress or a top they have to get rid of a piece of clothing, it helps them be more conscious of what they have and need. Encouraging girls to be more discerning about trends – to be more individual – and to make long-term purchasing decisions about clothes liberates them from being fashion slaves. Learning to sew, alter and mend their clothes can be a great creative outlet – for example, discovering how new buttons or simple beading can transform a jacket helps girls to develop their own style. As adults we also need to be as smart as advertisers, and give girls good scripts to combat the pressure to consume. The ways girls can express who they are is limitless. It's important we find relevant and inspiring ways to communicate this to them, so they don't derive their sense of worth from a dress or a handbag.

Make-over mania

Teenaged girls are more conscious of how they look now than perhaps at any other time in history. Every day of the week they are exposed to ads, sitcoms and the lives of celebrities, which constantly reinforce the message that image is everything. This pressure to conform to an ever-narrowing definition of beauty makes it hard for girls to value themselves for who *they* are. 'The normal pressures like being thin and having the right clothes, and things like that, these are huge for teenage girls. Personally it's quite a big thing,' said Joy, 16. Carly, also 16, agreed. 'We all judge each other heaps. Looks are really important.'

'Everybody wants to look better than they are, have a boyfriend, a better body. It goes with puberty and stuff. We're obsessed with having bigger boobs, a better body, better hair.' *Lilly, 13*

In their desperation to have the 'perfect figure', some teen girls are resorting to surgical procedures. Eager to make over their bodies, they have plenty of options, from breast enhancement, tummy tucks and chin implants to nose reduction and liposuction. Girls no longer have to wait to talk to a professional about whether surgery is a good idea as they can 'window shop' online. Many sites make procedures sound so straight-forward it doesn't seem that different from buying a new shirt or pair of shoes. The whole emphasis on these sites is how much better life will be once you've had one or more procedures.

On mybodypart.com, for example, there's even free make-over software where people can rate their bodies. Other sites have galleries where you can put together your own make-over wishlist. One site encourages browsers to 'look good, feel great', and has glamorous photos of busty women with handsome male partners, to emphasise what surgery can do. The first consultation at this clinic is free. Here potential clients have access to everything from payment plans to before-and-after photos.

'The idea of a permanent change to the body – made practically overnight – appeals to adolescents, people who are by definition shifting identity daily.' *Alissa Quart, author*[1]

Combined and/or multiple procedures, such as breast implants and modified noses, are gaining popularity. If a girl is having one procedure, then signing up for another doesn't seem such a big deal. Increasing numbers of parents are 'treating' their daughters to breast implants and liposuction for birthdays and Christmas, or for doing well at school.

MOTHERS AND DAUGHTERS UNDER THE KNIFE

Some mothers and daughters are choosing to undergo procedures together. On one website a prominent plastic surgeon invites browsers to view his mother/daughter 'transformation picture gallery'.[2] The choice of words is as seductive as the photos. Another site suggests: 'It sounds so much more fun to go under the knife when you have the company of a loved one, so that you can not only share the experience of the surgery itself, but also recover together and then celebrate the results at the same time.'[3]

Traditionally a mother's role was to nourish and protect her daughter, and help her develop a positive and independent sense of self. It's hard to see how sharing plastic surgery achieves this. As a girl reaches adolescence this often coincides with a time when a mother is confronting her own fading sexual appeal. This can be difficult for both to navigate. 'Now when we walk into a room together, all the eyes are on her, and I'm fairly sure no-one notices me. This hasn't been easy to deal with,' Jessica, 45, admitted. 'I want to protect her (my daughter) from attention that I don't think she's ready for, and at the same time I miss the attention myself.'[4]

With plastic surgery now well and truly out of the closet, teen girls are a growing market for cosmetic procedures. Reality TV shows such as *The Swan* and *Extreme Makeover* are perfect advertising vehicles, making surgery look normal, straightforward and risk-free. Perhaps the most disturbing aspect of cosmetic surgery TV is the underlying message that the best way to deal with body issues is to slice away those parts of the body that you don't like, and/or acquire parts that you do. Very little attention is given to the pain and discomfort of surgery, let alone the psychological consequences. With all this exposure to cosmetic surgery, girls can hardly be blamed for believing surgical procedures will solve their hang-ups, and deliver them the love and attention they crave.

'Today's generation of rampant teenage consumers have lived only in the era of supersizing: they know no other. They cannot distinguish between the proper size of breasts, bank accounts, or cola portions.' *Alissa Quart, author*[5]

As more and more celebrities resort to surgery, it doesn't take a huge leap of imagination for teen girls to equate figure enhancement with success. Every day of the week ads and magazine articles reinforce these beliefs. 'You've got to have breasts to be successful,' insisted Jenna Franklin, 15, who made world news when she announced she wanted breast implants for her 16th birthday because 'Every other person you see on television has had implants.'[6]

I WANT WHAT SHE'S GOT

The desire to look like someone else is another disturbing trend amongst teens. In one media survey conducted by Children Now, two out of three girls said they wanted to look like someone on TV. A third of these girls admitted to having 'changed something about their appearance to resemble that character'.[7] Sha, 19, who was featured on reality TV show *I Want a Famous Face*, openly confessed that she went on the show because she longed to look more like Pamela Anderson, and hoped to follow in her footsteps as a Playboy Playmate and actress. Looking back on the experience, she says, 'It was worth it because I love all the attention I have gotten, and it has made me feel so much better about myself.'[8] If we are to reverse this trend we need to find fun and funky ways for girls to celebrate their uniqueness in the media, on the net, at home and at school. Instead of fighting the media, we need to get them on board with campaigns that reward good content.

> **'I used to pray that my boobs would grow. Then I just thought, "What's the point when I can have implants when I want?"'**
> *Jenna, 15*[9]

PSYCHOLOGICAL CONSEQUENCES

When *Bliss* magazine surveyed girls aged 10 to 19, more than a quarter of 14-year-olds admitted to contemplating plastic surgery.[10] Often girls elect surgery in the hope their lives will improve, but as teen cosmetic surgery is relatively new, it's too early to gauge the long-term effects these procedures may have. Even if teen girls do undergo some form of psychological testing before surgery, current tests are not completely accurate because they are based on adult criteria. One long-term study of over 2000 women with breast implants is less than encouraging, as these women proved three times more likely to commit suicide in the immediate years following their surgery.[11]

'I have had problems with my body since I was 8. When I was 8, I thought that I was disgusting, and in writing my letter to Santa (the only way to get presents), I asked him for liposuction,' *Rein, 16*[12]

Experts are also concerned that girls are undergoing surgery while their bodies are still growing. 'Growth charts indicate that the average girl gains weight between the ages of 18 and 21, and that is likely to change her desire or need for breast augmentation as well as liposuction,' pointed out Diana Zuckerman, president of the National Research Center for Women and Families.[13]

The difficulty for today's teenage girls is that they see more beautiful women in a day than their mothers' generation saw during their teens, which then makes ordinary women's bodies seem abnormal.[14] Even beautiful women are frequently unsure of themselves, make bad decisions and spend their lives looking for the right partner, but teen girls don't realise this. They want to be drop-dead gorgeous, as they believe this will make them loved and adored. For girls to instantly and radically change their bodies doesn't teach them how to resolve self-esteem and other issues. TV, magazines and the internet are hardly the ideal reference points for girls considering surgery, but that's where most now go to for advice.[15]

While promoting a culture that celebrates difference may be inconvenient for manufacturers, variety is what makes life interesting. The simple fact is that most of us don't fit the marketers' moulds. Even the briefest study of what constitutes a beautiful woman in different cultures and periods in history would help girls grasp just how subjective and fleeting definitions of beauty are. This, along with a short project to find their own examples of why unconventional-looking women are beautiful, would help consolidate this message. Again this is a question of balancing education for careers with education for life.

Girls also need help in understanding and appreciating the richness of how different we all are, in language and images that appeal to them. Again we need to employ the tools advertisers use – catchy slogans that convey new ways girls can see themselves and others. It's not that hard to come up with ways to celebrate girls of all sizes, from curvylicious girls and perfect pears to girls who are sassy and slim. An ideal way forward would be to launch campaigns for girls to design ads that express these ideas. As there's so much disgust and self-loathing around women's bodies, it's up to women to fight this trend for themselves and for our girls. We can do this through our own attitudes to our bodies and clothes, by the way we talk about ourselves and others, and by encouraging girls and validating them for who they are.

It's in to be thin

It's not just stick-thin models that make girls self-critical. Teen magazines don't help, with page after page of ads featuring glamorous women, and editorials and visuals that examine celebrity hair, make-up, clothes and weight with forensic precision. The content in teen magazines would be laughable if its influence on girls wasn't so tragic. In one issue of *Girl-friend,* described by editor Sarah Oakes as 'a girl's guide to life',[1] readers were invited to vote on whether wearing only one stocking was 'totally fashion forward' or 'residing in skank city'.[2] The same month *Dolly* turned its attention to celebrity fashion 'victims', to who was 'stealing' whose style, and which celebrities had skin breakouts.

'There's too much emphasis on the perfect body and the perfect person, and what is normal.' *Sandi, 14*

Girls devour these details, because they so want to be where it's at. 'I love my magazines because you see celebrities look bad, so it makes you feel better,' Kiera, 17, confessed. As I talked with girls it soon became clear that the relief at seeing their icons under scrutiny is often short-lived,

102

as they struggle to maintain their girlfriends' love and approval by trying to appear cool at all times.

'Talking about people in terms of their looks is wrong, but any insult or bitching match always contains the word "fat".' *Mandy, 16*

Whether it's a trip to the movies or the shops, or a night out at a party, every detail is carefully thought through, because girls know what is likely to happen if they get something about their presentation wrong. This pressure is constant throughout their teen years, forcing girls to use every trick in the book to stay ahead of the pack. 'If you had a friend who was a bit fat and a bit uncool, you'd kind of feel better about yourself,' Joy, 16, admitted. 'And sometimes you might spend extra time with them because it made you feel good.'

THE IMPACT OF MAGAZINES

Links have now been made between the representation of thin models in magazines and eating disorders. In one study, the teenage girls who watched TV ads with skinny models were less confident and happy with their bodies than girls not exposed to these ads. Those who spent the most time and effort on their appearance had the least confidence.[3] The whole basis of advertising is to highlight people's inadequacies so they'll buy the products that promise them they'll feel better. It's interesting to learn that many eating disorder clinics won't allow glossy magazines in their waiting rooms, because of the negative effect they have on girls.

GIRLS UNAWARE OF THEIR REAL WEIGHT

Not only are girls obsessed with their looks, they can't accurately gauge their weight. Studies show that on average girls see themselves almost 5 kilos heavier than they are, which only makes the situation worse.[4] 'I've always considered myself fatter than my friends, whether it's true or not. I always go "I think I'm larger than her", but my weight is almost the same as theirs and sometimes I'm even lighter than them. I can't see myself in the mirror for a long time now. My views are totally distorted,' confesses one girl on her website.[5] It's important girls overcome their negative sense of self. If they don't it can lead to poor eating habits, drug and alcohol abuse, and mental health problems.[6]

This deep unhappiness girls have with their bodies comes at a time when models weigh 23 per cent less than the average woman. Only 7 per cent of today's young women between 18 and 34 are naturally likely to be as slim as a catwalk model, and a staggering 1 per cent are naturally as thin as a supermodel.[7] 'Our anxieties are very much about body image,' Whitney, 18, confessed. 'We have just been plastered with it through pop culture. There's so many kids with eating disorders, and it's happening so young. Even skinny, fit girls are down on themselves.'

One of the worst aspects of this obsession with looking perfect is that no-one ends up happy with how they look. Thankfully, not all girls are uncomfortable with themselves, and some have their own take on body image. 'I'm sick of telling healthy, attractive people that they are both healthy and attractive. I'm sick of offering out tissues because someone's gone up a clothes size,' complained Bea, 16. 'And I'm particularly sick of hearing about another f***ing diet which is going to be as ineffectual and pointless as the last one.'

The constant focus in magazines on getting into shape for the beach, for love, and for parties increases this pressure to be perfect. Many of the girls I spoke with have absorbed the messages about how they should look so thoroughly that they no longer recognised their need to be thin as an external pressure. 'It's more like you feel bad yourself,' Joy, 16, told me. 'It's not other people around trying to make you feel like that, but you look around and you see other girls, and you put that pressure on yourself. You see girls that are already skinny and already have like all the clothes that you want, and you look at them and you think,

"That's what I want."' Girls need to know where this pressure is coming from, and that the only reason they're being put under pressure is to manipulate them to buy. They need to be able to look at ads and advertorials and know what exactly is going on in the ads.

> '**I remember standing in front of the mirror as a small 5-year-old child, thinking that I was far too heavy. I started to diet at 6. I would eat nothing but fruit for several days, and then I would become "weak" and eat. My mother was dealing with her own eating issues at the time, and decided that not allowing food with fat to be in the house was the way to go.'** *Allegra*[8]

HOW PARENTS INFLUENCE HOW GIRLS SEE THEMSELVES

While teen body issues are fuelled in part by anorexic models and skinny celebrities, studies show that girls are also influenced by the way their mothers view their own bodies. In one 2000 survey by *Bliss* magazine of girls aged 10 to 19 with eating disorders, 90 per cent said their mother was insecure about her body.[9] Constant talk about weight and fad diets rubs off on girls. Expert in women's body attitudes Dr Jenny O'Dea agrees. 'It is essential that a mother realises that her words and actions influence her daughters — even from as young as 6 years old,' she advises.[10] Whether or not teenage girls show it, they still want their mother's love and approval.

No matter how confident teen girls seem, they are exquisitely sensitive to the world around them. What other people think about them matters a great deal. Dads also play an important role in how their daughters feel about themselves. If they're always going on about women's bodies, their girls will pick up on these messages, assuming that their bodies are what people will love and value them for. 'Pay attention to how you respond to the media images of sexy, thin women because your daughter is listening,' advises social worker Carleton Kendrick.[11] In spite of the many life choices available to girls, many never get the chance to embrace them, because they become lost in body issues. It's concerning to learn that the distress girls are experiencing around these issues is on the rise. Nicky Bryant from the Eating Disorders Association has seen an 'alarming' increase in callers aged 13 and under now contacting their helpline about eating issues, which she believes is caused by the media's emphasis on 'thin is beautiful'.[12]

This distress affects a girl's ability to embrace new experiences, be spontaneous, chill out and have fun. In one Dove Newspoll, one in four girls aged 10 to 14 preferred not to take part in certain activities, because of their concerns about the way they looked. This figure rose to over a third by the time they were aged 15 to 17.[13] As near-anorexic models dominate billboards and ads in magazines, the line between fantasy and reality has blurred. Girls are now seeing the bodies of real girls as abnormal, and spend every spare moment working on their bodies in the hope they'll look 'right'.

The issue of weight has now permeated almost every area of a girl's life. Even a day at the beach is no longer just about having fun in the sun. As the weather warms, girls worry about looking good on the beach. To reach their desired weight they often resort to crazy exercise regimes, crash diets, taking laxatives and anything else that will help get the weight off. And with magazines filled with bikini diets, and tips and tricks as to how to get this summer's perfect look, who can blame them?

If we are to give girls a strong sense of self as adults, we need to work a lot harder at getting them to appreciate and celebrate the fact that everyone is a different size. We do this best in casual conversations and comments, by celebrating our curves or lack of curves, loving the fact we have small or big breasts, and by making it clear that unhelpful comments about girls' bodies are unacceptable from women and girls, as well as from men. When we see ads that are detrimental to girls we need to make our voices heard. All this is about taking back the ground we have lost to the advertising industry.

Starving for attention

It's tragic that eating disorders are now so prevalent among girls that we now see them as a normal part of teen life. All the girls I spoke with had numerous stories of friends and classmates suffering from problems with food. These disorders not only rob girls of precious years of their lives, they can be lethal. Of all psychiatric disorders, anorexia has the highest mortality rate, as these girls are also very vulnerable to suicide.[1]

'Eating disorders are really quite a common thing, but you kind of get used to it – like that's the way it is.' *Missy, 15*

Bringing girls with eating disorders back from the brink can be a delicate process, because they need huge amounts of support and are susceptible to relapses, especially in their first year. One risk to recovering anorexics and bulimics are the pro-ana (pro-anorexia) and pro-mia (pro-bulimia) websites, created by other girls suffering these disorders. These sites give vulnerable girls the acceptance, belonging, and 'thin-spiration' they crave as Helen, a recovering anorexic, explains. 'If you visit (these sites) on a regular basis, you can start to feel like you belong to an elite club – especially since, by nature, anorexia is a lonely disorder. It becomes a competition of sorts – who can be thinner? Being the thinnest translates into being the best, and anorexics want to be the best at being anorexic at all costs.'[2]

Even websites that seem supportive can be dangerous for recovering girls, as they focus on the very issues they're trying hard to overcome.[3] A recent Stanford study indicated that girls who visit pro-eating-disorder sites are slower to recover than those who stay away from them.[4] Most worrying for parents and therapists is the way the web provides vulnerable girls with immediate, private access to an international community of girls suffering eating disorders, who spend their time spilling out their pain, anger and confusion to anyone who will listen. Girls do need to express how they're feeling – especially when they're in crisis. The problem with these forums is that there are no balancing views.

'Intake . . . B-NOTHING!! L-Fat free mushroom soup & an apple. EDIT!! D-Salad and fat free cottage cheese. BLAH BLAH BLAH BLAH BLAH BLAH!! Work out = 500 sit ups, 200 hip crunches, Dance 30 mins.' *TinyxTinks*[5]

EXTREME EMOTIONS

Pro-ana and pro-mia sites regard eating disorders as a positive choice, and emaciation the highest form of beauty. These girls don't want intervention. The lengths to which they will go to achieve and maintain their condition indicates how much self-disgust they struggle with. Pro-ana girls celebrate their weight loss on their websites with arty photos of emaciation and pain-filled poetry. Here emotions run high as they talk openly about their self-loathing and intense anger at parents attempting to monitor them, as well as their massive insecurities about their bodies. 'I hate everything about myself. EVERYTHING . . . I'll do anything to be thin. ANYTHING . . . .', says Amber.[6]

'If you don't like it then leave. This is our lifestyle and our choice. Yelling at me isn't going to solve anything. But if you really need to yell and be mad, go to therapy and leave me alone.' *Angelica*[7]

There are frequent online discussions with fellow sufferers about the value of one weight loss program over another. Mainstream diets are viewed with derision, because they're not regarded as serious diets. Pro-ana and pro-mia girls pride themselves on their ability to go without food. One website banner reads 'Respect yourself, put down the fork.'[8] Another says, 'I will achieve what I mean to achieve, whatever the consequences, whatever the cost.'[9] Yet another states, 'Hunger hurts, but starving works.'[10] These girls live on the edge. 'I have the willpower – I really think I could starve to death . . . if I let it go that far,' confessed Emily, 19. 'I am really tired of reading posts by all these weaklings. "I ate sooo much today. I am sooo fat." Isn't there anyone out there as strong as I am?'[11]

PASSING THEIR TIME

On 'Ana's Underground Grotto' there's a Starving for Perfections award, and a ritual for anas to celebrate their emaciation. 'Break open a couple Dexatrim capsules, or Xenadrine or whatever your thermogenic of choice is, burn it to Anamadim or dissolve it in a chalice (goblet) full of pure water (we all know water is our friend, right?) and offer it as a libation . . . If you are not too squeamish to do so, sign your pact in blood.'[12]

One of the main preoccupations of anorexic and bulimic girls is distracting themselves from food. The busier they are, the less they're likely to think about food. There are tips on how to handle this and other challenges that may tempt girls to eat. 'Clean something – your room, the toilet, your car, dog, cat, fishtank, garbage bin. The dirtier the better!!' Pippa, 16, advised. 'You will hopefully feel too repulsive to eat. THEN – take a shower and get nice and clean. Now you're too clean to sully with nasty food!!'[13] Ana websites include diary entries, details of daily food intake and exercise, photos of painfully thin girls, and tips on how to live on just a few calories a day. 'Today I have had ovaltine made with water (80 cals), a pickle (4 cals), and a dum dum (30 cals) and I rode my bike for at least 10 miles this morning. I don't want to eat anything else today. If I do, it will be a salad or something equally unsubstantial,' says WhiteNailPolish, who describes herself as 'never being good enough'.

'After binging on a fruit slice i feel stoopid and guilty, but i'll work it off in the ex class-thank god they're back on,' *pink_sparklygurl*[14]

These girls are often well informed about their condition, and have worked out their own ways to get around the resulting issues they face. 'Rinse your mouth out well immediately after purging. If you rinse with bicarbonate of soda or chew an antacid tablet immediately after purging it might help a little,' suggests Pippa, 16. When girls visit these sites they learn new ways to maintain their anorexia or bulimia, and how best to get around their parents and therapists.[15] Some sites include a gallery of photos of their ideal models, but there's no mention of Ana Carolina Reston, the anorexic 21-year-old Brazilian model who died of organ failure, or Uruguayan model Luisel Ramos, who lost her life due to heart failure.

'Hey everyone . . . im starting a week-long fast 2–8 feel free to join me!! id love some other ppl to do it with me . . . and just send me an IM or anything. Hope to here from a couple others?' *Whiteraven*[16]

It's hard to appreciate just how dark a space many of these girls have reached, until you hear what sufferers have to say. 'Anorexia robbed me of my ability to embrace life. It destroyed my relationships with family and friends and snatched away my dreams for the future. My world became a black hole of uncertainty and fear where self-loathing only served to drive me deeper into my illness. My lonely, painful existence was all I knew,' writer Melinda Hutchings told me.

'What exercise do u do that u love? cause i hate hate hate exercising, but if any of you guys have something that really works for u and ur seeing the results that make u happy, PLEASE SHARE,' *trying2bher*[17]

Anorexia is destructive for too many teen girls, who are trying hard to be perfect in every way. Unless parents understand and respect the often intense pressure girls are under to be perfect, no matter what, it can end up blighting precious years of their lives. Girls need to know that no-one is perfect, and that they're loved for who they are intrinsically. This message needs to be clear in the values promoted at home and in family conversations.

Control is a significant part of the anorexic mindset. The teenage years are stretching for almost everyone, and girls who become anorexic often feel their bodies are the only thing they have some control over. When parents realise this, with professional help they can work gently and positively to help their daughter overcome her sense of helplessness and develop her unique sense of self.

MOTHERS CAN HELP

Mothers play a major role in helping girls with their self-esteem. Bella,15, who has struggled with weight issues due to her medication, feels totally supported by her mother, and has a positive sense of self as a result. 'My mum is more like a sister – I can talk to her about anything, and it's not like a typical mum, like she is really good and she helps me with my weight,' Bella,15, told me. 'Like I've been an asthmatic my whole life – when I was 4 I stopped breathing. She had to take me to hospital and they put me on steroids for three years, so that like obviously it made me quite big. But ever since that she's been taking me to a dietitian. She goes running with me and whatever. She's one of my best friends just because of what she does, and not because she's my mum.'

As many psychologists are at pains to remind us, eating and related disorders are not normal. It helps parents to know that alongside eating disorders, their daughter may also be suffering from problems such as anxiety, depression or substance abuse. The good news is that eating disorders are treatable. It's important parents seek good professional advice as early as possible, because these disorders can cause other health problems, including heart problems and kidney failure. While girls with eating disorders often deny they have a problem and may resist getting treatment, parents must call on expert assistance.[18] Teen years can be trying for girls and their parents. Girls need genuine support that speaks to *their* concerns in ways that are meaningful to them. Respect and trust are central, if they're going to make their transition into adulthood with greater ease.

The first cut

As the self-hatred in girls grows, so too do the ways in which they express it. The number of teen girls who resort to self-injury has increased so much that cutting has been labelled the new anorexia. Psychologist Lisa Machoian goes so far as to describe teen girls self-harming as a 'contagion'.[1] While it's hard to know exactly how many girls are cutting themselves, because they do so in secret, it is now estimated that one in ten do so. My interviews bore this out. 'There is a stereotype like if she doesn't have anything on her wrists then she's fine – wrong! And girls will say that she doesn't have problems, she's making it up, but you don't know,' Sandi, 14, told me.

'I'd never seen cutting widespread till the 2000s. The media's got a lot to answer for with this. Then kids think, "Oh well, that's something to do."' *Rose, psychologist and school counsellor*

The girls I spoke with talked about self-harm as if it were a natural part of teen life. 'One of my really good friends used to sit at lunchtime and cut herself with a tuna tin lid, and scissors and everything like that,' said Missy, 15, adding, 'but she's so much happier now, it's a kind of maturity thing.' Evie, also 15, described how one of the girls in her year used to cut herself on her thighs so her parents wouldn't know what she was doing. When I asked Sandi, 14, why girls hurt themselves, she said, 'At our age you want to hurt yourself, you want that dress in the window, you want what she has, you want that pair of shoes, you want your mum to be like that.'

> **'At my school there's probably 50 per cent are cutting themselves. Not many of them show it. It's really sad. It's your mood swings. You're getting pressure from your family, fights with friends, then you think it's all your fault.'** Lilly, 13

CUTTING HAS BECOME THE THING TO DO

The tragedy is that the more normal self-harm appears, the more prevalent it becomes. 'I've never cut myself, but my best friend's cut me a few times 'cos she was angry, but I said she could because her body's already covered in scars. I just thought it would be the best thing to do,' confessed Tanya, 16.

> **'Scars in interesting places, or with interesting stories behind them are by far the sexiest. Consider making up some unbelievable stories to go along with your scars. See who will fall for them, and who will fall for you because of them.'** Karia[2]

Curious girls don't have to venture far to learn more about self-mutilation. There's plenty of material on the net. Here girls can read about the intimate details of celebrity self-mutilators from Princess Diana to Courtney Love. If they didn't know it already they'll discover how Christina Ricci used to burn herself with a cigarette, and how Angelina Jolie, also a cutter, wore a shirt with her first husband's name written in her blood to their wedding. Should girls log on to such sites as self-injury.net, they'll have access to everything from a 'gallery of pain' to lurid diary entries of self-harmers, the youngest of whom began hurting themselves at 4.

> **'Cutting was a big thing with girls 13 and 14. To me it now seems like a young girl's thing. I think in a way it's wanting attention, and maybe perhaps they feel like they're letting stuff out when they bleed.'** *Whitney, 18*

GIRLS ARE FAR MORE LIKELY TO SELF-INJURE

Boys are also known to harm themselves, but in far smaller numbers. One major study of students aged 15 and 16 revealed that girls were four times more likely to self-injure.[3] While girls who self-injure tend to cut themselves, some also resort to overdosing, burning or bruising themselves, pulling out their hair or picking at their skin and sores so they won't heal. Others break their bones, especially their fingers.

Often parents have no idea of this, because girls are careful to cover their injuries. Wearing long-sleeved tops and long pants on hot days may be cause for concern. 'I do have one friend who cuts herself,' admitted Ashlee, 15. 'She was wearing a long shirt and it was a humungously hot day. She was still hiding her scars even though the scars are almost gone. I think a lot of it is their home life. My friend's parents were divorcing – she just couldn't do it anymore. Girls do it 'cos they need something to get their mind off what's happening.'

The girls who cut themselves use a whole range of tools from razors and knives, to scissors and glass, or whatever they can find. They dress carefully to hide their mutilation. When asked why they self-injure, they talk about relieving their emotional pain, which ranges from depression and anxiety, to other overwhelming feelings. 'I did it. Like clockwork.

Every night before I went to sleep. Right across my arms, my legs and my stomach. I'd put on some loud music and just cry while I was thinking, "It's my own fault I'm how I am I should punish myself." But I wasn't doing anything about how I felt. All I was doing was creating ugly scars which made me look like a psycho,' admitted Mia, 17. 'There's a lot of cutting,' agreed Barbara, a child psychologist. 'I see it is as a release mechanism, also frustration. There's also a lot of copying. I was working with a young girl the other day. Girls were talking about it, so she thought she'd try it. It's almost like a badge of honour. They've heard how kids use this to get rid of angst.'

> **'Expanses of warm skin and a half-smoked cigarette glowing at my fingertips. It's not such a big step. The thrill of a new sensation, something you can do to yourself. An imprint, a stamp of possession. This is my body, here is proof.'** *Stand/alone/bitch*[4]

Self-harm often starts at around puberty, and girls from middle- and upper-class homes who lack self-esteem seem to be most at risk. Most have average to above-average intelligence, and just under half talk of experiencing physical and/or sexual abuse. Almost all feel unable to express their emotions, especially sadness, grief and anger.[5] 'Every now and again sometimes I get so angry or upset I get carried away with my own self-pity,' Sass, 17, confessed.

> **'I self-injured, starting at around 13, but only causing serious damage much later. Cut myself, burned myself (heat or chemical, either). I will always have the scars. I have stopped, but I still want to, regularly, when I'm sad enough or scared enough, or having trouble coping with how I am doing.'** *Wolfa*[6]

THE EMO CONNECTION

When I asked teen girls why friends and schoolmates cut themselves, a number said girls were influenced by the lyrics of emo music. 'Emo is probably the biggest thing of our generation, it's a more subtle version of goth, and it's really emotional, and it's gotten really big. A lot of them now say, "My life's so bad".' Sandi, 14, told me. Evie, 15, agreed, 'There was another girl who was right into the emo music, like real emotional music, very heavy and depressing, and as soon as she went with that (emo) crowd she starting cutting herself. And now there's the stereotype emo is cutting yourself. So many people I know have done it — probably around ten or eleven girls in my year alone, which is 119 girls.'

'There's a lot of people who are unhappy in our generation – a lot of people. Even guys are hurting themselves. I think it's changed because they have heavy emo music which is like "cut yourself", whereas that was never around. Cutting is a big thing.' *Evie, 15*

Full-blown emos are easy to spot with their red and black clothes, and ragged fringes worn on one side. Emos are not afraid of expressing their emotions, and are proud of their ability to cry. How much emo music, with its emotional lyrics, influences teen girls to harm themselves is hard to gauge. Professor Graham Martin, director of child and adolescent psychiatry at the University of Queensland, suggests the link between emo music and cutting is more likely to be because young people tend to seek out the music that matches their emotions.[7]

However, the teen girls I spoke with saw a clear connection between emo music and cutting. 'There's a lot of people who are unhappy in our generation – a lot of people. Even guys are hurting themselves. I think it's changed because they have heavy emo music which is like "cut yourself", whereas that was never around. Cutting is a big thing.' Evie, 15, told me. Whether or not this is the case, should a girl be heavily into the emo culture and has withdrawn from the family, it may suggest she's struggling with painful issues that could benefit from professional assistance.

CUTTING HELPS GIRLS FEEL IN CONTROL

Self-harm gives vulnerable girls a fleeting sense of control. These girls talk about its soothing effects, and how it helps them feel alive. 'I cut myself because I feel so much pain inside that I need a way to release it all,' admitted Chrissy, 17. 'So by cutting myself, it acts as an outlet for that pain, I guess, somehow.' For Alicia, now 17, it was peer group pressure that tipped the balance. 'I'd get made fun of for being smart. Getting As on tests. Stuff like that. It was devastating.' The first time she cut herself Alicia felt an immediate sense of relief. 'I remembered just having kind of this euphoric, everything's OK.'

'When I got angry with myself, I would scratch myself. I would scratch my legs and my arms, just to inflict pain on my body. Cause it was easier for me to deal with that than with the emotional pain. That was just punishment for myself.' *Sanne, 16*[8]

It's hard to get girls to talk in detail about their self-harm, except on the net, where there is no shortage of 'confessional' sites. 'I started self-mutilating when I was 5 years old. I'm not sure how it started, but I consistently pulled my eyelashes out all through the year,' admits Kandy, 16. It wasn't until her early teens that she began cutting. 'I started cutting my left wrist . . . I didn't get stitches, but I did get a large bandage on my wrist for a while . . . After that, I found my knife had disappeared mysteriously from my drawer and so then I played with a pin, making boat designs and smiley faces on . . . my arms.'

While self-harmers consistently mutilate themselves, their injuries don't tend to be life-threatening. Left unchecked, however, cutting is often linked with eating disorders and substance abuse. There's a lot yet to learn about cutting. While the girls who cut are not necessarily sui-cidal, cutting is their way of coping. Feeling pain, or seeing their blood flow, is often calming for them. Some experts suggest the relief comes from the rush of endorphins through the body caused by cutting.

When girls are cutting, normal teen behaviour – mood swings, angry outbursts, loving someone one minute and hating them the next – is often intensified. Finding a professional experienced in dealing with cut-ting is the best approach for parents. When talking with their daughter about getting help, parents are advised to tread gently. As their daughter is possibly feeling out of control, cutting may be the only time she feels remotely in charge of her life. Experts suggest parents broach the sub-ject by acknowledging their daughter is probably feeling distressed, and how hard this must be for her. Once a girl gets professional help, she will be given tools to help her stop cutting. Having positive ways to deal with the urge to cut is important. One girl made sure she was around other people when she was feeling vulnerable, so she couldn't cut her-self. Another would sit down and draw her feelings whenever things got too much.

'In the past five years, I have been concerned to see self-mutilation on the rise – mostly manifested by intentional cutting (usually on the forearm, but it can be anywhere), self-inflicted with a sharp instrument such as a knife blade, razor blade, even the end of a paper clip,' said counsellor Jan Sells. 'Last spring I spoke to a psychologist who works with adolescents . . . who concurred with me that the increase is alarm-ing. This spring it seems to be occurring in epidemic proportions. I hope parents and teachers will start taking a look at their students' arms.'[9] As well as helping girls who are cutting, we need to know why, when girls have so many more choices, they are harming themselves over and over, and in increasing numbers. One of the most important messages girls need is that no-one copes all the time, and that they are not alone.

Why girlfriends matter

Often parents feel frustrated when they try to help their daughters, because what their daughter's girlfriends think and say always seems to come first. Girlfriends are important to teen girls, because they are part of their generation. When these friendships work, they help sustain girls through their teenage years and beyond. With girlfriends, teen girls feel listened to and understood. Together they can dream, push the limits, chill out. One of the reasons girls rely on their peers rather than parents is because they are often more sympathetic and in tune with their concerns. Frequently, they're also more available than parents.

'I love my girlfriends,' said Kiera, 17, 'and I always get that constant support without them judging me. They help you carry your burdens and things like that – all the things that boyfriends can't do. You can call them at any time and tell them, "I need to talk".' Missy, 15, agrees, 'I've probably got eight really close best friends. It's so much fun. Like my best friend, we just like muck up so much. I just love them, and they're always there for you.' Girlfriends help Lilly, 13, keep things together. 'Friends are really important, because it's the bitchiest time of school,' she told me. 'They help back you up, and keep you happy.'

'My friends listen. They get me more than my mum. My mum knows what's best for me, but my friends get me.' *Sara, 18*

This doesn't mean parents are irrelevant, but girls do need to develop a separate identity. It's comforting for girls to feel they belong, especially as they are still coming to grips with who they are. When parents understand this, it's easier for them to be more relaxed about their children's intense friendships. However, parents still need to be vigilant, as the price of friendship for many girls is extremely high.

KEEPING GIRLFRIENDS HAPPY

Girls' friendship groups are tribal, in many ways. Each group has its own distinct identity with preferred music, dress, values and language. There are emos and goths, skaters, blondes, punks, geeks and nerds, the 'popular' group, sporty kids, and the losers, to name but a few. While groups offer girls a sense of belonging, they can also be a major source of angst, as there are often very strict rules about how girls should appear and behave.

'It's all about what clothes you wear, what mobile phone you have, what music you're listening to on your iPod, it's everything like that.' *Joy, 16*

Puberty is an intense time for girls, and is reflected in their complex relationships with each other. 'I went to an all-girls school,' Alana, 18, told me. 'There was a lot of bullying. Lots of cliques — for arty girls, sporty girls and stuff.' As she spoke, there was a real tension in her voice as she recalled past incidents. 'Being part of the group was based around what you had in common. And if you didn't look like what you were supposed to, you were subjected to taunts and bullying. It was a dreadful thing to experience. Even though you have friends around you, it didn't help – you were like on your own.' When they're bullied, often girls feel there's little they can do. 'There's lots of people I wish weren't in my life, like 210 people. I've spent five days a week, most weeks of the five years with,' admitted Air in one teen chat room.[1] Often it's assumed that the pressure on teen girls to look good and wear the right clothes is so boys will take note, but for most girls it's what their girlfriends think that counts. 'I think like a lot of people think girls only worry about boys, but I worry more about what other girls think of me, and I know a lot of girls do,' Evie, 15, admitted. 'Girls judge each other on looks straight away. You cannot like mental music or heavy metal music to be in a certain group, where you have to love it to be in a different group. You never find a group that has this kind of girl and that kind of girl, it's just all the same sort of people.'

'There's a lot of pressure from other girls. You want to fit in. You don't want to be an outsider. It's a lot about how you dress and how you look – you can't be too different.' *Whitney, 18*

Time and again girls told me how they had been ostracised by girl-friends because they were out of step on some minor detail. 'You have the queen bee, and you have the loser,' explained Sandi, 14. '[It works by] judgement, silence – no matter how good or caring your personality is, if you wear the wrong shoes, the wrong hat, they will say the meanest things.' This pressure is constant and touches almost every part of girls' lives. 'Girls want to fit in so much. If someone says they look fat, they won't eat as much,' said Lilly, 13. 'If someone doesn't like their hair, they'll change it. If someone says they talk too much, they won't talk as much. They'll change their attitude, until they think they're perfect.'

It's hard to imagine the stress this must create for girls as they work hard to get every detail right. One girl confessed to watching every episode of *The O.C.*, which she hated, to remain a part of her group. She didn't dare talk about other TV programs she watched, because they hadn't been sanctioned by her girlfriends. Once parents understand the dynamics behind these friendships, they can begin to see why girls can get so worked up about their looks and what they are doing with whom.

KEEPING PARENTS AT A DISTANCE

With their attention focused firmly on what their group expects of them, it doesn't leave girls much time to think about anyone or anything else. This, it appears, is how some girlfriends like it to be. A number of girls admitted to being reluctant to spend time with their parents from the age of 14 up, because they were concerned about what girlfriends might say. 'The pressure is probably not to be that close to your parents,' Joy, 16, told me. 'If you're really close to your parents and enjoy spending time with them, if you say like "I went on a day trip with the family", it's kind of like "That's weird, you should just be out with your friends."' This continual focus on what friends are thinking and feeling allows girls less time to reflect, to be themselves.

> **'There was a lot of girls bullying. Lots of like cliques – for arty girls, sporty girls. It was based around what you had in common. And if you didn't look like what you were supposed to you were subjected to taunts and bullying. It was a dreadful thing to experience, even though you have friends around you.'** *Alana, 18*

Frequently when girls do get rejected, they have no idea why their 'face no longer fits'. All they know is that it's devastating to be rejected. Psychotherapist Judith Asner warns the resulting isolation can make them more vulnerable to mental and physical illness.[2] Studies show that when girls are victimised they do tend to suffer more than boys.[3] It's important we understand this, so we can better appreciate how painful falling out can be, and help support our girls through unhappy times.

Seeing someone expelled from their group may be uncomfortable for the girls who remain. While they mightn't agree, they're unlikely to object in case the same thing happens to them. Expulsion is a powerful reminder to those still in the group that they have to play by the rules. Even the girls left in the group aren't off the hook. They have to continue to work hard to keep up with expectations, and so for many girls life becomes one long struggle to remain popular.

MAGAZINES ENCOURAGE A BITCHY MENTALITY

Bitchiness amongst girls mirrors the catty comments in teen magazines, where whole pages are devoted to taking celebrities apart. In one issue of *Dolly* there are the 'latest thrills, spills and chills inside celebsville'. In the same issue the Dollywood Gossip pages get stuck into Beyoncé, Kimberley Stewart and others for how they look on the dance floor. Nicole Ritchie and Mary-Kate get a black mark for 'scraggly hair', for rarely being seen 'without massive sunnies' and for having 'spent time in rehab'.[4] In this same issue teen readers learn that Christina Aguilera received a generous note from Jessica Simpson. This piece of trivia closes with, 'Maybe Jess could also have popped under her door a few tips of how NOT to let your marriage end in divorce.'[5]

> **'One friend is like so skinny and she thinks she's big, because she used to be friends with the popular group and they like totally put her down, so she stopped eating altogether.'** *Evie, 15*

ON THEIR OWN

Teen life has always been a process of disengaging from parents. The growing power of peer pressure and popular culture is hastening this process, without the safety net that good parenting provides. An important part of girls keeping up with girlfriends is staying constantly in touch through the net or by mobile phone. This endless communication leaves little room for today's teens to move. Until mobile phones, girls were at least able to leave worries about school and girlfriends behind, as there wasn't the same pressure to pick up the home phone if they didn't want to. Now they are accessible to others almost every moment of their lives, which gives them little chance for a wider perspective.

Acutely aware of the social minefield they tread daily, girls work hard on their appearance, clothes and accessories in an attempt to 'get it right'. It's a tricky world where no-one is as they seem. 'Girls judge each other on looks,' Kiera, 17, told me. 'Like as soon as you go to a party and you don't know very many other girls there, normally they won't talk to you. It's kind of like girl cattiness, and so like you kind of have to try to be extra bubbly so they realise you're not a threat or something.'

Keeping girlfriends happy can be a full-time job. 'With girlfriends you kind of have to dress all the same, and you can't really do anything differ-ent. That's why there's a lot of pressure,' explained Whitney, 18. 'If you're shy they say "Why are you shy?", or if you're out there, they say "Why are you out there?"' This was a theme girls spoke about over and over. 'Even if you change, you're still bullied, because you did what they asked without fail, and showed your inferiority,' said Alana, 18, despairingly.

'All this focus on ultra-high achievement at school or being party girls, is just another way girls put people down if you're not like that.' *Georgia, 20*

Teen girls inhabit an uneasy world of shifting alliances, where intim-acies and friendships are traded to stay safe or get ahead. Some of the girls I spoke with were honest enough to admit to their roles as victims and bullies. Most tried to put on a brave face, or found it too painful to go there. The awful thing is that even though they've been treated badly, most teenage girls desperately want to remain friends with the girls who have hurt them. The majority of girls do maintain the friendship, although there's a good chance of being hurt again. The terrible pain of betrayal or rejection wounds girls deeply. It can strip them of what little sense of self they have. Many carry these scars into their adult lives. When talking with women friends about being bullied as teens, the memory of that humiliation is still keen.

GIRLS HURTING GIRLS

It's uncomfortable to admit to the darker aspects of girls' lives, especially girls hurting girls, because we so want to celebrate their potential and the things they do well, but denial doesn't help them move on from destructive behaviour. The lengths to which girls will go to be accepted is exhausting, but what alternatives do they have when faced with social extinction? 'It's a major problem,' explained Evie, 15, 'because I've moved groups in my own school five times, and I've only been at school for three years. It's just because people that dominate groups push people away from them.'

'I think kids have gone backwards. They're into demeaning each other. It's not liberated to be abused and used by others, but that's what they do.' *Rose, psychologist and school counsellor*

Handling the ups and downs of being with girlfriends is so much easier for girls when parents help them gain a clear sense of themselves and what works for them. The stronger a girl's identity, the less likely she is to be pushed around, or overly dependent on friends. Self-confidence, however, takes time, and often there are plenty of bruises on the way. Seeing how parents handle tricky situations helps girls see how they could react. Mistakes can also be valuable, because girls learn that no-one gets it right all the time. Parents do their girls a big favour when they help girls see their blunders in this way.

126

As there's a lot of sensitivity around what girlfriends are up to with whom, parents can help their daughter navigate their way through relationships by showing them positive ways to let friends down gently when they don't want to do something. Teaching girls by example how to be generous about other people's successes and failures is also a great way to give them life skills. And when parents can talk about their own relationship dilemmas in conversation, it helps girls to realise that being around others has its good moments and its challenges.

When girls are encouraged to develop strong boundaries, they are less likely to be drawn into unfortunate situations, and more likely to cope when they do. This is not to say that parents don't ever have to intervene when bullying takes place. They accomplish far more by supporting their daughter to know herself, rather than micro-managing her life, or simply hoping everything will turn out.

As girls become more independent, some parents may feel concerned, resentful or abandoned. Parents are more likely to keep their daughter close by inviting friends into the home, making them welcome, and taking an interest in their lives. This way their daughter isn't asked to choose between her parents and her friends. Naturally, if friends are abusive or dysfunctional, parents must intervene.

Alongside time with girlfriends, parents have the right to insist on family time. When this is handled in a relaxed and inclusive way, girls are more likely to want to be a meaningful part of the family. And if a girl asks parents for time, it's vital that they carve out time to be with their daughter, even if there is a lot going on. Every time parents fail to respond, girls assume they're not interested, and are less likely to turn to them again. One of the best approaches for parents is to establish the kinds of things both they and their daughter enjoy doing – chilling out over a coffee, visiting markets, browsing a specialist poster shop, or painting pottery – and allow these to develop into enjoyable rituals they share. It doesn't matter if there's no deep and meaningful talk;

it's about shared moments of enjoyment, savouring each other's company. It helps if parents discover when and where their girls are most relaxed. When one friend realised her teenage girl was most chatty when they were in the car, she would invite her to come along when she was out and about, doing nothing in particular, and found it worked brilliantly.

While teen girls need to be around girls their own age, they also benefit from good relationships with a range of adults outside their immediate family – wider family, neighbours, family friends. When girls have grown-ups in their lives who have time to listen, empathise and encourage, they have more support and perspectives to draw on. It's also important we teach girls how precious their individuality is, and that differences between girlfriends doesn't have to mean disagreement. What is clear is that our girls need a wider sense of belonging and self-worth than most currently enjoy. They need an engaging, inclusive community that goes beyond their peers and is also there for them round-the-clock.

The bullying thing

As peer pressure grows, so too does bullying. In spite of some excellent initiatives in schools, bullying continues to take new forms. One psychologist I spoke with felt reality TV shows were having a direct impact on the amount of bullying taking place. 'They're about character assassination and chucking people away,' she said. 'Girls do the same through SMS messages and other ways. It's nasty, vindictive stuff, but these shows have made it okay.' Such shows as *Survivor*, *The Biggest Loser*, *Big Brother* and *Pop Idol* dehumanise contestants by exposing and humiliating them. This gruelling, psychologically cruel process pits participants against each other. Sometimes the judges or audience decide who stays and who goes. Sometimes contestants make that decision. It's a world devoid of true friendship, loyalty, sharing or kindness, where personal survival and winning are all that matters. In this environment, participants frequently do appalling things. And recently, *Big Brother* contestant Emma Cornell remained in the show's house, unaware that her father had died and his funeral had gone ahead without her. Reportedly this is what her family wanted. Teenage girls watch these shows and may be forgiven for assuming this is how people should behave in real life.

CULTURE OF CRUELTY

When trying to come to terms with some of the things girls do to each other, it's easy to lose sight of the fact that bullying is about power, and the need some girls have to exert their will over others to ensure they always come out on top. Girls' bullying can be hard for adults to pick up on because the pressure girls exert on each other can be extremely subtle. Unlike boys, girls don't tend to fight in the classroom, and there's normally no blood or broken bones, so their bullying goes largely unchecked. Often the girl bully is smart enough to appear to be an ideal friend or pupil, and to get on with her teachers and other adults.

For the girls the bully preys on, however, it's a very different story. They are acutely and uncomfortably aware of what this Queen Bee is thinking and feeling at any one time. There wasn't a girl I spoke with who didn't voice her concerns at how cruel girls can be. 'I think girls are vicious bullies,' said Ashlee, 15. 'They never come straight out with it.' When I spoke with Peta, 16, she described the experience of being bullied with chilling accuracy. 'It's not like hurting people physically. It's very mental,' she reflected. 'It's very much an emotional, kind of like breaking you down mentally. It does break people down very systematically until there's not much left.' Often girls feel they are in a no-win situation, as Alana, 18, pointed out. 'Even if you change, you're still bullied. Because you did what they asked without fail. Then you're seen as weak, because you showed your inferiority.' Frequently girls cave in, consolidating the bully's power, because they don't have the tools and self-belief to do otherwise.

THE EMOTIONAL PAIN

One of the most poignant accounts of how painful rejection from peers can be is from an online teen, BreeZ33. 'The first time i was ditched i was so upset, but got over it. then i was ditched again and found myself in a state of depression i have 2 take medicine now to keep me happy and barly go outside. You may think that this person caused you trouble, but it really hurts to be removed from someones life. I was recently ditched again and i dont really understand why, but its so painful. people move on but they never forget things, and i never will. I went to therapy for mi depression, and met people, and wen everything was goin good, one of mi new friends tried to kill herself over the fact that people didnt want to be her friend.'[1]

While we're aware that bullying is part of teen life, sometimes it's hard for adults to remember just how horrendous being victimised by peers can be. A long day at the office, or concerns about an elderly parent, can make an incident their child has suffered at school seem hardly worth worrying about. However, peer abuse has the same kind of impact as other forms of abuse.[2] While this is a challenging thought, it does help parents appreciate what their daughter may be going through if she is being bullied.

'I am depressed, actually now,' confessed Linley, also online. 'I have been picked on ever since pre-school, no one really liked me and they still don't. I do have friends, but I feel upset and sorry for them because they are picked on too. That was at my "post-old" school, and when i went to my "old" school last year, i was picked on and physically abused by people there – not sexually. I had no friends at this school, so I was a mute for the rest of the year, and acted fake so people would like me. Now I am at my new school, and I have real friends. Except I am still abused and it hurts because no-one realy likes me. i had hopes for each school, but whats the point? I hate my life.'

This seems to be Cherry's situation also. 'I had two friends who treated me like CRAP!,' she admitted. 'I NEVER thought of them as friends, they were my demons. Everyday I was worried and sick what was going to happen to me. What would they do? They ARE going to rip me up again. And every night after school I would cry, cuz of the horrible way they treated me. And I wouldn't eat, if I did I would get sick.

It's because I was worried SICK! Whenever I was with them, I could feel myself shake! I try telling them that they weren't being nice. They said they wouldn't again, but they DID! THREE years of that.'[3]

Girls do need to learn how to deal with difficult situations, so they can survive as adults, but this isn't an overnight process. Unlike adults, most girls are very dependent on each other. They live and breathe each other's joys, hurts and aspirations. Should they be threatened with expulsion from their group or cast out, this is more than some can bear. Learning to be confident, and how to counter attempts to bully can be a painful journey, albeit a necessary one. This again is why it's so important parents work with their daughter on her self-esteem from a young age.

NEW LEVELS OF CRUELTY

While every generation of girls has had to deal with bullying, it is reaching new levels of physical and psychological cruelty. The ways it manifests are also more covert, which makes it harder for parents and teachers to intervene. With the net and mobile phones, bullies no longer have to front their victims. They can set up abusive websites and send nasty emails and poisonous text messages to classmates or to the whole world without revealing their identity. It's very easy for girls to take or scan pictures of someone they dislike, manipulate these images, then post them on the net. What they do here is limited only by their skills and imagination. One study of teens online in the United States revealed that over a third had experienced cyberbullying. Over half the bullying took place in chat rooms. Next in line was the use of instant messaging to send cruel messages. Just over one in four teens said they were being bullied by email.[4]

'Girls think more about what girls think of them, rather than what guys think. Guys are not a big thing. Like you think about them, but you don't care. It's more about what another girl's going to think of you. Girls go into depth about each and every person.' *Evie, 15*

Now girls are being drawn into more 'out there' behaviour, there's a lot more information girls have to hold over each other. If someone 'misbehaves' at a party it's very easy for other girls to capture their moment of madness, then let everyone know. 'There's quite a bit of bullying,' one school counsellor pointed out. 'It's made it much easier for girls to find out what's going on in a bullying situation, because it's broadcast to everyone, but harder for the likes of me to minimise the damage.'

GIRLS HURTING GIRLS

While bullying is often verbal, some bullying is becoming extremely physical. 'Girls often announce they're going to bash someone up. They spread it around,' one teacher told me. 'They all come to watch. There's not a moral code that it's wrong to hurt or humiliate someone, then put what you've done on a website. There's no empathy. I think it's because a lot of these girls have no self-worth.' When talking with girls about bullying, some opened up about the confrontations, talking of the violent outbursts they'd witnessed as if they were perfectly normal.

Alongside physical violence, we're now seeing new forms of bullying on the net. One of the most shocking cases of cyberbullying took place recently in a small New Zealand community. When Sophie, 14, didn't seem herself, her mother became worried about her. Sophie finally admitted that Ben, a boy she had met on the net, had killed himself with an overdose. Prior to this, Ben had become increasingly depressed after his girlfriend had hung herself several months before.

Before Ben killed himself he had texted Sophie asking her to keep an eye on his friend Nancy, who was at Sophie's school. Nancy had her own problems, and had swallowed razorblades some time back. Sophie tried desperately to reach Ben in time. When she couldn't get hold of him she'd tried to reach Nancy without success.

After Ben's suicide Sophie became more withdrawn and uncommunicative. She texted Nancy constantly, because she was worried Nancy wasn't handling things, as she was now talking about killing herself. Through all this Nancy was out of touch with her family. Distressed and full of guilt, Sophie ended up taking an overdose of pills and bleach, and was rushed to hospital. Luckily she survived. Nancy was there by her side with flowers.

Sophie's attempted suicide brought her even closer to Nancy. Often they'd text late into the night. Then, just as the girls were planning to visit the beach where Ben had killed himself, Sophie's mum got a call from Nancy's mum, who revealed that Ben didn't exist, and that apart from one incident of self-harm over a year before Nancy was fine. The terrible distress Sophie was dealing with was over an imaginary boy Nancy and one of her friends had dreamt up. They'd even set up Ben's website and his RIP website.[5]

'Use of the internet really requires street smarts. It puts just about everything human beings are up to, from high-minded to horrific, at the fingertips of anyone, anywhere connected to it.' *Anne Collier, NetFamilyNews.org[6]*

More recently, two 15-year-old cheerleaders in Auckland were tricked into believing they were having online romances with boyfriends they'd met on the net. Their drop-dead-gorgeous beaux turned out to be fake. Another girl at their high school had simply scanned in photos of male magazine models and placed them on the net. This chilling ruse began in an MSN chat room. The girls thought they had no reason to doubt the identities of their boyfriends, as they were in regular contact. Over a number of months they received a range of presents, from teddy bears to T-shirts. Then the girls were persuaded to enter a suicide pact.

They received a detailed email from their 'boyfriends', which told them when and how to slit their wrists. Had one of the girls' mothers not found a scalpel under her mattress and the suicide email, these girls might well have gone through with their deadly pact. In a last bitter twist, before the offending girl left the school, she told classmates how she'd tricked the cheerleaders into believing they had online boyfriends, but made no mention of masterminding the suicide pact.[7]

Almost all the girls I spoke with felt there was nothing parents could do to help with bullying. 'It's something you have to work out for yourself, if you are going to gain the respect of the people who are bullying you. If someone else comes in, they're gonna to lose more respect for you,' Peta, 16, told me. Parents and schools have to turn this perception around. Some schools are now writing letters to parents, alerting them to the kinds of bullying happening on and off the net, and encouraging parents to be more aware of what is happening with their teens. This is an excellent first step.

WHAT PARENTS CAN DO

Sometimes girls bully to be more popular or to feel superior, or because they can see another girl is vulnerable. As victims often feel shamed by what has happened, they don't tell anyone. If a girl doesn't seem to be eating, is reluctant to go to school or out with girlfriends, or is having problems, it may well be due to bullying. When asked if anything is wrong, a girl might say there's nothing wrong because she feels humiliated at being bullied and worried that her parents knowing might make things worse. If parents sense their daughter is being bullied, it's important they tread gently to encourage her to open up. Getting older siblings to introduce the subject in a general way, or parents talking casually about their experiences of being bullied can help. Parents also need to talk to their daughters about how prevalent bullying is, so they don't feel annihilated when they are bullied. Experts encourage parents to keep their shock to themselves, and focus on nurturing their daughter and empathising with her, to help restore her sense of self.

If the situation is serious, then parents may need to intervene. This, however, should be a last resort, as girls do need to learn to stand up for themselves, even if the outcomes are a little rocky to start with. If parents and siblings help girls come up with positive strategies to deal with their bullying, then give them confidence to apply these measures, it will achieve far more than parents trying to solve everything. Where help is needed, parents need to be clear about the issues, before they approach their daughter's teachers or the school counsellor.

It is important girls know they have the right to talk about what has happened, and seek redress. Bullies are less likely to be drawn to girls who have a clear sense of self, so helping rebuild a girl's self-esteem is essential and will help her stay safe in future. Encouraging girls to come up with special catchphrases, such as 'no matter what others say or do, I'm still an amazing person', will help them when under pressure. Girls need to know they are best to stick close to good friends, move on from dysfunctional groups, and to avoid or ignore the bully. Emotionally intelligent answers will also be needed, so these need to be rehearsed. Pointing to the bully's best trait before making their position clear will surprise the bully and is a whole lot smarter than being verbally abusive. They might like to use a variation on this phrase, 'It's kind of tragic you're so talented, but so mean. When you stop being so mean, everyone will stop calling you malicious behind your back and notice just how talented you are.'

During their teenage years many girls do also participate in some form of bullying. Parents can help prevent their daughter getting involved in bullying by the values they display in the home. Households that recognise everyone is different, and are generous towards others, do far more for their girls than those who encourage gossip, constantly compete with friends, and enjoy putting other people down. Parents have an important job in teaching girls to respect other people's feelings, while helping their girls to be clear about their own needs and boundaries. Teaching girls how to talk about their needs and aspirations confidently without diminishing others is one of the greatest gifts of good parenting. Encouraging girls to move from a 'them and us' outlook, to being genuinely approachable and friendly to all their peers, whether they're close or not, is a good preparation for life. Those who are able to relate to a wide range of people have far richer experiences and less angst.

Girls also need to know that if they do bully, their parents will expect them to change their behaviour and apologise. This should be approached not simply as a punitive measure, but to help girls become more emotionally intelligent. When they get help in learning how to mend unfortunate situations, they get the chance to move on. If a girl has been part of bullying, it's essential parents talk through the anxieties and attitudes that caused her to get involved in bullying. Often bullying takes place because girls were showing off, trying to be popular, or worried about being left out if they weren't being mean. Empathising with these dilemmas, then talking them through, helps girls make better decisions. This way girls learn about the dynamics of situations and what presses their own buttons. If this is done well, over time girls will develop the confidence and skills to encourage girlfriends to be less mean.

It was interesting to note that the girls I spoke with who experienced the least bullying in their teens were at schools which actively celebrated difference. These girls attended performing arts and independent schools, which went out of their way to encourage girls to be themselves. Girls described the teachers at these schools as more like friends, and spoke repeatedly about how much they appreciated their support, and of how they hoped to stay in touch when they left school.

Sexy girls in a sex-saturated world

One of the main challenges for teen girls is coming to terms with their emerging sexuality. It's a scary, exciting, and confusing time. As they try to get a sense of where they are heading, girls are naturally keen to have all the information they can, to help them understand who they are and what sex is all about. In the past girls weren't expected to know much about their bodies or sex, which left them vulnerable because they were ill-informed. Now the opposite is the case. Peers expect girls to be sexually knowledgeable and experienced. Those who aren't are seen as 'uncool', 'repressed', out of the loop. From my research I have no doubt that peer pressure is one of the reasons why more girls are pushing the sexual boundaries. As one school counsellor pointed out. 'To be called a virgin is now a disparaging term.'

'Normally it would have happened around 18, 19 kind of thing, now it's happening 12, 13, 14. Parents have no idea, not at all. We're very good at keeping secrets.' *Peta, 16*

FINDING OUT ABOUT SEX

At present much of the information girls glean about sex is from magazines, TV and the movies. Local figures are hard to come by, but one Canadian Pediatric Society paper suggests that as many as two out of three teenagers rely on the popular media for information on sex.[1] This is less than ideal, as often sex in the media is presented as immediate, exciting, casual and risk-free. Rarely does anyone get pregnant or end up with a sexually transmitted disease. According to child psychologist Rina Guptha, this is happening at a time when sexual imagery in the media has become 'much more intense, and more complex and confusing'.

When girls access the media, they learn almost nothing about the subtle differences between sensuality and sexuality, understanding and expressing desire, the importance of intimacy and boundaries, and life beyond instant gratification. While access to the internet, films, sitcoms and magazines may help girls fill in the gaps, often the information they have access to is far from than ideal. Too often their anxieties and fragilities are not dealt with in a way that is helpful or empowering, so they simply struggle on. Take this extract from one online teen discussion, for example.

'after my boyfriend has fingered me, like a few hours to a day after i always start my period, is this normal?' don't_know

'are you sure its your period? and not just bleeding from him fingering you?' Lea

'if he's a bit too aggresive maybe its just cause of that. You're still a virgin right??? so most likely to be cause of that it ain't your period.' Perfect_Wings

'yer i am still a virgin and, no, it isnt just bleeding. it is a propper period and like i have stopped him doing it so much now, but like i used to go round his, like on every weekend and a period would have just ended and i would have another one, OMG is this seriously not normal???????' don't_know 'i know i used to do it to vicki not long after her period, and i still ended up with trace amounts on my hand, yuk.' young gun.[2]

While don't_know was asking an important question about her body, it was only partially addressed in this forum. The deeper anxieties that lay behind her question were not picked up on. Access to good, relevant support and information was a concern that teachers, school counsellors and psychologists spoke about over and over.

SEX EDUCATION

When and what to tell girls about sex is a complex issue. What came out of my discussions with girls was how uncomfortable many felt with the way sex education is approached, especially at school, because they saw their teachers as 'old' and 'out of touch'. 'They try to be trendy, but they try too hard. It just didn't feel right,' said Georgia, 20, when looking back at her school days. 'It's awful having teachers who've taught it year after year, telling us we've got to accept our bodies. It's a bit of a cringe.'

In spite of many advances, sex education concentrates on the mechanics of sex, and on a girl's vulnerability to rape and pregnancy, but neglects to deal with the situations and pressures girls face. Teen life is very different from what it was a decade ago, let alone what happened when a girl's parents were young. Girls need to know how they can express their desires, be clear about their boundaries, counter peer pressure and sustain positive relationships. Those teaching sex education need to understand that navigating sexuality is a whole lot more complicated than it was for previous generations. Telling them to respect themselves in a society that shows little self-respect or restraint just doesn't cut it. Teachers need a more detailed understanding of the scenarios girls are subjected to, so they can speak directly to these situations.

Not all girls are pushing the boundaries, but even those who aren't talk of the immense pressure they are under to do so. In many ways girls are damned if they have sex, and damned if they don't. 'There are many kids who are okay,' one school counsellor agreed, adding, 'but you also get the young girls who are climbing out of the window and meeting guys. Then things tend to escalate. They're asked to do things sexually they don't want to do. The guys do these things to girls, then call them sluts. Other girls get to know, and so sometimes the girls have to stay with the group of boys because there's nowhere else to go.'

One of the problems for today's girls is that everything everyone does is openly discussed and bragged about. So even the girls who aren't involved in risky sexual behaviour are well aware of who is doing what with whom, and often in great and graphic detail. Again teen chat rooms are a good indication of the kinds of discussions that are commonplace amongst girls.

'We have got a lott of whoress in my school,' explained Annabel, 16, in one chat room. 'They give handjobs and get fingered on the bus or in class. and a girl a few years above me got caught on the surveilance camera having sex with 4 different guys in some storage closet. and she had a bf, and she got pregnant by one who wasnt her bf.' Those taking part in this discussion were quick to come back with their stories, including Suzi. 'I know all kinds of girls who have gotten fingered/given hand jobs in class as lectures were going on, but nothing to that extent. Although at the local bowling alley, they had to keep extra surveillance on the bathrooms, because 14-year-old girls would give blow jobs for a few bucks.'

While not all discussions in chat rooms do push the limits, many do. Now and then there are girls such as Haley, 16, with more balanced views. 'I don't understand the teenagers that not only drink/do drugs/ have sex/engage in promiscuous activities and then BRAG ABOUT IT. Are they that stupid? Who really wants to hear about their bedroom adventures with the captain of the football team?'

'Everything you've ever thought about or are feeling is on the net.'
Abbie, 17

ATTRACTED TO HARMFUL SEX

What is concerning about the material discussed openly on the net is that it can give girls an appetite for the lurid, and make harmful and violent sex appear normal, if not expected. This is the first generation of girls who have had access to all the information the web contains, including a whole range of material they may not be ready for. As Abbie, 17, pointed out, 'Everything you've ever thought about or are feeling is on the net.'

All the teachers and psychologists I spoke with were concerned about the sudden escalation in sexual activity amongst girls, and at a much younger age. Girls are naturally curious about sex, and drawn to more explicit material. The prevalence of 'out there' material erodes a girl's right to make her own independent choices, as increasingly she feels she has to be primed and ready for sex. It's interesting when surfing the net to see again and again how teens nudge each other to cross the line on teen websites. Here's an excerpt from a storyline on one site I came across. Storylines start with a thread (phrase or sentence), then others add their threads to make up a story.

'im hurney i need u,' cynthia12

'so he went down on her and sucked her for 5 minutes. She moaned from the pleasure and he . . .' **steph**

'lowered himself into her mouth . . .' White Raven

'but he was eating mcdonalds so he,' dimSUM

'spilt chips all over her tits,' White Raven

'he was about to all the way bu he needed some ketchup so he,' coolgirl91

'drove to ur grandma's house and got some ketchup from her period stain so he,' dimSUM

'could eat the fries off his girl's chest. she was just lying on the bed with the dirty bedsheets, waiting for him to return. Then she got an idea . . .' Holly[3]

LIVING IN A SEXUALLY SATURATED WORLD

So where else, apart from the net, does this increase in sexual activity come from? We've already seen how much girls from very young ages are becoming sexualised. When you immerse yourself in the world of teen girls, you quickly see how much sexual content they have access to. One study of kids aged 8 to 18 revealed that they spent a staggering six to nine hours a day with some kind of mass media, most of which they viewed in their bedroom.[4] 'Fashion is number one in magazines,' Evie, 15, told me. 'Then all the sex sections that everyone reads. People may say, "oooh yuck", but like they read it. There's the girls who say I'd never read that, but they read it. It's a new sex position or whatever.' Every day, girls can also read about and watch the antics of teen icons on- and off-screen. Their world is one of exposed nipples, enhanced boobs, butt cleavage and low-rider jeans. As these images are everywhere it can and does affect the way girls look and behave.

Daily girls can read about and watch the antics of teen icons on and off screen. Theirs is a world of exposed nipples, enhanced boobs, butt cleavage and low-rider jeans.

Many girls are so desensitised to sexual material, they have no idea of the impression they create when wearing skimpy clothes or behaving in a certain way. Girls need to understand the signals they send out, just as boys need to be clear about what is acceptable behaviour. Again, parents need to take a more active role. One teacher told me that the principal of her school sent some girls home on their out-of-uniform day to put on more clothes, as they had arrived at school wearing very short skirts, and tops that were more like bras. One would have thought their parents would have been grateful. But when the principal rang one mother, she accused him of being a pervert, so that was the end of out-of-uniform days. According to this teacher, still in her 20s, it was an uphill battle to get some parents to pay more attention to these kinds of problems. They either agreed with their kids that they looked cool, or found the situation amusing.

NOTHING MUCH HAS CHANGED . . . OR HAS IT?

I suspect one of the problems for parents coming to terms with what their girls are exposed to is that they assume teen life is pretty much the same as when they were teenagers, except that perhaps it's a little more risqué. Others are so busy trying to hold down jobs, pay the mortgage, and do everything else they do, that they never seem to get their heads around these issues. This is frustrating for parents and their daughters. It is also frustrating for teachers who try hard to hold the line, often with little support from parents or the community. What parents do need to know is that there is no comparison between how teen life was for them and how it is now for most girls.

> Parents assume teen life is pretty much the same as when they were teenagers, except that perhaps it's a little more risqué.

Whether or not parents make an effort to get up to speed with what is going on, their girls still have to deal with the issues they're confronted with almost daily. Expecting them to cope without proper back-up can make life impossibly hard. The interesting thing is that girls sense things should be different. One young teacher, who deals a lot with at-risk girls, told me that when she asks girls if they'd allow their children to do what they do, the answer is always a categorical no. 'Parents need to judge their children carefully, and do what's best for the children, and not because other parents are doing something,' Chelsea, 18, insisted. 'Children are growing up too quickly. At the time I hated Mum for holding the line, but like now I'm so grateful.' Every girl I spoke with said the same thing.

Even the young teachers I spoke with were shocked at the sexual conduct of some of their pupils, because they see girls struggling with issues they shouldn't be worrying about at their age. One teacher told me how a 14-year-old girl had asked why sex went on for so long in the movies, when the sex she had was over so quickly. This teacher has also talked to 14-year-olds who've had up to twenty partners, including several in one night. She finds this heart-breaking, because these girls are so young.

> One teacher told me how a 14-year-old girl had asked her why sex went on for so long in the movies, because for her sex was always over so quickly.

The sexual boundaries continue to be pushed. According to sex educators in schools, the latest thing for girls is to be with girls, kissing and touching each other, to get boys interested. Along with this faux lesbianism, teachers are also aware of a growing interest amongst some teens in threesomes. 'From what the girls say, the boys will think nothing of asking, "Can I have sex with your friend at the same time as well?"' one teacher told me. 'The way things are, it's like it's prudish to say no.'

SEX SELLS

Girls are influenced by celebrities, advertising and magazines, sitcoms and movies, and reality TV. They are torn between a desire to be their own person and the constant, and often overwhelming, attention given to their icons. They see how many column inches Britney gets for not wearing knickers, and how Paris Hilton's celebrity status rocketed after the video of her having sex with former boyfriend Rick Solomon hit the internet. They are well aware of the amount of interest Lindsay Lohan got for being bruised 'all over' from her pole dancing workout in preparation for her role in the thriller *I Know Who Killed Me*.[5] Or how much the media made of Christina Aguilera when she appeared dressed in a skimpy schoolgirl's uniform licking a lollipop. While they may be personally more reticent, teenage girls understand that the more sexily they behave, the more attention they'll get.

Girls see how many column inches Britney gets for not wearing knickers, and how Paris Hilton's celebrity status rocketed after the video of her having sex with Rick Solomon hit the internet.

What was once off-limits is now mainstream. For girls to be referred to as 'hos' and 'sluts' is no longer such a big deal – for some it's almost a badge of pride. Swept along by the music and mesmerising graphics on MTV, often girls fail to see the extent to which the lyrics of rap music, for example, denigrate women and can promote violence towards them. On the Ninja Dude site tagged as 'celebrity gossip with a kick', where teen idols *The Pussycat Dolls* are celebrated as 'the sluttiest music group around'. While browsers familiarise themselves with the band, there's also the chance to check out three full-screen photos of Ashley Robert's knickerless crotch. The only time Ashley is referred to on this site is as the 'leg spread chick'.[6]

'There's a lot of people doing it. They're just starting to realise now that everyone's doing it . . . There's lots of pressure, and it's in all the magazines we read. Magazines, television, the media.' *Kiera, 17*

PIMPS AND PORN STARS

Teen celebrity Jenna Jameson and best-selling author of *How to Make Love Like a Porn Star*, is now one of the latest waxwork figures at Madame Tussaud's. You only have to enter 'men's' sites to see how much some men applaud Jenna. Askmen.com heaps her with praise, stating, 'Well, she's a porn star and she's hot. But what we really like about Jenna is that she's probably the single person who's most responsible for bringing porn into the mainstream.'[7] Jenna also has one of the most popular sites on MySpace, so she's immediately accessible to her teen fans.

As what constitutes sexy becomes more explicit, there are few boundaries to protect young girls as they grow up, which helps explain why half the 12-year-old girls Joan Sauers surveyed for her book on the sex lives of teenagers had seen some form of pornography.[8] Girls know that the more 'out there' the behaviour around them, the greater the expectations are for them to 'deliver'. 'In some ways it's a bit of a worry porn is what sex is meant to be about. It takes expectations of boys to the extreme,' Whitney, 18, told me. 'I think that's why rape and sexual abuse is more common now. Porn expresses women in a very different way. I hate the way they like represent themselves like so skankily.'

'What we really like about Jenna (Jameson) is that she's probably the single person who's most responsible for bringing porn into the mainstream.' *Askmen.com*[9]

Another teen icon is hip-hop/rap superstar Snoop Dogg, whose popularity is such that he made the cover of *Rolling Stone* with the headline *America's Most Lovable Pimp*. Like many in his genre, Snoop Dogg's lack of respect for women is breathtaking, but few challenge his behaviour or views. 'I wasn't a gorilla pimp where I was beatin' the girls up,' he explained when talking about his life as a pimp. According to Snoop Dogg, he was simply offering a service, 'providing you with opportunity 'cause I know so many motherf**kers who like buyin' it.'[10]

I WANNA BE SEXY TOO

If sexy's where it's at, then that's what some girls will aim for. Knowing this, advertisers push the importance of girls being sexy at every opportunity, because this is a surefire way to grab their attention. This then becomes part of the way girls see themselves. It influences their whole way of thinking, including the products they are attracted to, as you can see from one blog, where a teen girl tells of shopping with a girlfriend.

'I bought a bottle of perfume, that she only picked up because the bottle said "pick me up, I purr". So she picked it up and we spent about twenty minutes giggling over it. Turns out the perfume smells reaaaallly good. It's called Sexy Little Things and my god it's orgasmic.'

This interest in being sexy may seem harmless enough, were it not for the fact that the sexualisation of girls is taking its toll. 'What troubles me is that it's like girls don't feel they have any rights,' one young teacher confessed. 'It's like they want to be objects to be desired.' She went on to tell me about one of her students, aged 14, who went off with her girlfriend in a car full of boys, who got her to take her top off. The girl didn't want to, but did so because she didn't want to look 'silly'. The boys took a photo of her with their mobile phone and sent it to other kids. When this teacher pointed out that she'd been assaulted, the girl was so focused on appearing 'with it', she'd no sense that her rights as a person had been violated. 'These girls are terrified of being isolated and not being seen as cool,' this teacher explained. 'It was like she could only see herself as how boys were seeing her.'

'I don't think parents have much of an idea what's going on. They think "I drank alcohol, went to parties, had a boyfriend when I was young, so it's okay". But it's all changed. Girls are having sex with a number of boys. When they're drinking they're vomiting and passing out.' *Jayne, teacher, 28*

This in-your-face sexuality is present in almost every form of media teen girls have access to. At the back of *Dolly*, read by girls aged 10 to 15, is a directory advertising a range of text messages, including 'Free Hot Hunks'. The opportunity to 'Hook up to a Hottie' is only an SMS away. It's difficult to see what benefit young teen readers get from 'Safe, Fun and Flirty' messages, or the chance for a 'Free Camera Phone Chat', but it does help explain why just under three out of ten teenagers in Joan Sauers' survey admit to having phone sex.[11]

148

Sex lives of teen girls

Teenage life is a time of curiosity and experimentation. Girls will seize on whatever information they can get. Too often they're caught between their parents' attitude to sex, which fails to acknowledge their daughter's emerging sexuality, and a culture that glamourises streetwalker and gangsta looks and makes strippers look chic. When girls don't get the chance to have important and meaningful conversations about sex with their parents, it's hard for them to be clear about boundaries they are comfortable with. They may end up doing whatever their peers expect. 'I do see a number of girls sorry they've got into sexual situations they weren't happy with,' one school counsellor told me. 'Often these girls are desperate to be accepted. Boys say, "You've got to give us head to be accepted", so they do and are shunned.' This was a frequent story. A number of teachers and counsellors spoke to me of the 'Monday morning syndrome', where girls arrive at school totally devastated by an experience, generally sexual, they had when out with their peers over the weekend.

Life can be doubly hard for girls who physically mature early, because they sometimes look or act more mature than they are, and mix with an older crowd. Often these girls attract attention they'd rather not have.

'I have had guys as old as 60 staring at me since I was 11 years old,' complained Melissa, 14. 'It's not my fault that I developed earlier than most girls. I am sick of being seen as an object and not a person. I hate that males see me as an object and other girls hate me for it. I want to be seen as the intelligent girl I am.'

In an effort to make sense of their emerging sexuality, these girls are often drawn to the sexual content in magazines, movies, and on TV, and to listen to sexual content in music. Early-maturing girls are also more likely to interpret what they see in the media as approving of teens having sex. One American study warns that for early-maturing girls the media can become like a 'super peer', and that their exposure to more adult sexual material could have the same effect as hanging out with older, sexually active girls and boys.'[1]

'There's a lot of girls aged 13 and 14 who are very sexually aware. They're the ones who are going out with boys who are older – 15, 16 and 17.' *Rose, psychologist and school counsellor*

It's important we don't forget that TV programs and teen magazines are there to make money, and sex is a great way to boost circulation and lift ratings. In the past, magazines and programs were much more circumspect, because they feared a parental backlash. Now parents are so tired and distracted, often they have no idea about the content in TV programs or magazines, particularly for young teenagers. If parents were to voice their concerns, all this would change, because magazines don't want bad publicity, and nor do the outlets that stock them. Parents need to be on the case.

Teens do need to take risks to learn and grow. Positive risks can help girls gain a greater sense of themselves and where they are heading. But as adolescent psychiatrist Lynn Ponton warns, often the media promotes risk-taking as glamorous and fun, blurring the lines between 'normal, exploratory' conduct and destructive behaviour.[2] Helping expose girls to positive risks is a world away from girls being exploited by clever marketers hungry for the bottom line. Actively teaching girls in school how to see through the many sexualised images they are subjected to would be an excellent step.

WOMEN STEPPING UP

It's tempting to blame men and boys for the exploitation of young girls, yet the majority of people who work on teen magazines are women. And while there are plenty of women working in ad agencies and merchandising, no-one seems to be holding back there either. When concern was expressed about the effects of media saturation on teenagers to Betsy Frank, executive vice-president of research for MTV, she couldn't see any problems. 'Kids are exposed to a lot of media; nobody is going to deny that. That said, kids are exposed to a lot of things in their lives, and everything we've seen says that the kids are growing up just fine,' she declared.[3] Why are we not surprised she would take this line?

It's not in the interest of the media to hold back on the content they deliver, unless popular opinion demands they do so. This means parents and lobby groups need to be vigilant. They need to be watching TV programs, and looking at the magazines their daughters are reading. They also need to be aware that young teenagers are often desperate to be older than they are. Given the chance, many will bypass magazines for girls their age and head straight for *Cosmo* and *Cleo*, especially where there are older sisters around. Here they can learn about everything from clitoral stimulation and vibrators to penis rings and anal sex.

It's not just magazines whose content is questionable. Too few parents are aware of the obscene, often violent language of rap lyrics, or the highly sexual bumping and grinding on MTV clips, which leaves little to the imagination. It's not until you take a good hard look at MTV that you realise how 'in your face' it is.

ORAL SEX ISN'T REALLY SEX

Access to this material does have consequences. There is a growing concern by many adolescent health experts about teen girls' participation in a whole range of sexual activities, including oral and anal sex, because these professionals are having to deal with the physical and psychological consequences. As in so many areas that affect girls' lives, things are moving quickly. Georgia, 20, commented on how different teen life is for her sister, who is just three years younger, in the sexual issues she and her friends are now struggling with. One doesn't have to look very far to see how the boundaries are being pushed way beyond anything previous generations of girls experienced. 'There's a lot of relationship expectations, and much younger,' one school counsellor and psychologist told me. 'I get a lot of kids as young as 12 who are allowed to go to parties with alcohol. Things happen that they can't control. Then we see the fallout on Monday morning.'

Girls are participating in oral and anal sex to please boyfriends so they can still say they are virgins. 'Oral sex seems to be an acceptable entry point for a lot of girls and not classed as actually having sex,' observed one detective. 'It seems to be an expectation on the part of the boys. If the young girls don't adhere to the apparent norm, then everyone hears about it, and the girl's reputation is shattered. Ironic, isn't it? I would have hoped, as a father, that by not doing it, that would be good!' Some girls are now taking part in 'rainbow parties', which is oral sex with a twist. Here girls wear different-coloured lipsticks or lip glosses. As they give boys oral sex, they create a 'rainbow' effect on the boys' penises. The different colours enable everyone to see who has been with whom.

Increasingly sex between teens is casual and random. Aided by the growth in early drug and alcohol use, the constraints a girl would normally contemplate before having sex are being eroded. Some of the girls, who have got into the swing of things, may even have a 'friend with benefits' or a f**k buddy – a boy they like as a friend, with whom they have no-strings-attached sex whenever they feel like it. Others are attracted to edgier situations, such as 'randoming', where they see a guy they like the look of, but have never met, and make a beeline for him in the expectation they'll have casual sex.

While some like to argue these developments are all part of the liberation of girls, when talking to counsellors dealing with the fallout, a different picture emerges. Now many girls are getting involved in a whole range of sexual activities they're uncomfortable with, if not devastated by, simply because they're afraid of appearing repressed. The pressure teen girls experience around sex isn't just from boys. Girlfriends can exert a huge influence over what a girl does.

Not that boys are complaining. 'Rainbow kiss is a oral sex party game,' explains Slight, on the net. 'All the girls put on a different shade of color-ful lipstick and the guy with the most colors on his dick by the end of the night usually wins a drink or something along those lines.'[4] There are no prizes, it seems, for the girls – apart from the very real risk of sexually transmitted diseases. Again, you only have to cruise the teen chat rooms to get a better sense of what girls are up to and how they are feeling, as you can see in this exchange:

'ok so today i gave my boyfriend mine and his first blow job . . . while i did it i felt fine and everything seemed to go pretty well. but afterwards i felt really guilty and just like we had done something wrong . . . or something we're not supposed to . . . i dont know i guess it doesnt really make all that much sense . . . did anyone else feel this way?? does this mean i wasnt ready or is that normal?' Xxthatshotxx

'its normal to feel that way. glad you had fun,' samisam

'i really think this is a question ur gonna have to answer for urself,' greatescape11

'maybe you're sad cuz it didn't meet your expectations?' Meghank91 'honestly i felt like i had an open pit in my stomach after the first time i did it. dont think about it too much,' princessshortyluv

'And now the question that is on everyones mind; did you swallow?' Meep123[5]

RISING SEXUALLY TRANSMITTED DISEASES

These activities aren't risk-free. Between 1995 and 2005 diagnosed cases of chlamydia here rose fourfold. The largest increase was in adolescents and young adults.[6] Similar trends are apparent in many countries across the western world. What is chilling is that girls who contract chlamydia aren't always aware they have been infected, because sometimes there are no symptoms. Left untreated, chlamydia can cause infertility. The sudden increase in oral sex is taking its toll. According to adolescent health expert professor David Bennett, the current generation of girls may turn out to be the most infertile in our history.[7]

> Girls who contract chlamydia aren't always aware they have been infected, because sometimes there are no symptoms.

Recent research suggests there may be a link between oral sex and oral cancers. Health professionals were puzzled by a rise in oral cancer amongst young people, especially as many of those suffering cancer didn't smoke and weren't necessarily heavy drinkers. Researchers at the Johns Hopkins Kimmel Cancer Centre found that those infected by the human papillomavirus (HPV), which can be transmitted by unprotected oral sex, are thirty-two times more likely to develop oral cancers than those not affected by HPV. The study also indicated that regardless of whether someone is infected by HPV, if they have had up to five oral sex partners, they are 3.8 times more vulnerable to oral cancer, and 8.6 times more likely to contract oral cancer if they have had six or more oral sex partners.[8] If this trend continues, it is thought that

HPV-associated cancers will overtake those caused by tobacco and alcohol use.[9]

> **'The current generation of girls may turn out to be the most infertile in our history.'** *Professor David Bennett, adolescent health expert* [10]

SEXUALLY AGGRESSIVE GIRLS

I suspect part of the current difficulties we have in coming to terms with what is happening with teen sexuality is in our outmoded stereotypes, such as 'only boys want sex' and 'girls are looking purely for love'. Not all boys are hanging out for sex, and increasingly girls are making the first move. While I was researching my book *What Men Don't Talk About*, a number of teen boys spoke to me about how sexually aggressive girls had become, and how they wished they could have more genuine relationships with girls. They also talked about how often their heartfelt gestures were passed over, because many teen girls have become 'Britney wannabes'. I'm not suggesting for a moment there aren't plenty of boys willing to take advantage of girls, but we can't lay all the blame at their door. Girls also need to step up.

> **'There's two ways they can look at it – that they're sluts, or that they're heaps grown up and "I know what I'm doing". After like "the first one", girls do tend to have lots of partners. After that first time you're a lot more lenient, morals get pushed down, because you've been there, done that, who cares.'** *Carly, 16*

WHAT CAN GIRLS DO?

As everything becomes more confused, it's much harder for girls and boys to find their way forward. 'One teen girl was telling me she liked a boy in her year, but she didn't want to go out with him, because she didn't want to have sex,' one young teacher told me. 'Today for a lot of girls there's nothing about having an understanding about how far a relationship can go – it's unheard-of.' In a world where there are few boundaries, skewed attitudes creep in, which do little to protect or enhance the lives of girls.

'Luke and I were together for at least six months before he even laid eyes on my boobs,' explains Lola in a teen forum, 'and that was only because I was unconscious in hospital having my vomit-drenched clothes pulled off me in front of him (it's been years and he sees them regularly now). *No-one* I've slept with before him ever saw my boobs naked.' [11]

Girls without clear boundaries are vulnerable to sexual predators. When they aren't aware of their rights as human beings, too often this abuse continues. When one young teen girl told her teacher that she'd been subjected to sexual abuse at home, the language she used was very revealing. 'One of my girls was 14 when she told me her mother's boyfriend would have sex with her,' this teacher explained. 'That's how she described it – not that she'd been raped, just that they'd had sex.'

While many teen girls remain reluctant to have intercourse, having oral sex is less of an issue. Local figures are hard to come by, but in one extensive study by the US Centers for Disease Control and Prevention in 2002, over half of girls aged 15 to 19 had given or received oral sex. Of the girls aged between 15 and 17, 38 per cent had received oral sex, while 30 per cent had given it. [12] The researchers proposed that girls may be taking part in oral sex because they are more aware of this option, or because they don't see oral sex as real sex. Or perhaps it's their way of pleasing their partner without having intercourse. Too few girls realise that unprotected oral sex isn't risk-free. They have no idea the majority of all sexually transmitted diseases occur in the 15 to 24 age group, or that in addition to chlamydia they may end up with herpes, syphilis, gonorrhea, or HIV. [13]

Parents do need to understand the climate their girls are inhabiting, so their conversations can be more relevant. Trying to be cool helps no-one. It may make parents feel good, but it's embarrassing to teenagers. Teaching a girl to value and celebrate herself is a great start. Girls also need good information. Being prepared to talk about things that at first may feel awkward is important, as it gives parents the chance to explain why boundaries matter, and why instant gratification and having sex simply to please others offers girls very little in return. Girls also need to feel parents respect them and trust them to make good choices. When parents are approachable and supportive, girls are more likely to talk to them if they have done something they regret or are unsure about.

Loss of identity

When young girls are sexualised, their focus shifts from thinking about who they are and what they want to do with their lives, to how to please and get the most attention. The more sexy a girl is, the less she's viewed as person with feelings, needs and vulnerabilities. She's simply another object of lust. 'What's most worrisome about this age of blasé blowjobs isn't what the girl may catch,' reflects journalist Caitlin Flanagan, 'it's what the girls are most certainly losing: a healthy emotional connection to their sexuality and their own desire.'[1]

One high school teacher I spoke with voiced the concerns of many. 'When you talk to girls about sex, they don't have sex for pleasure or because they've got a special boyfriend. Most of the time it's just spread your legs for a boy. That's happening younger and younger. When I first started teaching in 2000 there was a sense of wanting to be sexy, but in the last three years it wasn't common for girls to be having sex at 12 – it was more likely at 14. Now it's more common at 12. It's like they want to be wanted and loved in that moment, and that's enough.'

One of the difficulties with a sex-and-shopping culture is that from a young age, girls become accustomed to having everything now. Living in a world of instant gratification, they never get to experience the deep joy and excitement of anticipation. Their latest experience soon flips into boredom and disappointment. We need to work much harder at enabling girls to feel good about becoming a woman, at a much more profound level than the preoccupation with botox and big boobs allows.

> 'What's most worrisome about this age of blasé blowjobs isn't what the girl may catch, it's what the girls are most certainly losing: a healthy emotional connection to their sexuality and their own desire.' *Caitlin Flanagan, journalist*[2]

FACING THE FALLOUT

When a girl identifies with sexualised images, she naturally thinks looking and feeling sexy is the best way to be. Studies show that these images do girls no favours, as they can make girls anxious and ashamed of their bodies, and can trigger depression and eating disorders.[3] When girls identify with these images it can also make them more vulnerable in sexual situations. The belief that they should be ready for sex any time, anywhere, can make them reluctant to speak out about what they don't feel comfortable with.[4] If a girl is driven to be sexy because this is the only way she feels she can gain love and approval, it can also make her more likely to choose inappropriate sexual partners, and to tolerate abuse in relationships.[5]

WHEN BEING SEXY IS ALL THAT MATTERS

When girls focus on being sexy to the exclusion of all else, their life choices narrow, as does the way others view them. Everywhere girls look, sex is portrayed as exhilarating and fun, which is true, but it's only part of the truth. Being a sexy girl does not guarantee the love, belonging and acknowledgement that teenage girls crave. Girls need to know that the sexy girl image can imprison and diminish them if they're seen as commodities, not people. One of the saddest stories in recent years is that of former Playboy bunny Anna Nicole Smith, who was abandoned by her father as a little girl, and married and a mother by the age of 17. When her husband walked out, Anna Nicole worked in topless bars to make ends meet. In an effort to get ahead, she resorted to plastic surgery, having two implants in each breast. Anna Nicole used every inch of her sexuality to help attract the love and attention she craved.

Sadly, what people remember her for is her over-the-top behaviour and comments, marrying an oil tycoon 60 years her senior, flashing her breasts and knickers in Nashville, and pulling her dress down to her waist at the inaugural MTV Australian Video Music Awards. No sooner was her tragic death announced than a string of former lovers surfaced, eager to get a slice of her multi-million-dollar estate. The fallout didn't end there. Her son Daniel died at 20, and her little baby Dannielynn was at the centre of a very public paternity dispute.

> In one *Girlfriend* survey 28 per cent of girls who participated had caught sexually transmitted diseases, and a staggering 58 per cent had regretted their last sexual encounter.[6]

WHERE'S THE INTIMACY?

Today's girls may know a whole lot more about sex, but there's precious little talk about intimacy, which is tragic, because intimacy is the x-factor in relationships. Intimacy is what takes a relationship deeper, and helps it grow. Psychotherapist Roger Horrocks has worked with many adult clients who have enjoyed great sex in their relationships, but still sought therapy. He puts this down to what he calls 'a deep sense of incompleteness or deprivation inside'. 'They are not suffering from a lack of pleasure in their lives,' he states, 'but are still suffering from a very early lack of holding, containment, nourishing, which impairs their capacity for intimacy and fulfilment as adults.'[7] This is a crucial observation and one that parents and sex educators need to take on board. While sex is special, it's only part of our lives. When we portray sex as the single most important life experience, we short-change everyone.

Our brave new world of in-your-face sexuality isn't delivering girls the joy it seems to promise. When *Girlfriend* magazine, whose readership stretches from girls aged 6 to those in their mid-teens, conducted an online survey into girls and sex, it revealed that one in four participants had had sex before they were 14. Twenty-eight per cent of these girls had caught sexually transmitted diseases, and a staggering 58 per cent had regretted their last sexual encounter.[8]

Psychologist Michael Carr-Gregg, who specialises in adolescent mental health, is concerned that a lot of girls appear to be going straight from 'toys to boys', and he is right to be concerned.[9] To understand intimacy, first girls need to know themselves. They need to understand what feeds and intrigues *them*, what brings *them* genuine delight. Many of our teen girls never get this chance. They are constantly distracted from thinking about themselves by the need to appear sexy. Again parents have an important role in helping girls experience intimacy and nurture by creating this kind of environment in the home, and by respecting and empathising with the complexities of their daughter's changing needs as she matures. There can never be too much communication.

While not all girls succumb to these pressures, it's hard for them to be their own person, because of the pressures from peers and advertising, TV, magazines and movies. The girls I spoke with who were most comfortable with themselves and their choices were actively involved in youth groups attached to local churches, or had a strong group of close girlfriends, who were clear about what they would and would not do at parties. The way these girls described how they held the line at peer gatherings made it sound as if they were in a war zone. As they talked about girlfriends 'sticking close', 'watching out for each other', 'arriving and leaving together', this gives us some sense of just how intense this pressure can be at parties or other gatherings. Having good girlfriends made all the difference to their ability to be themselves in these situations.

The girls in active youth groups enjoyed these groups because they got to discuss *their* issues. 'It gives me more self-confidence. I know who I am, and I know I don't have to change myself to be who people want,' Kiera, 17, told me. 'I can be myself and if they still don't like it, then that's okay.' One of the reasons the girls I spoke with benefited from these programs was because they were with kids their own age, and because difficult issues were debated openly with team leaders, who were only a few years older than they were. The girls felt the team leaders understood their issues and were able to offer good advice. Having voiced their concerns, they felt much clearer about how to handle difficult decisions. Girls who went to independent and performing arts schools felt similarly able to be themselves, because individuality was prized. Recent research backs this up, indicating that girls need assistance in gaining good social skills, so they can counteract the very real pressure they experience from peers.[10]

> 'It's definitely like support. You have people around you that kind of have the same beliefs and the same expectations of yourself – not to go around and get wasted and like sleep around. You have a group of people that you can relate to.' *Joy, 16*

This valuable feedback offers us some powerful clues as to the way forward in discussing sex in schools. I feel there is a place for well-trained young teachers to take on this important role, to help dissolve the generation gap, so girls feel more comfortable about raising their issues around sex and sexuality and getting the support they need in a way that is relevant and meaningful to them.

THE PROTECTION OF GOOD MEN

To help girls make positive choices around sex, they also need good male role models. Without this, it's hard for girls to know what they have the right to expect from men and boys. Two long-term studies in the United States and New Zealand discovered that the girls with the most teenage sexual activity had fathers who had left home before the girls turned 6. Next were girls whose fathers left later on, followed by girls whose fathers remained at home. The girls in homes with absent fathers saw mothers struggling with relationships, and this, along with the destabilising effect of losing their own fathers, was thought to prompt girls to be attracted to 'early and unstable bonds with men'.[11] Solo mothers can't be expected to parent alone. Girls can suffer profoundly from 'father hunger'. If a girl doesn't see her father, good male friends and relatives can play an important role in teaching her about men and boys through family interactions and conversations.

One teacher I spoke with said that many of the at-risk girls she deals with lack a good, stable relationship with their father. If girls don't have engaged fathers in their lives, then it's clearly important for them to have other good male figures they can interact with. If girls don't have this support, they become vulnerable as they have no idea how to behave towards men. As this teacher pointed out, 'Some girls cling to male teachers. Or they get flirty because they don't know how to act around them.'

When girls only know about sex and not about intimacy, they are more likely to engage in passionless encounters, which offer little joy or respect. Teen girls need to know they have a whole lot more to offer than being sexy. There is little point in trying to turn the clock back or pretending our rapidly expanding multi-media doesn't exist. What we need to create for girls are better media choices that are hip, informative and fun. The Media Project, a nonprofit advisory group, has been working with the media for two decades to get good educational content on sex written into TV shows. This is a valuable first step as so many teenagers turn to the entertainment media to get their information about sexuality and sexual health.[12]

Highs and lows

As the world of teen girls continues to change rapidly, so do the girls themselves. The kinds of things girls aspired to three or four years ago no longer figure. Almost every day of the week, young girls are treading new ground. While this constantly changing landscape is exhilarating for many, teen girls are finding it hard to cope. The number of girls suffering from drug and alcohol abuse is on the rise, as is the number of girls who are depressed.

Not only are girls drinking earlier and more than their mothers and grandmothers, they are drinking to harmful levels, and more so than boys.[1] Binge-drinking has become a 'girly' thing to do. 'All the stuff in the media about alcohol, it's not an exaggeration,' Whitney, 18, told me. 'It's normal to get smashed every weekend. It's okay as long as you're not driving and hurting anyone.' Ashlee, 15, agreed. 'There's a lot of drinking and drugs goes on. You just do it for fun. When we do, we're not thinking about our futures and stuff. Once everyone's "out there", it's fine because everyone's doing it.'

'You don't just walk home one day and say, "I'm going to take a pill" or "I'm going to drink". There's something that builds up. I remember two years ago, thinking I'm never going to drink or smoke or anything, or sit with anyone who does anything like that. But you can't run away from it, it's everywhere.' *Rachel, 14*

With this heavy drinking come new challenges. Teenage binge-drinkers have been found to be four times more vulnerable to rape, date violence and attempted suicide than their peers, and five times more likely to have had sex with one or more partners, and to use drugs.[2] Binge-drinking occurs at a critical time in a teenage girl's development when her brain is being shaped, and it can affect her memory and ability to learn. 'Girls drinking alcohol at an early age is an entry point into the drug-taking world,' said one of the detectives I spoke with. 'They often get the alcohol from older siblings, or in a lot of cases their older boyfriends, as they seem to be seeing boys that are a lot older, and also ones that have been in a bit of trouble. It seems to be a thrill for them to be with guys that are classed as "bad boys".' He went on to explain that a routine part of police work now is picking up intoxicated young girls off the ground at concerts and other gatherings, and taking them home or to hospital. 'The only people who seem shocked are the parents, who had no idea what their young daughter was up to,' he told me.

This experience is also true for cab drivers, who are dealing with very drunk girls on the weekends. A number of drivers confessed they were reluctant to pick up young girls late at night, because they're so inebriated, often they throw up. The drivers then have the unenviable task of cleaning their cab and trying to get rid of the smell of vomit before they can get back to work. Some cab drivers can also be sleazy. If she takes a cab when drunk, a teenage girl may not be as safe as she'd hoped.

'I don't think parents have much of an idea what's going on. They think "I drank alcohol, went to parties, had a boyfriend when I was young, so it's okay." But it's all changed.' *Natalie, teacher of 7 years*

When you talk with medical staff, an even darker picture emerges. They are concerned about the numbers of intoxicated girls being admitted to emergency units. One in 20 of our school-age teenagers is now drinking 50 drinks per month. Some girls are so drunk they can't maintain their own airways. These girls have to be monitored closely, as they can die if they roll back or vomit. The girls admitted are often aged 12 to 14. 'You just feel so helpless,' said one accident and emergency nurse. 'It's really distressing.' She went on to tell me how vulnerable these girls are to rape. Sometimes their parents weren't even aware they weren't at home.

This nurse had a whole catalogue of distressing incidents she has witnessed, including one young girl who was picked up alone in a local park after dark. She was soaking wet and incomprehensible, and had no ID. When staff took off her wet clothes to warm her up, they discovered she had no knickers. When the facts were assembled, it became clear she had been raped. The girl had no memory of this. 'A lot of girls say their drinks have been spiked,' this nurse told me. 'Some have, but often the tests show it's just the amount of alcohol they've drunk. They often forget how much they've had after three drinks.'

The nurse went on to tell me about the terrible accidents some of these drunk girls have had, including serious head and other injuries, because they've fallen or jumped off something too high up. If they are drunk, they are also far more likely to get into a car with friends who are intoxicated. They also get a lot of young girls asking for the morning-after pill after a night of binge-drinking. These situations are shocking and real, and are taking place in our hospitals week after week. Parents need to talk to their daughters about the very real risks they face if they binge-drink. Being more open, by staying calm and not giving way to your own anger or distress, encourages girls to be more frank. Relating anecdotes about what is happening to other young girls in a conversational way is the best approach. It's equally important parents show respect for and interest in teen culture, so their girls don't feel defensive about their generation.

ALCOHOL AND UNPLANNED SEX

Girls who binge-drink are cause for concern as they are more likely to have unplanned sex and forget to use condoms. Some don't even remember who they had sex with or where, which makes them targets for further abuse because predatory peers know they are frequently out of it. One study of girls aged 14 to 21 who had unplanned pregnancies revealed that a third of these girls had been drinking when they had sex. Nine out of ten hadn't planned on sex.[3] Georgina, now 17 and undergoing rehabilitation, began drinking when she was 13. She was soon drinking up to 12 breezers and cruisers in a night, and would then move on to vodka and bourbon. She had frequent blackouts. 'There's been a lot of times when guys have taken advantage of me and it was scary because sometimes I would wake up in the middle of it,' she recollects. 'I'd kind of come to and realise what was happening. And that was really upsetting and very scary. Sometimes I knew who they were and sometimes I didn't.'[4]

Georgina's story is not an isolated one. Recently a 17-year-old girl who lived near me was deliberately intoxicated by peers, then filmed while being gang-raped. Afterwards her 'friends' dumped her on her doorstep, knickerless and barely conscious. This girl had no memory of the incident, and wouldn't have given it a second thought, had not one of the boys showed her the footage on his mobile phone. By this stage the footage had also been circulated to school friends.[5] These scenarios are harmful to girls on many levels. They do nothing to give them a healthy sense of themselves, and the trauma stays with them for a long time.

'Girls way too young now drink, like at 15. They drink every weekend until they throw up in the gutter.' *Alana, 18*

'I don't think parents have much of an idea what's going on. They think, "I drank alcohol, went to parties, had a boyfriend when I was young, so it's okay." But it's all changed. Girls are having sex with a number of boys, and getting into sex acts with other girls to attract boys. When they're drinking they're vomiting and passing out,' one teacher told me.

Every girl I spoke with had her own stories about girls and alcohol. 'Girls do binge-drink,' said Abbie, 17. 'About 50 per cent of girls in my year do it. They've been doing it since they were 16. Most girls have fake IDs or they borrow their sister's ID, and go out every weekend and get rat-arsed. Often it's because they've screwed up their marks, or they don't want to go to school any more – it's more about escape. They generally binge-drink together, and like look out for each other.'

Teens who drink before they are 15 are four times more likely to become alcoholics in later life.[6]

For an increasing number of girls, binge-drinking is what they do most weekends. The girls I spoke with talked openly about how they constantly saw girls projectile vomiting, or passing out and having to go to hospital to have their stomachs pumped. 'I didn't go to parties until I was like 16 – except for sleepovers with pizza and lollies. But like at my first party people were vomiting and stuff,' reflected Sara, now 18. While this behaviour has become commonplace, many girls still find it troubling to watch. 'It's scary, especially when you're not doing it – it's overwhelming what you see,' Ashlee, 15, confessed. Alanna, 18, agreed. 'When things are out there, I often don't like it. I don't want to be part of it.'

WHEN DRINKING MAKES GIRLS VULNERABLE

To drink as much as boys may seem a great expression of girl power, but it's not the reality. Few girls realise how vulnerable they are when they drink. When John Toumbourou from the Murdoch Children's Research Institute conducted an extensive survey of young people in both the US and Victoria, Australia, he discovered that those aged 12 to 13 who had more than three glasses of alcohol in a year were more likely to be binge-drinkers by the time they were 15 or 16.[7] Other studies suggest that teens who drink before they are 15 are four times more likely to become alcoholics in later life.[8] Again, many older teen girls expressed their very real concern about how much young girls are drinking, and about the resulting situations they find themselves in.

Often a girl's self-esteem does take a dive during adolescence, and having a drink has become one way to relieve this anxiety. 'A lot of the time it's to feel more confident in social situations,' said Whitney, 18. 'For me, drinking can loosen me up a bit.' As with sex, girls are often more worried about saying no because of what peers might think. 'Once a few people do it, it catches on,' Ashlee, 15, explained. 'It's another "fitting-in thing". A lot of people feel pressured, worrying, "Am I doing something wrong by not doing it?"' If a teen girl drinks to overcome stress and anxiety, she is more likely to reach for a drink whenever she feels pressured or down as an adult.

Sleepovers are the perfect way for girls to disguise what they're up to. They know this and use them to give them the freedom they need to do their own thing.

Girls are not only drinking more, they are very good at concealing what they do. 'A lot of kids [girls] have been drinking from 13 and 14. A lot of parents didn't know they were drinking,' Joy, 16, told me. This wasn't an isolated comment; almost every girl I spoke with said the same thing. 'Parents don't know. Half the time girls make a way of getting away from their parents, so that by the time they go home they're sobered up or whatever. It's easy to do it,' said Evie, 15.

Sleepovers are the perfect way for girls to disguise what they're up to. They know this and use sleepovers to give them the freedom they need to do their own thing. One of the ways for parents to take control is to make sure their daughters come home at night, or that they are only allowed sleepovers with friends whose parents are equally vigilant. While it is inconvenient to have pick-ups late at night, at least parents know their daughter is safe. Smart parents will keep their own up-to-date list of phone numbers for their daughter's friends and their parents, and will make a point of getting to know them.

DRINKING TO GET DRUNK

The whole culture around drinking has shifted. Now more and more girls are drinking simply to get drunk. Even in Europe where alcohol has been an integral part of meals for centuries, teens now regard drink more as a mood enhancer than a beverage. Nations such as Scandinavia, Italy and Portugal are also struggling with teen drinking issues. In Spain the numbers of teens admitted to hospitals has doubled over the past ten years. Between 2000 and 2003, emergency departments in Germany saw a 26 per cent rise in teens suffering from 'coma drinking'. Half these admissions were teenage girls.[9] This level of drinking has real and lasting effects. Doctors are increasingly concerned to see teenagers suffering from the kind of liver damage normally associated with adults who drink to excess.[10]

'Lots of people are taking drugs and alcohol. Parents don't know because their kids wouldn't tell them, and on the news you only hear the most extreme cases, so they think you're just on a little cruiser.' *Carly, 16*

GIRLS AT RISK

When girls drink they are at risk on a number of levels. As their body fat to water ratio is higher, they are less able to process alcohol than boys, so the alcohol entering their bloodstream is much stronger than for a boy drinking the same amount. Research also shows that girls are less able to process alcohol, because they don't have the same levels of the enzyme in their stomachs which breaks down the alcohol. The more they drink, the more they compromise this process.[11] Basically every drink a girl takes is equivalent to two drinks for a boy. Medical experts don't have enough information yet to know the full impact of regular drinking on girls. What they do know is that it can disrupt their growth and puberty.[12] Again this is something girls need to understand from parents and teachers.

> **'Girls who get drunk every Saturday night and every Sunday night, come to school and can't remember what they did at the weekend, and they'll have jokes about how much alcohol they drank or which drug they tried.'** *Peta, 16*

Sometimes parents invite their underage girls to have a drink at home, to help teach their teenagers to be responsible about drinking. Unfortunately, this often has the opposite effect; already familiar with drinking, the girls then enter a peer culture where heavy drinking is the norm. Studies have shown that the earlier a girl drinks, the more likely she is to have problems around alcohol in later life.[13]

IT'S JUST A BREEZER

One of the greatest areas of concern regarding teen girls is alcopops, or 'breezers', because while they may look and taste like soft drinks, these drinks frequently have a higher alcohol content than most beers. There are now dozens of alcopop products on the market. Parents who feel comfortable buying their underage daughters breezers are breaking the law, and might be less inclined to do so if they knew how potent they are. Now there are also a number of 'black label' brands available that are even stronger – the average alcohol content is around 5 per cent.[14]

'Girls love breezers like Smirnoff Ice Double Black. We used to call it carnage, because you could get drunk really fast. Girls like it because it tastes nice, but it's lethal. You tend to think it's just a breezer, so it seems okay, but it's not.' *Georgia, 20*

Medical professionals are unhappy about breezers because they encourage girls to start drinking and introduce them to other forms of alcohol. Not so the companies who produce alcohol, because while most teenage girls don't like the taste of wine or beer, they like breezers. That's why such spirits as vodka and white rum are used as the base for breezers, because they're more suited to teen palates. The sweetness of the additives in cruisers and breezers helps mask the strong taste of the alcohol.

The price of breezers also makes them attractive for teens. For the cost of a couple of drinks in a pub, girls can purchase a pack of breezers that will last the night.

There's a whole range of appealing and seemingly innocuous flavours to choose from, such as apple, peach, raspberry and lime. Archers Aqua, tagged as the first ready-to-drink (RTD) product 'to singlemindedly target females', offers products like the Frutini – a blend of wild cherry, apple and banana.[15] If you read some of the ads, you could be forgiven for thinking girls were simply having fruit drinks. The price of breezers also makes them attractive. For the cost of a couple of drinks in a pub, girls can purchase a pack of breezers that will last the night.

WHY GIRLS LIKE TO DRINK

There are many reasons why more girls are drinking so young. Seeing celebrities who are constantly wasted normalises this behaviour. Having an older sister or brother who drinks can also double the amount teen girls drink.[16] All these influences make it that much harder for those who don't want to drink to make their own decisions. 'There's a lot of pressure,' Missy, 15 admitted. 'I know some friends that go to parties like that, and it's like they hold a Bacardi Breezer the whole night or whatever, and like don't drink it, but do it to look like they're in with it.'

Teenagers are the new growth market for alcohol manufacturers. There are over 400 alcopops products on the Australian market, and in 2006 alone 16 million litres of alcopops were produced here. This was a 9 per cent increase on the pre-mixed spirits sold the previous year. In comparison, beer and wine sales grew by just 1 per cent over the same period.[17] The recent report 'Ready to Drink?' prepared by the peak association for general practitioners stated that teenagers are now consuming alcohol 'at levels that cause significant health and social harms'.[18]

Alcohol ads play a key role in encouraging girls to drink. In one recent National Drug and Research Centre survey, just under three-quarters of those aged 14 to 15 felt Bacardi Breezers were being marketed to them.[19] The likelihood of a girl drinking rises the more she sees alcohol ads, as does the amount she is likely to drink.[20] It's not just exposure to these ads which is detrimental to teen girls, so too is the content. Almost all the alcohol ads show women having a great time and associate drinking with having fun and being sexy, suggesting that it's the girls who put themselves out there who get the gorgeous guys. This encourages girls to drink to prove they're grown-up. And if a girl is nervous about projecting the right image, then having a few drinks seems like a good way to loosen up, which in turn makes her vulnerable to predators.

Again, one of the best ways forward for parents is to keep the lines of communication open with their girls, by being honest about how they feel about teenage drinking, while acknowledging the pressures girls face from friends and peers. Encouraging older siblings to be mindful of how they talk and behave around a young teen is also important. The more girls are able to see alcohol ads for what they are, the better decisions they are likely to make. Self-esteem is important here also. The greater a girl's sense of self, the more comfortable she is likely to be with making good choices around drinking.

Walking on the wild side

It's not only alcohol girls are into. The numbers of teen girls using drugs is also on the rise. One site for girls suggests that girls are fifteen times more likely than their mothers to have begun using illicit drugs by the age of 15.[1] 'You can't run away from it, it's everywhere. Everyone thinks it's cool,' Sandi, 14, confessed. These comments were echoed time and again by the girls I spoke with. The worries parents had about girls smoking in previous generations seem almost laughable when compared with the constantly evolving drugs now on the market. Too few parents realise how much drugs are now part of teen life, and that some girls work hard to keep it that way.

It's not just illegal drugs parents need to be aware of, there's also a growth in girls using prescription drugs. As the numbers of girls on medication grows, prescription drugs have become a 'natural' part of life. It's not a huge jump for some girls on prescription drugs such as Ritalin to share or sell their or their family's drugs so friends can get high. These can include everything from cough medicine to painkillers. Operating below the radar is easy for these girls, whose parents have no idea this might be happening. The internet provides a wealth of information on everything from how to pass drug tests, to which drugs to mix for new highs. It's also an ideal way for girls to order prescription drugs direct.

In my interviews with girls it was clear they rarely, if ever, told their parents about how often they were exposed to drugs. 'It's a huge scene,' said Evie, 15. 'I've been offered drugs so many times it's not funny.' This was also Lilly's experience. She is 13. 'There are more drugs in school than parents realise,' she told me. 'Drugs can happen to anybody. We lost one of our friends to it. She took marijuana. She lost her friends, her boyfriend. She went really weird. She's no longer at school. She's got like bipolar. She's really, really moody. She's 15.'

We all celebrate girls embracing life, and wouldn't have it any other way, but there are concerns. Studies suggest that girls are now using illegal drugs as much as boys, and that they have surpassed boys in the numbers smoking cigarettes and using prescription drugs.[2] This is happening at a time when their bodies and brains are still developing. Teen girls aren't completely unaware of the risks they face, but somehow this isn't enough to help them make better choices.[3] When I asked them how many teens were seriously wasted at parties they said between 40 and 60 per cent.

One detective explained how drug-taking amongst teen girls escalates, especially when girls mix with older peers. 'They start with alcohol then move on to cannabis, then methylamphetamines and or ecstasy,' he told me. 'A different set of girls move to amphetamines. Ecstasy is a socially acceptable drug; it seems they don't have any idea what they are actually taking. If they did they might rethink this. Ecstasy means they don't have to drink alcohol (lots of fattening drinks) and only drink water. It stops alcohol putting the weight on the young girls, by only having water and an E or two, and dancing all night.'

'I go to parties and they're smoking pot and drinking, and their parents are completely unaware. Like kids are growing marijuana

plants in their parents' backyards and some parents are oblivious to it. They go crazy and don't know when to stop, because they're not old enough. Probably like 40 per cent or higher (of girls) are out of control at parties.' *Kiera, 17*

When you talk with drug counsellors, school counsellors and child psychologists who work with drug users, you find the majority of young people get involved in drugs through friends and acquaintances. Some girls come on board out of curiosity and peer influence. For others it's a way of leaving their anxieties behind. Regardless of the reason, girls need to be reminded that the risks they take can compromise their physical and mental health, especially as drug-taking and drinking alcohol tend to go hand in hand. As with all these challenges, it's important parents can talk with their girls about drugs, and that they're not afraid to get help if there is a drug problem. While it may be embarrassing or distressing to have a daughter in this situation, if parents don't get her assistance, nothing is likely to change. Parents also need to be sensitive to the reasons why their daughter has taken this route, and take positive steps to help her deal with the wider issues she may be struggling with.

Drugs find their way into girls' lives in seemingly innocuous ways. 'My friend keeps her drugs in little Extra packets, and the other day I went to have a mint, but I'm a bit scared now. It's very big at school,' Peta, 16, told me. Most of us don't like the fact that drugs are readily available at school, on the street, at parties. Trying to gauge the extent of the problem is a challenge for parents and professionals, because there are so many ways girls can operate below the radar. Even the girls with real problems can be hard to spot, and thus help. In one study paediatricians only managed to accurately assess substance abuse in one out of every ten adolescent patients they saw, and failed to recognise dependence in any of these patients.[4]

GIRLS WANT TO DO THEIR OWN THING

Alcohol and drug initiatives have been less than effective, because they still haven't addressed the reasons why girls get into substance abuse. That's why lectures from parents and teachers continue to fall short of the mark. This generation wants to know for *themselves* what is what. 'Even though there are all these horrendous ads on smoking and stuff on the screen this hasn't made any difference to children at all, because children still think "that's never going to happen to me" – that's after thirty or forty years of smoking. I'm only going to do it while it's cool, then I'll stop. I think they have that "I'm never going to die" attitude to everything,' Peta, 16, told me. Morgan, also 16, agreed. 'I get sick of all the "be yourself" messages and the "don't do drugs". I know they're meant to help, but anyone who was going to do drugs seriously or conform to the norm would not change their mind just from seeing a couple of commercials that they'll probably make fun of later.'

> **'Yeah, teenagers find drugs and alcohol really attractive. We're like growing up and we want everything that 20-year-olds and stuff have done – we want to be like part of it. Doing that makes me think I'm grown-up. It's like "Oooh, I'm at a party and I'm drinking and that person over there is smoking, and that person is on drugs."'** *Carly, 16*

'Alcohol has always been there, but drugs more so now, because it's like our parents say we can't have it, but they don't know most of the effects of the drugs, so how can they tell us what to do when they haven't been there? We've got to try this for ourselves, we need to know what's happening,' Peta, 16, insisted. When teen girls need advice about substances, the overwhelming majority ask their friends.[5] Girls turn to each other because they share the same experiences and issues, and because their friends are available for them all the time.

HANDLING THE PRESSURES

During their teens girls start to lead far more intricate social lives. As we've already seen, popularity and being part of a group informs much of what girls do, because the attitudes, values and expectations of their girlfriends are important. Studies suggest that girls are more vulnerable to peer pressure than boys.[6] With so much riding on relationships, it's no surprise that they resort to alcohol and/or drugs to increase their confidence and lose their inhibitions.[7] 'A really close friend of mine got ruined by drugs. She takes them often; you can't talk to her any more because half the time she's out of it,' Evie, 15, told me. 'She's concerned about what other people think of her – so she has to keep on taking them.'

Stress is now recognised as another reason why girls drink, smoke, and use drugs.[8] My interviews with teen girls bore this out. 'All the kids are getting big into alcohol and stuff, they use that to forget about their problems, instead of talking things through. They'd rather get drunk and forget about it, kind of thing,' said Joy, 16. Uppermost in the minds of many girls was the need to escape their anxieties. 'Drugs and alcohol are fun,' Carly, 16, explained. 'There's nothing like worrying you or anything.' This takes us back to the amount of pressure girls now face, and how few places there are for them to chill out and relax away from friends, mobile phones, the net and shopping centres. We need to work harder to help reduce the stress in girls' lives, so their teen years aren't so pressured.

SHOPLIFTING

Shoplifting is also part of teen life. A number of girls talked about shoplifting simply for the thrills. While local figures are hard to come by, three out of four teenagers who shoplift in the States are girls.[9] Shoplifting is popular because it's a 'cool' way for girls to prove they've got what it takes. That's how Tracy wins the friendship of wild girl Evie in the film *Thirteen*. After her shoplifting spree, Tracy then steals a woman's wallet to cap the experience off.

'Shoplifting's really in,' Sandi, 14, confessed. 'You think you're so cool, because you're not paying for something. Friends of mine will take sheets and not pay for them, whether they want them or not. Like then they started like getting sheets, then taking them and returning them. They didn't want them, and went and got a video game. They will think of anything not to pay – even if it's two dollars.'

'I had a girlfriend. She used to nick stuff all the time, because her parents were like, "No, no, you don't need that stuff." She'd steal Billabong and RipCurl clothes, and stuff like that. She knew how to take the tags off, because they don't put dye in the tags – there's too much risk of damaging the clothes.' *Georgia, 20*

There's a whole range of reasons why girls shoplift. For some it's the desperation to have things, or to get back at 'the system'. Others do it to please friends, or to relieve their hurt, boredom or despair.[10] The more girls are immersed in a world that sells to them constantly, the more they want, and what they can't afford, they steal. 'With girls it's mostly about clothes,' one girl told me. 'They steal from each other, like at school, or money from their parents.' Shoplifting isn't always related to a girl's ability to pay for the items she steals. Doing something risky creates an adrenalin rush, which can become addictive. Experts also talk of the exhilaration girls experience from getting something for nothing, and how shoplifting can seem like a reward.[11] Should a girl be shoplifting, parents need to understand what is going on for her and that she may need professional assistance. It may be a silly mistake, or it may suggest there are deeper issues that need to be examined and resolved.

There are many risks girls take during adolescence. It's a natural part of growing up. What they don't understand is how vulnerable they may be when they do cross the line. Every second movie or DVD girls see depicts risky behaviour as fun and exciting. When taking risks girls feel pumped up, alive. Some parents encourage this behaviour, because it takes them back to the excitement of their own teen years. While it might give parents a boost, it doesn't do much for their girls.

The very real influence parents can have in talking through issues with their daughters can't be underestimated. One girl I spoke with resisted the temptation to shoplift with friends because her parents had discussed the issue with the family. They pointed out that while it was understandable that a starving person might steal food, it would shame their family if a member did so, because they were not needy.

PRAISING GIRLS FOR GETTING IT RIGHT

When faced with the fear of daughter's binge-drinking, shoplifting or taking drugs, it is tempting for parents to focus on what their girls might do wrong, and ignore the fact that they're battling big issues. The girls I spoke with didn't feel their parents understood their pressures, or gave them enough credit for the good decisions they did make. Our girls do need to be told what they're doing right, because as Joy, 16, pointed out, 'Maybe sometimes they aren't grateful enough if their kid is heading down the right track, or realise how hard it is to stay on the right track.' Even though they may act as if nothing touches them, they ache to be acknowledged and respected.

Girls need more support that speaks to *their* lives and concerns. They also need boundaries, not just to protect them, but so they can learn appropriate behaviour. Studies indicate that when parents supply positive boundaries, they assist that part of their daughter's brain that understands limits to develop, so their daughters can learn to make appropriate choices for themselves. Many girls do struggle to please their parents and girlfriends, to grow up slim and beautiful, be popular and successful, and come to terms with sex. With less pressure and more relevant support, theirs could be a markedly different experience.

Depressed

With all the pressures on teen girls, it's hardly surprising that depression is on the increase. One report indicates more than 15 per cent of our school-age girls are unhappy, and that one in five are experiencing such high levels of psychological stress that it's almost more than they can take.[1] In another study just under six out of ten girls admitted to feeling stressed out 'all the time' or 'sometimes'. Worries about their weight, body image and overall appearance were the main causes of their stress.[2] As we look at what's going on for teenage girls, we return to the issue of overstimulation. Their constant access to music videos, iPods, magazines, sitcoms, movies, mobile phones and the internet is a rich diet of entertainment and information by any standard. Add to this the pressure to succeed at school, the wider challenges of war, climate change and future job prospects, and it's not hard to see why life mightn't always seem so rosy for teen girls.

'I was so depressed this last summer and I didn't know why. I was depressed enough to the point where I started cutting myself. It felt so good to get my anger out though. I tried to hide my scars

from my mum, but she found them and her and I got into a huge fight. I had even planned to kill myself. I had it planned out that I was gonna hang myself, but I never got to, because my mum found my scars and put me into counselling. I hated the counsellor, but she actually saved my life.' *blondebrat*[3]

MANIC LIFESTYLES

There's also the question of lifestyle. Teen girls do tend to live at break-neck speed. Their daily schedule, which often reflects the manic lives of their parents, allows them little time to draw breath. As a society we have come to equate action with motivation. On the surface their many commitments look good, because girls seem to be getting on with their lives. We praise them for being self-starters and for their ability to fit so much in. But when you talk to girls, you quickly realise that often this way of living doesn't feel that fulfilling.

Just because today's girls lead busy social lives and seem self-assured and in control, doesn't mean they find it fulfilling, or that they are mature yet. 'We are really insecure and self-conscious, and we over-think things,' Whitney, 18, admitted. And while today's teens may seem more confident and worldly-wise, often their life experience is quite narrow. If they're not locked in their bedrooms, they're out with friends who pursue the same interests. They socialise with the same people, watch the same TV programs and movies, and read the same magazines. Teen girls need their own friendships and forms of expression, but these activities alone are not enough to prepare them for life's many and varied challenges. Yet again, access to strong friendships with a favourite aunt or family friend, who shares your values and whom your daughter can trust, can be invaluable in helping them gain a wider perspective, beyond the expectations of peers or parents.

A FRAGILE SENSE OF SELF

A number of school counsellors also spoke of the inability of today's teens to deal with failure, and of the high level of distress girls experience at the disintegration of close friendships. They found the response girls had to these situations was often out of proportion to the problem, especially when compared with girls in previous generations. 'I deal with a lot of depression and anxiety,' one counsellor told me. 'There's a lot of pressure. Their coping skills aren't great.' This fragility isn't just down to the girls, as this counsellor was quick to point out. 'A lot of them are starting from a shaky foundation, because their parents are separated and they're in blended families, or parents are working and away for an extended time.' This pressure can also come from academic and/or socially ambitious parents, or those who fail to put in place positive boundaries by becoming overly controlling.

Recent research has found that depressed people are far more sensitive to other people's emotions than the average person.

Behind their self-confidence there's considerable anxiety around a whole range of issues girls face, from how they come across to peers, to what adult life might bring. In one recent chat room where the topic was loneliness, Shani expressed anxieties that many girls talk of, 'I am going through a lot at school with rumours, fights, friends misunderstanding and bad grades. Every decision that I make seems to be absolutely wrong. I have nobody to talk to about anything. Everybody is either too busy or just doesn't want to talk at the time (including all my friends). Then they always seem confused when I tell them that life is just too hard at the time. I feel so enclosed and alone.'[4]

Our girls are under all kinds of pressures, and we need to appreciate this, so we can help improve their ability to cope. The many hours of homework and constant school assignments can be crippling, and allow girls little time to relax. They need to know that everyone feels unhappy and overwhelmed at times – this can help them re-evaluate and be sure they're not taking on too much, and that they're doing what they love, getting enough sleep, and so on. It helps when parents are honest about their own shortcomings, and can empathise about how uncomfortable it is to be sad or stressed out. We do live in fearful times, so this also needs to be taken into account. How adults react to issues such as terrorism and global warming will also colour how girls see the world. Conversations which constantly focus on doom and gloom don't encourage girls to feel optimistic. Clearly if a girl's depression is ongoing, seeking professional help is best. While local figures are hard to come by, the number of girls in the US aged 10 to 19 using anti-depressants between 2005 and 2006 was up by more than 9 per cent, as compared with less than 1 per cent for boys. Over this same period, the girls who took prescription drugs to help them sleep rose by about 12 per cent.[5]

SENSITIVE TO OTHER PEOPLE'S FEELINGS

While we may assume it's the girls who have become isolated from their parents and peers who are most likely to be depressed, research suggests that depressed people are very sensitive to other people's emotions, and unable to process these emotions, so there is no resolution for them.[6] At this age girls often feel responsible for other people's emotions, especially those of their parents, which can contribute to their depression. Teenage fragilities often coincide with a parent's fragilities – fear of retrenchment, health problems, less energy and confidence as they age, and caring for elderly parents. It's good for girls to understand there may be other concerns that are causing pressure in the family, so they don't feel they are to blame for everything. This helps girls start to glimpse the complexities of adult life, and to see how these issues can best be navigated.

Should a girl seem unable to shake off an encounter or situation that has disturbed her, this may indicate to parents something more is going on that she may need help resolving. Another finding suggests that adolescents who bully, as well as those who are bullied, are at an increased risk of depression and suicide.[7] This is a very different take on bullying amongst teenagers, and underlines the importance of gaining a greater understanding of what is going on for the victims as well as the perpetrators.

It can be difficult for parents to know how best to support girls, as girls who are depressed or suicidal are more likely to turn to friends, the net or the media for answers, thus cutting themselves off from the best means of support. Girls need parents and other adults so they know they're not alone in their depression, and can gain access to professional help.

According to depression expert Professor Ian Hickie, the huge emphasis in popular culture on the individual is also adding to teen isolation, because it deprives young people of a sense of community, where there is access to a range of people and support in times of need.[8] This isolation is made all the more acute with the growing gap between teenagers and adults, which can make girls believe adults can't help them, or just don't care. 'No teachers will come up to you and say, "How are you? What are you doing? What have you been up to?" It's more, "Have you done your homework?", which is really degrading, 'cos it's like they don't care,' said Sandi, 14.

'Sometimes it helps you to talk about it, but sometimes it kind of gets you down even more to talk about it.' *Joy, 16*

SUBSTANCE ABUSE

Clear links have been made between binge-drinking and depression. In studies of adult drinking patterns, women who binge-drink are shown to be more vulnerable to depression than men.[9] There is no reason this would be any less true for girls. It's not just the changes in body chemistry, which can spark depression in girls who binge-drink. Drinking lowers their inhibitions, encouraging girls to do things they'd never normally do. Once they have sobered up, these girls then have to face the consequences, making them even more down on themselves. Without good support and the opportunity to think things through, these mistakes can seem like the end of the road.

The drug scene is a whole lot more complex than it was. New drugs are appearing on the market, and 'old drugs' such as marijuana are no longer as innocent as they once seemed. With hydroponics, marijuana, the staple drug of the Sixties, has morphed into a drug that is far from benign. Hydroponically grown marijuana has higher concentrations of its main active ingredient, delta-9-tetrahydrocannabinol (THC). The chemicals and fertilisers used in propagation are also thought to be damaging to users. Increasing numbers of young people are reporting psychotic episodes after short-term use of this substance, as marijuana changes brain function. The younger a girl is when she begins smoking, the more profound these changes are likely to be. When marijuana is smoked during the teen years, it can also trigger depression, suicidal thoughts and schizophrenia, and can lead to addiction and mental health problems in later life.

Ecstasy, also popular amongst teens, has its risks. Long-term use has been shown to impair thought processes and memory.[10] It too is linked with depression, because it depletes the brain's serotonin, which enables us to feel happy.[11] In one study of girls who take drugs, a third admitted to having suicidal thoughts in the previous fortnight. Another 3 per cent agreed with the statement 'I want to kill myself.'[12]

In trying to understand what is going on, there's the important question of how mature teen girls are. As Barbara, a psychologist and school counsellor, points out, 'Often I feel they're forced to grow up so quickly, because of the information they have access to and the society they live in, when they're little kids still.' What Barbara has found is that frequently these girls don't get the support they need from parents, because parents are at a loss as to what to do. Or parents don't realise how vulnerable their daughter is.

Parents need to be aware of the kinds of pressures to drink and take drugs their daughters are likely to be subjected to. Acknowledging these pressures and talking about what can happen when girls step over the line helps girls consider their own boundaries more closely. Parents do need to be much more aware of drugs, so their girls don't see them as out of touch, and therefore unable to help or support them. Good parenting is about protecting girls, not about being popular. Unless informed conversations are taking place at home and at school, girls will look elsewhere. Here's one forum where a participant asks about whether they should smoke marijuana:

'i'm high right now so i guess there's my opinion,' MourningAir

'i use it, but I don't recommend that *you* do the same,' Branflakes

'i luv weed . . . sry. but i do,' XxredcutsxX

'weed is awesome. I wish i was high right now,' Derailedjet

'well i think if u are goin to do any so called Drug u should do weed it make u feel good and it dont have side effects like those other stupid ass drugs and its not so addictive. u neveerrr go to rehab and see someone their because they are addicted to weed. Weed is that best!!!!' chyk4nv[13]

When dealing with girls with depression, sensitivity is crucial. What might seem like a minor event to an adult may push some girls into a severe depression. All it might take is for a girl to be dumped by a boyfriend, fail an assignment, or say or do something she bitterly regrets, to plunge her into despair. Girls who are vulnerable to depression already have a fragile sense of self. They live on the edge. One failure or disappointment can cause them to disintegrate. It's so much easier when parents understand just how fragile girls can be, as it gives them a much better idea of how to respond.

Suicidal

When depression deepens, some girls are left feeling that suicide is the only way out. In late April 2007 two 16-year-old girls, Stephanie Gestler and Jodie Gater, were found hanging from a tree at the foot of the Dandenong Ranges. Depressed, isolated and unable to face the future, these two young girls had come to the end of the line, so they killed themselves.

When the police examined their websites, they discovered that in the months leading up to her death, Jodie had posted three suicide poems on her MySpace website, and just prior to killing herself, she added the plea, 'Let Steph n me b free'. In her last blog, Stephanie admitted she needed someone to talk to. Described as a quiet girl who spent time listening to music and surfing the internet, Stephanie seemed like a regular teenager battling the usual issues.

Life hadn't always been so dark for the girls. Stephanie had enjoyed her own circle of friends. But when she became interested in the emo culture and dress, her friends deserted her and the bullying began. From all accounts the bullying was pretty intense for Stephanie, with no resolution in sight. It also appears that Jodie had been struggling. Not long before the girls killed themselves, Jodie had changed schools and moved in with her father and his new partner. She had been having counselling. When the girls went missing, there were real concerns for their safety, but no-one imagined they were at risk of suicide.

This story is tragic on many levels. Much has been made of the girls' attraction to emo music and culture, but their situation is more complex than this. While no-one seems to have picked up on just how desperate these girls felt, the fact is that they had made several cries for help. The tragedy lies in part with the medium they had chosen to express their angst. As children of their generation, it was natural for Jodie and Stephanie to go on the net and tell the world how they were feeling – that's what girls their age do. The unfortunate thing is that cyberspace is the last place most parents go to when trying to work out what's happening with their daughters.

What this case highlights yet again is the growing lack of communication between generations. As we've already seen, teenage girls are acutely aware of this divide. I suspect girls feel this gap more intensely than boys, because they are encouraged to consider what other people are thinking and feeling. Also, cyberspace doesn't play a large part in parents' lives outside of work. Most have no idea about emo culture, or the other subcultures girls are attracted to. However, even a basic knowledge of adolescent subcultures helps parents understand what their daughters may be battling with or trying to express.

The net offers girls many wonderful opportunities for communication, knowledge and friendship. But when teen girls become isolated from their peers the net is often a desperately lonely space. As their parents appear to have no real understanding of their world, their issues, it's not hard to see why girls may think they're left with nowhere to go. This is not to suggest that Stephanie and Jodie's parents were to blame for their suicide. Like most parents, no doubt, they too have been swept along by the massive changes in teenage life, technology and popular culture. It's difficult for adults to know what is going on with teenagers, because we're all treading new ground. But had these parents understood more about teen sub-cultures, and the importance teens place on their websites and blogs as a way of expressing themselves, perhaps the outcome for Stephanie and Jodie might have been different.

CRY FOR HELP

Having sat in on a chat room recently, I can't help but wonder how many teen cries for assistance get answered satisfactorily. When girls are in an acute situation, sympathetic cyberfriends aren't enough. There's also the vexing question of how girls feed off each other's crises, only to end up emotional wrecks themselves, as can be seen by this exchange:

'I've been really depressed lately about everything,' said Molly, when referring to her own suicidal thoughts. 'And the only person I feel I can really talk to is my best friend. She has helped me through all of my major problems. But this one I just can't leave alone. I hate my body and practically everything about my life. I just feel like wasting my life and not doing anything about it.'

A number of girls were sympathetic, then Lana pitches in, clearly distressed for Molly. 'Please dont become suicidal! please! really, i dont ven know you but I implore!!, please dont kill yourself! not joking! im serious! your life is a precious thing and it DOES have meaning! you are not wasting anything! every moment is worth something and you must not let time just meaninglessly slip out of your life, second by second by hour by hour by weeks and so on! i beg you, dont even think about even thinking about suicide! it breaks my heart when people say that! your life is worth a LOT more than you think!'[1]

It's time we recognised how much our popular culture has become addicted to pain and dysfunction, and how suggestible our teens are. While it's important people talk about their pain, it isn't helpful when they define themselves by their woundedness. This preoccupation with pain is evident in the number of teen sites that are dark and disturbing. You can see this in the graphics, usernames and online signatures teens use. 'I speak and no-one hears me, I stand and no-one is looking, I speak but no-one listens, I explain but no-one is understanding,' reads one signature. 'I miss the days when I was happy, instead my days are filled with darkness. There is no light that helps me go on,' says another. 'Is life really worth living?' asks yet another.

GIRLS WHO TRY TOO HARD

While we tend to assume the girls who take their own lives are withdrawn or out of control, often the girls who do so are right into life. These are the girls who work hard to be accepted, to get on with their peers, to achieve. What makes these girls vulnerable to suicide is their level of anxiety and insecurity. As they expect so much from themselves, they constantly fall short of their expectations. When we add to this the aspirations parents, teachers and society hold for girls, it's not hard to see why for some this pressure is too much.

In the West we pride ourselves on our material wealth, compared to the rest of the world, and assume this translates to mental health. It's worth noting, however, that research suggests suicide is more likely to take place in emotionally fragmented societies than in poor ones.[2] Growing up in broken families with minimal community involvement or support makes the gradient a whole lot steeper for too many of our girls.

It's suggested that for every teenage suicide, there are more than a hundred unsuccessful attempts. Even a fraction of this number is too many. We need to work harder on the mental health of our girls, by nurturing their sense of self. This is hard to do in a 'sex-and-shopping' culture. I have no doubt that it is the emptiness of this way of living that compromises the happiness of our teenage girls. Should a girl seem distant from family and friends, lose interest in her appearance, seem despairing or guilty, change her eating or sleeping patterns, give away her favourite possessions, or suddenly seem happy after being down, parents need to seek immediate professional help. Or, if they feel intuitively something isn't right with their daughter, it's far better to take action than wait and see what happens.

Suicide doesn't only affect the girls who take their own lives. It is devastating for the teenagers left behind. In some cases a suicide can prove lethal for peers, who are tempted to take the same route. While certain teenagers are more at risk of copycat suicides than others, now schools and health professionals are aware of how suggestible peers can be. A number of studies indicate the danger of reporting on suicides in the media, because it lessens the taboo around suicide.[3] So, if a girl has a friend who has killed herself, it's important parents stay close, so they can gauge how their daughter is faring.

Now the coverage of teenage suicides is handled with extreme care, so copycat or cluster suicides don't result. Broadcasters avoid glorifying or sensationalising suicide in the media, and refrain from giving undue details of the suicides they do report.[4] The internet, however, is much more difficult to police. Experts are worried that it is intensifying the risk of suicide contagion, because of the factors we have examined. That said, the net can also be a positive influence. Just under 1500 MySpace users now have a link on their profiles to Lifeline to encourage those who are feeling down to get help. This is absolutely the direction we need to be going in.[5]

Violent girls

Everything about girls' lives is changing. When we think of teen violence, we tend to think of teenage boys. However, now teenage girls appear to be becoming more violent. A 15-year-old girl on a playing field in Berlin was attacked by a group of girls who punched her face, knocked her over, then burned her arms and cheek with a cigarette when she refused to give them money. The girls were aged 13 to 15.[1] In Brooklyn an 11-year-old girl was stabbed to death by a 9-year-old girl after an argument about a pink rubber ball.[2] Near Perth in Australia, two 16-year-old girls strangled their friend with a speaker wire, then placed her in a shallow grave under her house. 'Sunday morning me and her woke up, and we were just talking, and for some reason we just decided to kill her,' confessed one of the girls.[3]

'I think it's from a musical influence like hip-hop. Girls feel like they have to have this big, bad, don't-mess-with-me-or-I'll-kick-your-ass attitude – "It doesn't matter if I'm a girl, I'm still gonna beat the crap out of you."' *Amanda, 18*[4]

A 17-year-old Muslim teenager on the Gold Coast was charged with stabbing her mother to death and severely injuring her father over issues about her non-Muslim boyfriend.[5] A month later a 14-year-old girl, accused of stealing boxes of soft drinks, stabbed a 21-year-old man.[6] And when police found 53-year-old Sydney taxi driver Youbert Hormozi, his injuries were so critical they thought he'd been run over. He was attacked and robbed by 14-year-old girls armed with a knife. They wanted his mobile phone.

In London, 14-year-old Chelsea O'Mahoney liked to go out with a group of boys to beat up druggies, homeless people, or whoever crossed their path. These random attacks, which they referred to as 'happy slapping', culminated in assaults on eight men in an hour, including the horrific beating of 37-year-old bar manager David Morley, whose injuries were so severe, he too looked like he'd been hit by a car. His friend Alastair Whiteside, also attacked, watched helpless as David was literally beaten to death. Chelsea captured the beatings on her mobile phone. She had planned to post the footage on the net.[7]

GIRLS ARE BECOMING MORE VIOLENT

The gap between boys and girls is narrowing when it comes to violence. Over the last decade, the numbers of girls in their mid- to late teens involved in assault here has risen by 32 per cent.[8] Some parents have become so desperate about the violence they are experiencing in their own homes, they have been forced to take out apprehended violence orders. In 2005 over a third of the children aged 10 to 14 served with an apprehended violence order in New South Wales were girls. And over a third of teenagers in their mid- to late teens who had apprehended violence orders taken out against them were also girls.[9] 'Girls aged between 14 and 20 have become more aggressive,' one detective told me. 'They are not afraid to physically fight in an almost turf war mentality. They fight over boys, gossip, and as a result of drug taking, they're increasingly paranoid.'

'There are quite a few aggressive girls that weren't there before. They get into fights with each other, threatening one another. It can get really nasty.' *Rose, psychologist and school counsellor*

According to Harvard professor Deborah Prothrow-Stith, the ways boys and girls express their anger have now converged. She believes the increased violence in girls is reinforced by the fictional images of violent women in the media.[10] 'Now, we are seeing a pattern where they are more likely to act out aggressively,' she explains. 'There is an attitude among them that they need to be like boys – you need to give it and take it just like the boys.'[11]

Girls resort to violence because they feel threatened, or because they don't know how else to handle difficult situations. Their violence is directly related to the way their brains work. As our brains develop, we learn to control its more primitive aspect that lashes out or takes off in threatening situations. When this development doesn't happen, girls continue to operate in survival mode – taking out others as the first line of defence. Parents have a central role here. Girls who are raised to see violence as wrong tend not to resort to it.

WHEN ASSERTIVENESS TURNS TO VIOLENCE

An important part of growing up is learning to stand up for yourself. We encourage girls to put themselves out there, to have the courage to speak up, but it's important they learn that assertiveness and aggressive or violent behaviour are not the same thing. This doesn't mean girls can't benefit from knowing how to defend themselves. Many girls benefit from and enjoy martial arts classes. Here they learn how to handle and protect themselves without having to be violent or aggressive towards others. The argument that because some boys are violent, girls have the right to be violent, isn't helpful. Ultimately violence serves no-one.

'There are programs aimed at teaching girls to be assertive, to believe in themselves . . . That's great if it's done appropriately. However, some families don't understand the difference between aggression and assertiveness.' *Marlene Moretti, The Gender and Aggression Project*[12]

HAS GIRL POWER BECOME AN EXCUSE TO BE VIOLENT?

Violence is not empowering, and it's inappropriate in almost all situations, regardless of whether you're a boy or a girl. It's important parents reinforce this message by their own attitudes and behaviour, and by teaching girls how to resolve tricky situations without making them worse. Basically this means teaching girls emotional intelligence, so they don't lash out or behave in other inappropriate ways when they are in unfamiliar or threatening situations.

The problem we now face is that the ability to 'kick arse' in any situation has become a symbol of girl power, further blurring the lines between acceptable and unacceptable behaviour. We need to get girls to understand that violence isn't a sign of power. Schools report that girls are leaving behind the traditional ways of fighting, such as scratching and pulling hair and punching, and are causing more serious harm.

'Sometimes there's like catfights,' Lilly, 13, told me. 'If ever there's like two girls fighting, everyone's there like a magnet. It takes a while to break it up. There's like one girl, she's the queen. She started a fight and got punched in the face. The ambulance had to come, because they were both bleeding and in pain.' She went on to tell me how as soon as there's a mobile phone message saying that there's going to be a fight, everyone turns up. The teachers I spoke with backed this up.

Again we see the connection between drugs and violence. 'The girls who move on to methylamphetamines become extremely aggressive with others, in particular other girls and the police,' one detective told me. 'They are less likely to commit burglaries, in my experience, but will shoplift and bag-snatch — take a handbag off a chair or out of a shopping trolley, as opposed to a direct snatch from a person,' he explained.

According to psychology professor Marlene Moretti, who has done extensive research into violent girls, girls are already under pressure as they enter adolescence. She sees the growth in the aggression in girls as connected to the wider challenges they're trying to deal with. 'They're competing for social status and trying to be attractive. Wanting to feel part of a group, they can drift into groups of girls where they feel they can compete. Often that means being involved in aggressive behaviour with each other.'[13]

'I think it's just kinda fun, kinda like showing off. You just use all your strength and take somebody down.' *Dolores, 16*[14]

VIOLENT HEROINES

Alongside the impact of violent movies on girls is the explosion of a strong voyeur culture, as expressed in reality TV, Xanga, MySpace, YouTube and blogging. Now some girls are celebrating their violence by posting it on the net. Many don't think twice about capturing their violent behaviour on their mobile phones and circulating it to friends, or simply posting these clips on the web. Video games don't help, as killing zones on the body are often detailed, and those who take out the most opponents are rewarded.

Every day teens are being offered scenarios that are more graphic and real, and way beyond the comprehension of most mums and dads. Take this mobile phone game just out: 'Experience the feel of cobblestone streets, machine gun bursts, and light saber pulses right in your mobile. Or feel the asteroids hit and bounce off your star ship and get the sensation of fighting for control as you approach the speed of light. Before games were boring, just graphics and sound. Now you can feel the action, even with the sound turned off,' it promises.[15]

Paediatrics professor Dr Howard Spivac has no doubt that the amount of violence in the media encourages girls to be violent, and teaches them that 'fighting is appropriate and acceptable when dealing with hurt, pain, anger and conflict.'[16] For at-risk girls, the kinds of heroines found in such movies as *Charlie's Angels* and *Million Dollar Baby* are like role models. These girls are drawn to heroines who are able to handle themselves in dark situations. It's not just vulnerable girls who love kick-arse heroines; the wider public is mesmerised by them as well. Some of these women, like Uma Thurman in *Kill Bill*, are very bad girls — that's part of their enormous attraction. While many girls are unaffected by these movies, in the absence of good education and more positive role models, at-risk girls find it much harder to distinguish between fantasy and reality. With so little to fall back on in threatening situations, they lash out.

'Unless we do something about this (violence), we are going to see girls going down the same path that we have seen men and boys going down for the past several decades.' *Dr Howard Spivak, professor of paediatrics*[17]

While the increase in violence in girls is in part down to the media, for a number of girls it's also due to neglect and abuse at home. On a chilly November night in 1997 Reena Virk, 14, from Manitoba, was repeatedly beaten and burned with a cigarette, then made to remove her jacket and shoes. She was beaten again, then drowned. Seven girls and one boy took part in this horrific killing. When award-winning Canadian writer Rebecca Godfrey researched this terrible incident, she found that most of the girls involved in this horrendous killing had come from violent homes. Two had fathers who had been murdered.

What struck Rebecca was how out-on-a-limb these girls were. 'There was nobody who came through for them, like a social worker or a program,' she said. With an absence of guidance, these girls were left to find their own way forward, and like so many girls they turned to the media for their role models. 'The pop culture they were interested in was glorified violence, which influenced their sense of what was glamorous and powerful,' she reflected.[18]

> **'Girls haven't learned any rules of engagement. They underestimate their own power. Group violence gives them permission, and they often go way overboard.'** *Patricia Pearson, researcher*[19]

Often abuse and neglect helps form the violent tendencies of at-risk girls. Violence becomes their way of dealing with issues and getting the respect of their peers. The media gives this violence shape. When these girls attack they intend to harm. Some are so shut down emotionally that they rarely show remorse for what they have done. They see their victims as deserving what they get.

> **'With the Reena Virk case, these same girls had attacked another girl several weeks before in a similar way, setting her hair on fire. In this attack, one of the girls was a kickboxer. You wouldn't have seen that 20 years ago.'** *Rebecca Godfrey*[20]

When I was talking with one teacher, she too confirmed that girls are getting more violent. She went on to tell me of one fight that almost got seriously out of hand. 'One of the powerful, popular girls got a group of girls together to wait for a girl they didn't like on her way home,' she recounted. 'The girl was held down and badly bashed. A concerned parent drove past and saw what was happening, leapt out of her car and grabbed the girl. As soon as they were in the car, all the students gathered around the car and started rocking it. The woman had no option but to risk running someone over as she drove off. The kids then picked up rocks and were throwing them at her.' It transpired the chief bully had been molested by her father for a number of years. 'What we see with girls fighting, is that it isn't a fair fight like there is with boys — two fighting together. It's about power and humiliation,' this teacher told me.

VIOLENT GIRLS AND ABUSE

One of the most dramatic findings to come out of research into girls in the criminal justice system is the high rate of abuse many have suffered while growing up. One study found that over seven out of ten girls had experienced at least one, if not several, kinds of abuse. Even more shocking was the discovery that many of these girls were suffering post-traumatic stress disorder symptoms as a result of their abuse.[21] Dysfunctional families and parents with criminal backgrounds were also key risk factors in causing girls to become violent.[22] It is now thought that as girls are brought up to be more sensitive to relationships, especially close relationships, if these relationships break down it may have a more dramatic impact on them.[23]

Another study indicates a high level of risk-taking and neglect amongst girls in custody. Thirty per cent of girls in one survey talked of experiencing high if not very high psychological distress. Just over one in four had never used condoms, or used them less than half the time they had casual sex. More than half these young women had injected drugs in the twelve months prior to custody, while just under one in four had seriously considered suicide.[24]

The increase in aggression in girls mirrors the increasing violence in society. By the time a teenager reaches 18 it is estimated they will have seen around 200 000 acts of violence. This includes a staggering 40 000 murders on the news and in films.[25] Violence is a learned behaviour, which is now reinforced by a steady diet of violent movies and video games, where the female heroines are sexy and extremely violent. Part of their sexiness lies in their ability to bring others down. Lara Croft and her equivalents take no prisoners, and their fans love them for it.

As our family and community structures continue to crumble, it should be no surprise that many of our girls are not getting the protection they need to thrive, and have become casualties of this fragmentation. Theo Padnos, who taught literature to adolescents jailed for a range of crimes including murder, discovered it was the myths which underpinned violent movies, as well as the violence itself, which attracted the adolescents he was working with. Although he was teaching boys, his findings could well have some relevance to violent girls. The boys he taught were so disconnected from family and community, they no longer believed they had a future. In some ways their violence was an attack on the meaninglessness of life. It was their only way of fighting back at a society that didn't seem to care. Violence helped them make sense of a world in which they feel left out, ignored, unimportant.[26]

Part of the way forward in dealing with the growing violence in girls surely has to do with addressing the breakdown in families and communities. As Pulitzer prize-winning writer and journalist Ron Powers points out, 'Children crave a sense of self-worth. That craving is answered most readily through respectful inclusion: through the reintegration of our young into the intimate circles of family and community.'[27] Yet again we get back to the critical importance of belonging and acknowledgement. Girls also need more protection. Apart from their family, they need community to experience a wider sense of belonging and support. When we fail to provide these elements, we fail our girls.

Secret lives

The decline in family and community support has forced some girls to lead their own separate lives to a level that can leave them extremely vulnerable. This trend is helped along by pop culture, which engages girls because it is relevant and fun. However, pop culture can be limiting for girls as it's often the only lens through which girls view the world. Most teen girls don't know that pop culture is big business and is largely manufactured by adults, who feed off their anxieties and aspirations to get them to consume. Pop culture also draws girls into a complex landscape of choices way beyond a parent's protection and influence. Girls like pop culture because it offers them a sense of belonging. It does this in part by actively encouraging girls to operate independently of their families, as they're much easier to sell to once they're beyond parental influence.

'We're just plastered with pop culture, with TV and music and everything. It's really intense. Like it's the only thing we really know.'
Whitney, 18

Girls love secrets, and with the help of pop culture they have their own secret language, which helps ensure their interchanges remain strictly private. Take the message 'ru f2t? imo it's nbd. ssdd. sc icbw. omg g2r. suitm spst. otb. bff'. While it makes little sense to most adults, our teens know exactly what it says: 'Are you free to talk? In my opinion, it's no big deal. Same shit different day. Stay cool, it could be worse. Oh my God, got to run. See you in the morning, same place same time. Off to bed. Best friends forever.'

At first glance these developments may not seem to be such a big deal. However, they're nowhere near as innocent as they appear. There are now hundreds of abbreviated and new words in the teen lexicon, which enable girls to have a secret life with peers that overtakes all the other significant, balancing influences in a teenage girl's life. There are helpful acronyms such as 'prw' (parents are watching), and 'pos' (parents over shoulder), for example. If they're referring to porn, it's spelt 'pron', so parents don't blink an eyelid. Should they get a 'booty call', it may well be an offer to have sex or '53X'. If they're 'off their face' and 'crazy drunk', they are 'crunk' or %*), so most parents will be none the wiser. And while references to 'swimming' may seem innocuous, they're just as likely to mean 'off their face' as a trip to the pool or beach. If she's planning to 'hook up', a girl may well be planning sex rather than networking. And if she's attracted to risky sex, she may well be up for a threesome or '3SUM'. The secret language of teens is such that adults don't even notice what's going on right under their noses, as they don't know what to look out for. If you go to www. urbandictionary.com, you can see how many words and abbreviations there are. This language is growing all the time.

The secrets girls share manifest in hundreds of subtle ways, and may include anything from their choice of username to the 'wallpaper' they have on their website. It doesn't take a genius to see that a girl who calls herself XxredcutsxX online is likely to be cutting, or that someone whose site wallpaper is decorated with pills may well be into prescription drugs. Often parents are in the dark, because they don't see the world this way, which is exactly what at-risk teens are banking on. The same is true of screensavers on mobile phones. The choices available to girls don't just include fluffy animals and pretty scenery. Websites are also a growing concern for parents. Smart girls who want to keep their 'real' online presence to themselves create a 'front' website with everything parents would want to see, so they don't look any further.

'Since I was 12, the main thing that's changed is the internet stuff. Social networking sites: you have to be a part of them, especially MySpace and, more recently, Facebook.' *Klara, 16*

Having a secret life beyond the reach of parents and other authority figures is something most teen girls long for. Using their own secret language, messages and signals are all part of girls finding their own way. The solution is not to ban girls from interacting with peers, but to give them a strong framework and sense of self, so they are able to evaluate what is offered them more realistically. Similarly, while technology has its dangers, it also has a really important and valid role in teen lives. Once parents understand its limitations, parents can help their girls fill in the gaps.

When I spoke with Dr Joe Tucci, CEO of the Childhood Foundation in Australia, he was concerned at how new technologies were drawing teens away from parents and closer to their peers, which meant that often girls were lacking good information to draw from to solve their problems. When parents are aware of the challenges their girls now face, alongside good family conversations, there are other good resources for them to access. NetSmartz.org has excellent material for teens, and parents, on cyber issues, including videos of teens who talk about unpleasant net experiences they have survived. Kids and teens are encouraged to tell their own stories and seek advice here. NSTeens.org also deals with net issues in a lively and contemporary way through comics and video clips. For up-to-date information for parents, it's hard to go past www.NetFamilyNews.org.

SOCIAL WHIRLWINDS

Because the teen world is changing continually, it demands girls' constant attention. This explains in part why girls are big socialisers, and why when they're home they're continually texting, chatting online or catching up with magazines and TV. While this never-ending activity drives many parents mad, few succeed in slowing their girls down. 'My mum doesn't understand the whole aspect of socialising,' complained Alana, 18. 'For us it's a huge thing. Like we do it a lot. Times have changed. It creates a lot of friction between me and my mum, because she doesn't realise I need to go out, even though it's kind of a lot.'

For our girls, the influence of peers is constant and intense. That's why being in the loop at all times is essential. Should they feel their status is in jeopardy, they will use whatever resources they can to cover their tracks. After deciding to give her family a break from TV, Debra was surprised to discover her young daughter, who was barely a teenager, had been reading the TV guide so she could look like she knew what was happening in the TV programs her girlfriends watched.

The less secure girls feel about themselves, the more vulnerable they will be to peer pressure. When parents can understand and empathise with these pressures, attempts at positive discussion are less likely to end up in a screaming match. There also have to be smarter ways to draw girls into a more profound sense of belonging through community activities that feed their passion, more proactive websites for girls, and a wider choice of good literature to engage them.

'Mom may be cool, but she can wait – not quite the same as that special friend with news to share.' *VibeTonz-Enabled Mobile Phones*[1]

The explosion of new technologies has made it much easier for girls to lead double lives. Girls are eager to embrace these hot high-tech items, because clever marketers know how to ensure their products hit the mark. 'We're always up on everything. We always have the new phone, the new iPod,' said Whitney, 18. 'We're a great market for these things. They make it enjoyable. The way they market to us is fun.' These gizmos don't just generate big bucks. They are also the perfect vehicle for advertisers to reach girls direct with more opportunities to purchase.

Aware of teen girls' desire to lead their own lives, many smart marketers are quick to capitalise on their need for privacy. One recent example I came across was a mobile phone company encouraging girls to 'Rev up ringtones. Indulge your inner mix-master and synchronize the sense of vibrations with music. You can get ringtones with touch sensations and match them to each of your friends' calls. Kind of like a secret handshake.'[2]

EMBRACING THEIR HIGH-TECH WORLD

The ways teen girls can access pop culture continues to grow with the availability of laptops, mobile phones, iPods, MP3 players and so on. On the net alone, there are dozens of virtual worlds and teen forums to sign up for, and a whole range of social networking opportunities from MySpace, Xanga and Facebook to CyWorld, Tagged, Flickr and Friendster, to name but a few. On YouTube girls can watch movies, TV programs, music videos and clips.

All these opportunities help explain why girls are so busy. The net can soak up several hours a day. 'There's hotmail where you can get messages from friends,' Lilly, 13, explained. 'MSN where you can meet friends from all over the world. Bebo, invented before MySpace, and MySpace where you can put information about yourself and get new friends, put pics of you and your friends. It's pretty cool.'

It is thought that by their mid-teens most kids have watched around 15000 hours of TV alone. This is often more time than they have spent with their parents or friends.[3]

When girls register for access to teen sites, chat rooms and forums, they connect them to their email, MySpace page, MSN and other links, so they don't have to log in and out to keep up with friends. 'I can have up to eight pages open at a time,' Abbie, 17, told me. Like most of the girls I spoke with, she loves time on the net, even if it does eat into her time to do other things. 'Often I start off looking for something for an assignment, then get distracted,' she admitted.

Many of today's girls have been living separate lives from their parents' from quite a young age. These new mediums enable them to take this separation to new levels. Even the influence of TV cannot be under-estimated. It is thought that by their mid-teens most kids have watched around 15 000 hours of TV alone. This is often more time than they have spent with their parents or friends.[4]

While girls do need to be independent, what is concerning is the number of experiences and influences girls are subjected to that their parents know little about. Most of the girls I spoke with had stories about operating extremely successfully under the radar. Mobile phones and the net take the hard work out of organising a secret rendezvous with a boyfriend, or a clandestine party in a local park once the family is asleep. Staying in touch with parents by mobile phone can give parents the illusion that everything is fine, when this may not be the case.

'You cannot put a device in your child's hand if you don't know what the capabilities of that device are. [Mobile] phones are a perfect example. We will be seeing many problems in the future with the web-enabled camera phones that just about all teens now have. Parents have to speak frankly with their kids about the potential risks in attracting adults online who may have sexual intents toward their child.' *Detective Frank Dannahey*

WHERE ARE THE BOUNDARIES FOR GIRLS?

Girls do need more freedom as they mature, but as social analyst Richard Eckersley points out, freedom is only meaningful when they are pushing out from a structured environment. For girls who have grown up without boundaries, freedom is pretty meaningless, because they have nothing to judge it against, or retreat to if things get tricky.[5] A number of teachers and school counsellors spoke to me of their frustration at parents, who have steadfastly refused to set any boundaries for their girls until they were 14 or 15, by which stage it is too late.

While there will always be girls drawn to risky behaviour, the huge popularity of reality TV shows and the constant coverage of the crazy lifestyles of teen celebrities has meant that in a few short years unacceptable and dysfunctional behaviour has almost become the norm. As Alana, 18, pointed out to me, 'Now it's cool to be doing crazy things. There are no secrets. Everything's on public display now. It's accepted. It's the norm. It's kind of the way things are.' Add to this the impact of new technologies and parents' ignorance of what teens can do with these devices, and suddenly we see how much more vulnerable our girls are. While they are growing up, our teenage girls still need protection, and to know where to go to get good advice.

Even the best of parents can find themselves in unenviable situations. Recently a friend discovered her 12-year-old daughter had been photographing herself semi-naked with her mobile phone, then sending the pictures to a boy down the road. Like many parents, my friend had no idea her daughter was taking these kinds of photos, let alone where she was sending them. When buying a girl a mobile phone, parents need to ask themselves whether she needs to take photos. If so, they need to educate her on what can happen if she does take 'silly' photos.

As someone who is well versed in internet predators and abuse, Detective Frank Dannahey reminds us that while parents tend to only learn the features they need on a device, teens learn every feature. Often parents aren't aware of potential problems, because they don't know what a mobile phone or computer is capable of. They have no idea how to download a photo off someone's website, or how to share this photo with others at the click of a mouse. 'In my parents' internet safety programs I always say that teens embrace technology and often use it in a dangerous way,' Detective Frank Dannahey told me. 'When adults fail to come to terms with technology, they are allowing teens to police themselves online.'[6]

Girls need to know how vulnerable they are when they do go it alone. Sometimes they are reluctant to talk to parents about issues because of the over-the-top reaction they might get. But where there is family or wider community support, they are more likely to use it. When parents can be open about the challenges of teen life, this helps break down the differences between generations.

ADDICTED

Parents aren't always conscious of how addictive these new technologies can be for teens. Today's girls have grown up with the expectation of being entertained round-the-clock, and these mediums make this possible. In one study, almost eight out of ten teens admitted the media was addictive, especially video games, TV and chat rooms. This was borne out in my interviews with girls. 'I spend a lot of time on the internet. I have a number of accounts like My Space, Facebook, email, downloading music, and MSN – except I took it off because I spent way too much time on it. Looking up stuff also takes a lot of time,' Abbie, 17, told me. Lilly, 13, agreed, 'Yeah, it's addictive,' she admits, adding, 'but you can send messages to friends quickly.' This addiction has now been recognised by psychologists as Internet Addiction Disorder (IAD).

'I'm on the computer a lot talking to friends, going on to websites, checking out new music. I'm on it almost every night for a couple of hours maybe. It does make me stay up when I should go to bed. I mainly stay up late talking to friends.' *Ashlee, 15*

Most girls said that time on the net did often mean they didn't get enough sleep, and that they struggled to get homework and chores done. 'I do use MSN quite frequently,' Sara, 18, admitted. 'I go through phases where I go on MSN all night – it's a huge distraction.'

It's not just the net that can soak up a lot of time. Now that girls can contact each other round-the-clock, many leave their mobile phones on overnight. They'd prefer to take a call in the middle of the night than be out of the loop. 'They come to school tired because their mobile phone rang at three in the morning,' one school counsellor told me. 'They feel they have to be connected 24/7. They're scared to miss out in case something's happened and they're left out.'

When I spoke with girls they freely admitted this was the case. 'I couldn't live without my phone, because I'm an incredibly social person,' Sara, 18, explained. 'I love being able to contact people and for people to contact me.' She feels anxious whenever she inadvertently leaves her phone behind, and has on occasions sneaked home to get it. 'I keep it on 24/7, which is probably bad, but I like being contactable. Someone rang me in the middle of the night at like 3.30am or 4.00am to check I'd got home okay the other day, when I was in like a deep sleep, so I yelled at them, but that's only because I was so asleep.' This need to be contactable all the time adds to the very real problem of sleep deprivation we examined earlier.

One option for parents is to have internet access blocked at certain times, or after their girls have been on the computer for a designated time. Having girls place their mobile phones in a central spot in the home before they go to bed is a good idea also, as it helps them have a good night's sleep. Reminding girls of the health issues they may be vulnerable to from lack of sleep – early-onset diabetes, weight gain, attention problems, depression, finding it hard to cope – helps them see why parents are taking these moves to protect them. Reinforcing how much a daughter means and how much they appreciate her ability to make good decisions helps build her independence and self-esteem.

BEDROOM CULTURE

Not all girls are heading down the wrong track, but increasingly they are leading significant other lives, and often with very little experience in how best to protect themselves should they get into trouble. When I asked one young teen what girls her age worried about most, she said it was going out to places she didn't have permission to go to, and hanging out with the wrong crowd. She enjoys the thrill of doing this, but also found it hard to say no to her friends. Again this lifestyle was made all the more possible with ready access to the net and mobile phones.

The vulnerable situation many girls find themselves in is heightened by the teen bedroom culture. When they are at home, girls spend most of their time in their rooms, where they often have access to a whole range of technologies and information without supervision. In one American survey of 10- to 17-year-olds, over a third of those using the net said they had been exposed to unsolicited sexual material in the last year alone. This was in spite of the better filtering software in their homes.[7] It is concerning how often girls will talk about complete strangers they meet on the net as if they were close friends. All this is happening way beyond the knowledge and protection of parents, and as we'll see, girls' attraction to secret lives can lead them to some pretty dark places.

As new technologies are appearing constantly, it's vital parents keep up to speed. Encouraging their girls to show parents new features on the computer and mobile phones helps parents reinforce their interest in their daughter's life, and also indicates they're not as out-of-touch as they may appear. Reading more widely and participating in parents' forums on the net will also assist them to fill in the gaps. Having internet access in a communal place in the home, and only allowing home users access to certain settings, chat rooms, games and voice-over internet protocol programs, are excellent measures to further protect girls.

In spite of their growing maturity, girls need this support. Research shows that the teenage brain is still a work in progress, and with the additional pressure of fluctuating hormones, it is hard for teens to read situations accurately and respond accordingly. Access to good teen forums, plenty of constructive family debate and more life education at school and beyond it, helps girls over this hurdle, so they are free to pursue their passions and to work towards the futures *they* dream of.

Alone in cyberspace

As computers and the internet are so much a part of our lives, it is easy to assume it's always been this way. But five or six years ago teenagers weren't surfing the net. Older teens are very aware of this. 'Everything's changed with the internet and googling,' Alana, 18, reflected. 'None of it was around when I was like 9, or not that I remember.' A number of girls brought this up. 'When I was 12, it was a bit odd using the internet regularly, and having my own email address,' Alex, 16, recalls. 'Can't believe that was only four years ago.'

> Because the web seems safe and anonymous, it gives girls the confidence to do and say things they wouldn't otherwise.

There are many reasons why cyberspace has become a big part of girls' lives. For some the web is the perfect way to overcome their loneliness or shyness, or to prove they've got what it takes. Because the web seems safe and anonymous, it gives girls the confidence to do and say things they wouldn't otherwise. 'We're more at home with the computer than face to face. It's very different talking to friends online,' Ashlee,

15, told me. 'There's like no emotion. You can't tell what a person is feeling. It's easier to say something on the computer than in real life.'

This sentiment was shared with many of the girls I spoke with. 'Often it's hard to relate to people in real life,' said Abbie, 17. 'But like with YouTube you can have people you confide in, you can be popular, you can have a belonging. You can have friends that are a million miles away who know more about you than your friends at school.' This was how Alana, 18, felt also. 'I like MSN,' she explained. 'It's a good way of talking to 50 billion people at one time. I guess at our age it's easy to get obsessed. You don't have to see people. You don't have to be in the same room as them. Unlike if you're talking with someone face to face, it gives you time to think before you reply.'

THE CHANGING FACE OF FRIENDSHIP

Experts are now speculating as to whether this new way of connecting with friends on the net will change the nature of friendship, and the ways people will interact with each other when they grow up. When girls are on the net, they're far more in control in relationships than in real life. They can log on and off at will. People have to wait to be invited into chat rooms, and can be banished in a moment. In cyberspace there's no need for patience or negotiation, or to consider someone else's point of view. You can move on at the click of a mouse. Girls who are more technically savvy can block people without them realising it on such sites as MSN, MySpace and YouTube. There are concerns that with the amount of time spent on the net, teens are missing out on building basic social skills, and that this can then erode their self-confidence in face-to-face situations, because they're not sure of how to behave.

'While there are fast ways to connect with others, girls are feeling very lonely. They're connected night and day, but emotionally they're not connected.' *Barbara, school counsellor and psychologist*

216

On the net there's little need for empathy or working through situations, all of which help girls develop as individuals. The growing lack of empathy girls are displaying concerned the teachers and school counsellors I spoke with. If girls only have superficial connections with others, they don't develop emotional intelligence. It's hard then for them to consider other people's needs, fragilities and expectations, making it difficult to communicate effectively with the people around them.

As Barbara, a school counsellor, pointed out, 'This is the irony. While there are fast ways to connect with others, girls are feeling very lonely. They're connected night and day, but emotionally they're not connected.' Dr Joe Tucci agrees. 'You have more control of relationships in cyberspace – it's not real life. It doesn't help shape the skills required to deal with conflict and resolution that you need to have meaningful relationships in adult life. The more mediated your relationships are in virtual space, the more you run the risk of practising blunt strategies to deal with situations in real life.'[1]

All the girls I spoke with loved having cyberfriends, and the fact that these 'friends' were from all around the world. As they live in a popularity-focused culture, it's no surprise that the numbers of friends they had were extremely important to them. However, while girls may have a whole bunch of friends on the net, these contacts are a long way from true friendships. Some of these friends may care, but they're not around to provide the stuff that real friends are made of – human warmth, loyalty, empathy and being there for someone through thick and thin. And so ultimately these 'friendships' can make girls' lives more isolated.

BEING WHOEVER YOU WANT TO BE

One of the great attractions of the net is that you can be anyone you want to be. This can be very appealing to teen girls struggling to find their own identity. By taking on another persona, girls are less likely to work on their real-life identity – to explore their potential, to be excited about what kind of woman they hope to be. When you look at some of the net names, graphics and signatures girls use, you get a sense of their desperation to appear grown-up and in control. It takes little more than a quick random search to find some of the heavily sexualised identities a number of girls are using. The less sure a girl is of her own identity, the more she will search for one outside of herself.

'I had a lot of phases when I got addicted to MSN, and talked with strangers for a very long time. I was up until midnight, or sometimes past it, but not always, otherwise I'd be dead.' *Alana, 18*

The internet has now become one of the many ways girls can push their boundaries. 'It's one of the things that I argue gives it a kind of excitement as a place to live out your fantasies and experiment with aspects of yourself,' says MIT professor Sherry Turkle, an expert in the impact of new technologies. 'But it also means that when you meet people online they're not necessarily who they say they are.'[2]

If you're a girl with few friends, then the opportunity to assume a different identity in chat rooms and virtual worlds, or on your own website, can have a huge appeal. Here you can be all the things you're not in real life – outrageous, fearless, in control. The net offers girls the chance for a complete makeover – a new body, new name, new identity. On the net girls can be as mature, intelligent, sexy and 'out there' as they want. As girls embrace these online identities, many start to take on a second life that is more real to them than their everyday life. 'They (teens) do less face-to-face talking, less phone talking, less playing outside than any other generation, and because of that, the internet is real to them,' says internet lawyer Perry Aftab, 'but the risks aren't.'[3]

The net offers girls the chance for a complete makeover – a new body, new name, and new identity.

NOT-SO-SECRET CONFESSIONS

The desire to have their own private lives is nothing new for teenage girls. This is something all girls yearn for. Previous generations of girls poured out their secrets in personal diaries, which they hid from parents and siblings. Now they spill out their anxieties and aspirations on MySpace, Facebook and YouTube, or on their personal blogs, without any idea of who they might be exposing themselves to. This mightn't seem such a big deal were it not for the subjects girls choose to talk about, or the situations some find themselves in.

STRANGER DANGER

Studies indicate that often teens are happy to provide their information to complete strangers, as they don't feel it's important to know the true identity of the person they are chatting with. They do so even though it's on the web, where they are most exposed to inappropriate violent and sexual material.[4] When you sit in chat rooms or teen forums, you see how easy it is for girls to be manipulated into situations they might not be ready for, or that are not what they expected. The following interchange in one teen forum gives some sense of the kinds of situations girls can face. There were several people in this forum. I have pruned back the chat to the central players – two guys and the girl who appears to be taking their 'bait'.

'C'mon girls . . . let's see 'em. Post pics here of your cleavage for all the horny guys on TH. Suggestions: Low-cut shirt. Squeeze em together with your arms, hands, or whatever (let someone else take the pic if possible). get them to look massive. i don't want to hear any BS like "mine are too small". use what you got! There will be no complaints unless they are gay or just retarded.' Phuck buddy

'I'm tempted rofl.' Omfgidc

'Are you telling me that if there are a few girls who post their cleavage pics on here . . . you wouldn't be happy about it? hmmmm? Just sit back.

Shhhhh . . . and watch the show.' Phuck buddy

'This would be a beautiful thing if we could just get a little female participation. cmon girls step up.' Van 18

'LOL @ people talking about my boobs. i haven't decided if i'm freaked out or flattered. aha. Rofl' Omfgidc

'Try to be flattered – itl help u sleep at night especially if u decide to participate.' Van 18

'I've participated enough in loads of other threads involving tits.' Omfgidc, who then backs off.

WHEN THE NET GETS DANGEROUS

Girls who are less discerning may not realise they are being carefully groomed to do things they had no intention of doing when their cyber-relationship began. All it takes is one conversation to reach a different level and suddenly a girl becomes vulnerable. For some girls this means having to beat a hasty retreat. Less savvy girls may well find themselves in over their heads. Twelve-year-old Shevaun Pennington from Lowton, England made world headlines when she vanished with her American ex-marine boyfriend, Toby Studabaker, 33, who had come to police attention for previous incidents with underage girls. Before she took off, Shevaun spent a lot of time on the net at home. But as everything seemed fine, her parents felt they had had no cause for concern. After several tense days and an international police hunt, Shevaun was located safe and well, even though she'd skipped the country. Studabaker was charged with abduction and incitement to gross indecency.[5] What the fallout for this young woman has been, only time will tell.

Thirteen-year-old Kacie Woody wasn't so lucky. As she lived in the country, most phone calls were charged at long-distance rates, so Kacie turned to the internet as a way of chatting with friends. In the summer of 2002 she met Dave Fagan, a drop-dead-gorgeous 18-year-old, who lived on the other side of the country. They were in a Yahoo Christian chat room at the time. Dave wasn't Kacie's first online boyfriend. Like many teens, Kacie was shy until she got to know people.[6] Not long before Kacie was abducted, Dave's aunt, who lived nearby, fell into a coma. Dave came to stay with his aunt until she died. Kacie was at a girlfriend's place the night Dave rang to say his aunt was getting worse. During the conversation the girls heard someone moving around outside, and ended up barricading themselves in the bedroom.

Some days later, Kacie vanished. Police managed to track down a David Fuller from out of town, who was registered at a local motel. Fuller had drawn attention to himself by flying off the handle when his internet connection wasn't working. Telephone records showed he'd been in touch with Kacie. By the time Kacie was found, she was dead. She'd been sexually assaulted, then shot in the head. Kacie never went off without telling people where she was going. Tragically for her, the night Fuller abducted her, her father, a police officer, was out, as was her brother.[7] These are extreme cases, but girls need to know the very real risks of engaging with strangers on the net. Even the briefest visit to www.mycrimespace.com or www.netsmartz.org will give parents an idea of the kinds of situations that are happening over the net.

Sometimes girls can be victims without inviting any attention. When high school champion pole-vaulter Allison Stokke got a call from friends, she was shocked to discover her photo was all over the internet. Someone had photographed Allison at a meet, then placed the photo on the net. A short video of Allison at another meet was posted on YouTube, and received thousands of hits. Then popular blog WithLeather.com got into the act, posting another photo with the following introduction: 'Meet pole-vaulter Allison Stokke. Hubba hubba and other grunting sounds.'[8] Allison has now been subjected to a barrage of crude and creepy calls. It's almost impossible for her to go out without being recognised. The tragic thing is that Allison wasn't doing anything other than enjoying her sport. The fact that she was young and attractive made her vulnerable.

Whether it's abuse by friends or strangers, girls need to fully understand how careful they need to be about their language and personal details, as well as the sites they visit, because ultimately nothing is private on the net. If parents are concerned about what their girls have been doing on the net, they need to take a look in the history menu on the internet toolbar of their computer. Here they will see where their daughter has been over the last few days. Taking a look in the favourites menu will also give them some idea of where she has been spending her time. If their daughter spends hours surfing the net and her history is empty, this may be cause for concern, as their daughter has deleted the sites she has visited.

Parents then need to decide how they are going to deal with this. Sensitivity is the key. The more open and understanding a parent's discussions, the less girls will have to be secretive. At the same time, girls do need a separate life. Encouraging them to keep a journal, or put together private scrapbooks of their life and experiences, is a safer and more imaginative approach.

Getting into porn

It's important parents recognise not all net activity girls undertake is innocent. Some girls actively surf the net for porn sites from their early teens. How much porn is being accessed by young girls is hard to assess. What we do know is that increasing numbers of girls are visiting porn sites and/or getting access to pornographic DVDs from friends' parents' collections. Some girls are doing this because they're curious. Others want to know how to attract boyfriends or keep them interested. 'The internet just opens things right up,' one teacher told me. 'I've had girls ask me in sex ed classes, "Miss, is that like what you see with porno stuff?"' The net is saturated with sexy language and graphics, and normalises obscene behaviour, which makes porn seem fine. While local figures are hard to come by, NielsenNetRatings suggests that one in five girls aged 12 to 16 in the UK view net porn at least once a month.[1] With the refinements in technology, girls are now able to access porn from their mobile phones.

After years of being exposed to sexualised images in advertising, and seeing sex in films and on TV, for some girls porn is the obvious next step. For a growing number of girls, talking about porn with their peers seems exciting and super-cool. Other girls look at a few sites, find them dull and move on. 'I think we're a bit de-sensitised to sex with all the movies and there's porn,' one girl told me. 'It doesn't really interest me seeing revolting older blokes doing stuff – it's just boring.' Even if girls don't know how to access porn, it's not hard for them to find out how, or to get help covering their traces, as this cyber chat reveals:

'i was wondering if i watch porn on the internet can my parents find out? and where do i go to watch it?' anonymous

'they can,' maghank91

'clear history and be careful about it, and they'll never find out,' Biskitz

'yes they can check through the history,' playboyfreak

'it wouldnt be that hard for them to find out so be careful lol. an i dont want to tell you where to get any just for that reason,' princesss-hortyluv[2]

PORN SITES AND MEN'S MAGAZINES

Some argue that girls visiting porn sites is no different from reading men's magazines. However, it's hard to come to that conclusion when you see what's readily on offer. Sexual material on the net is far more graphic than most men's magazines, and often depicts live sex acts. As one major report into teen pornography on the net points out, 'It is easy to find on today's internet not only images of naked people, but also graphically depicted acts of heterosexual and homosexual intercourse (including penetration), fellatio, cunnilingus, masturbation, bestiality, child pornography, sadomasochism, bondage, rape, incest, and so on.'[3] These acts are not just a stepped-up version of the subjects seen at the movies. Here sex is captured in the most graphic detail imaginable. Nothing, absolutely nothing, is left to the imagination.

While the full effect of girls' exposure to porn is still to be seen, studies of adults accessing porn show this material can be desensitising and addictive. Adults addicted to porn find it hard to be in 'normal' relationships, as they seem pedestrian by comparison. There's a need for parents and schools to work actively to counter the very real damage porn can do, because it allows girls to assume that abusive and violent sex is normal, and just as importantly, that there's little if any room to say no. The teachers I spoke with expressed their concerns at the way in which pornography is now seen as mainstream. They were worried that it can encourage girls to focus on what might be sexually appealing to potential partners, not what feels right for them.

NielsenNetRatings suggests that one in five girls aged 12 to 16 in the UK view net porn at least once a month.[4]

It's not just the fact that girls are watching porn that is cause for concern. Now they're becoming less inhibited about what they will post on the net. 'Teens post photos, especially the inappropriate ones, to say "hey, look at me,"' said Detective Frank Dannahey. 'Want to get noticed online, especially by males, post an inappropriate photo or video and you'll have lots of online friends. I would bet that if you looked at teen females on MySpace who have the most number of online "friends" in their friend list, you'll find the teens' webpages to be very provocative.' Teens know this and see it as a ticket to instant popularity.

'MySpace.com is the hottest thing on the web right now. We have an opportunity to show people a unique and one-of-a-kind perspective of what our industry and lifestyle is really like, and we intend to take them there.' MONSTAR, 'adult' journalist[5]

Technology guru Andrew Kantor agrees. 'Now anyone could be a porn star – or at least feel like one – without leaving his or her home. It's the world of teenage-girl "models". And it's huge. These girls, who have sites with names like *something*model.com or teen*something*.com, are still in high school – younger than that in some cases – and essentially pose themselves the same way adults do. The difference is, they keep their clothes on, mostly.' In a desire to be popular and to make sure they get noticed, too many girls are eager to seize the chance. 'These girls have found a niche and they're all over it,' Andrew Kantor points out. 'No magazine, porn or otherwise, would publish photos of 15- and 16-year-old girls, let alone the 10- and 11-year-olds who also have such sites, even if they keep the naughty bits covered. But the girls don't need a publisher because these days *everyone's* a publisher.'[6]

> **'Now anyone could be a porn star – or at least feel like one – without leaving his or her home. It's the world of teenage-girl "models". And it's huge.'** *Andrew Kantor, tech guru*[7]

SEXY GIRLS IN CYBERSPACE

'Picture a teen girl who is unpopular in her high school. Online, she can have thousands of friends very quickly, if she is willing to compromise some of her morals and good judgement,' says Detective Frank Dannahey. 'Another factor in this is that young teens desperately want to be like older teens. What better way to do that than to duplicate the riskier behavior that older teens often engage in? I am shocked, quite frankly, in seeing some of what middle-school-age teens that I know have posted online.'

'The youngest girls I have seen posting inappropriate material are in the 11- to 12-year-old bracket. Photos of this age group are generally focused on posing in underwear or inappropriately touching other pre-teens in the photos. What's especially concerning is that many of the pre-teens/teens are not aware that the "silly" picture or video they were just in will be uploaded to an online site by a friend, most often without permission. Most disturbing is the new trend for young teens to be part of online webcam sites in which they are streaming live webcam video of themselves for anyone to see.'[8] You don't have to look very hard on the net to see what's on offer.

'If parents saw what was filling the gap (in sex education), it would destroy them.' *Catherine Harper, Scottish Women Against Pornography*[9]

SHEDDING THEIR INHIBITIONS

Today girls want to be celebrities and they want it for keeps. It's almost as if they feel that if they're not 'out there' they'll cease to exist. This desire to be adored is fulfilled much more easily on the net. By daring to share some aspect of their lives, they have the chance at instant popularity. For these girls, the bigger the audience, the better. Those who are street-smart take this further by encouraging viewers to show their appreciation by purchasing them gifts from online stores.

However, as there's a lot of competition on the net, girls who want to 'make it' can only do so if they're prepared to push the limits. In a few short decades we've gone from parents concerned about neighbourhood creeps peering through their daughters' windows, to girls inviting a world of strangers to watch them pose or prance around their rooms in their bras and knickers, or stark naked. A recent headline, 'Looked at, Not After' (referring to Lindsay Lohan), sums up the situation many teenage and younger girls are now finding themselves in.

YOU'VE GOT THE POWER, BABY

It can be heady stuff when teen girls discover the effect they can have on men and boys. For many girls it's exciting, a bit scary, and flattering to get this level of attention. Translate these feelings into what is now possible on the net, and the ways in which our girls are more vulnerable becomes obvious. Even though they may be articulate and confident, most girls are extremely naive about who is likely to be watching them on the net and why.

Annette, mother of Bridget, 13, blames the media. 'Girls are automatically exposed to more sexualised images in the media, from TV and MTV to Facebook pages. They're posting images on the net like what they have seen in the media,' she told me with real concern. All too often girls are not aware of the numbers of adults out there in cyberspace ready to stalk and/or groom them. As social analyst Richard Eckersley points out, with all this stripping and masturbating in front of webcams, it's almost as if teens don't feel real unless they have a virtual life.[10]

'I found photos of a topless teen student from our local high school who had posed for the photo for her now ex-boyfriend. The girl had no idea that the boyfriend kept the digital photo and sent it to some of his friends after they broke up. Unfortunately, stories such as these occur on a regular basis to teen girls all over the globe.' Detective Frank Dannahey[11]

For parents to consider their daughter may be accessing porn can be fairly confronting. Having early discussions with girls about porn helps equip them to make good decisions. It is important parents explain that in porn, sex is often violent and uncaring, and that many of the girls in porn films do so because they have been sexually abused, live on the streets or have a habit, and that these films perpetuate their abuse. It helps for parents to remind girls that good sex is about caring and not treating a person like an object. Girls also need to know that people who get hooked on porn find it hard to express the warm and nurturing feelings that make relationships special.

Once girls know that some porn sites can add themselves to their favourites or desktop, and be hard to get off their computer, they may be less inclined to enter these sites. It's vital they also know that some of these sites have software that substitutes an overseas server for the family one, which can then accrue hundreds of dollars in phone calls. There is software to block these sites; however, as there are so many places determined girls can access porn, parents are best to educate girls about the dangers before they head down this track, or to get professional help if it is more than a passing curiosity.

Making it big on YouTube

It's interesting to look at the story of Tasmanian YouTube star Emmalina, one of the most popular cam girls ever. This teen racked up literally thousands of hits with her video blog entries, which talked about everything from her pet guinea pigs to yoga. After only three months Emmalina made YouTube's most subscribed list. International media coverage followed.

Although Emmalina launched herself on the web under a pseudonym, a hacker soon found his way into her computer, accessed her private files and posted them on the net. Then someone else discovered who she was, and posted her real identity online. Emmalina wasn't prepared for this level of intrusion, or for the hate mail and sleazy older men. Bruised, Emmalina retired from the net.

Once girls have enjoyed this level of attention, however, life without it can seem pretty dull. Emmalina's now back as one of YouTube's stars, along with Lisanova, LucyinLa and Nohogirls. 'I'm a kooky attention whore,' she admits. 'I love attention, I love the internet and I love technology – thus I am here on YouTube. I'm just your average chick with no particular claims to fame, but I'm cute in a psychotic sort of way.'[1]

Thousands of visitors continue to log on to Emmalina's video blogs. Now she knows the score, Emmalina is pushing the envelope, to ensure she remains in the spotlight. These days, discussions about guinea pigs have made way for such topics as Filthiness and Vulgarity, Deux Dancin' and Messy Shit Webgrrrls. There wouldn't be many net-savvy teens who don't know Emmalina's story or what she's up to, or who don't long to receive the attention she has received.

'Risk is exciting. I should probably clarify, Luke and I are of course still together and I love him very much, even though he's messy! We planned TOGETHER for me to have sexy fun with a girl. I like girls.' *Emmalina, 19*[2]

PRE-TEENS GETTING IN ON THE ACT

On MySpace, Xanga and YouTube, you can now watch dozens of young girls putting themselves out there, literally for the whole world to see. The surprise is just how young some girls are. Even a cursory exploration of YouTube reveals girls such as 'Lolipop', who looks to be around 8. In her clip she slowly makes herself up, with seductive close-ups of her reddening lips.[3] Then there are other young girls such as Fuzzyblur, who couldn't be more than 10, gyrating for the camera with a Stitches shopping bag in front of her. It's unlikely that these girls have any sense of the impact their behaviour may have on some of the adults surfing the net. Clearly their parents have little idea, either.

'I would say that at this moment in time, those who are online who are attracted to children or teens are applauding the fact that they don't have to run the risk of getting caught enticing kids to post inappropriate images/videos. The kids are doing that for them.' *Detective Frank Dannahey*[4]

A SEXUAL PREDATOR'S DREAM

At present these new forms of expression on the net are at a very early stage of their development. We need to be asking where they are going, because things are escalating fast. 'I have seen more [inappropriate] photos than I care to, and there is no lack of that type of content,' says Detective Frank Dannahey. 'Having done undercover work online in the past, I saw that online sexual predators would entice girls into posing or posting images of themselves or friends. Not any more. Teens willingly post inappropriate material that is easy for anyone to come by online. I would say that those who are online who are attracted to children/ teens are applauding the fact that they don't have to run the risk of getting caught enticing kids to post inappropriate images/videos. The kids are doing that for them – mostly unaware that someone, namely an adult, is using their images in a sexual way.'[5]

One of the cases he recalls was of a 13-year-old girl, who sent a number of 'child pornography-type photos' to her boyfriend, aged 16. These photos ended up on a public webpage that named her boyfriend. This 13-year-old had taken provocative photos of her genitals with a mobile phone cam, then sent them to her boyfriend's email account. He looked at the photos, but didn't delete them. A friend using his account went snooping and found the photos, which he downloaded to show male friends. Another boy didn't like the boyfriend, so he copied the photos, then set up a website naming the boyfriend, and posting his girlfriend's photos there. When Detective Dannahey interviewed the devastated 13-year-old, she asked if anyone had seen her photos, and if there was a possibility that someone had copied them or kept them. He was of course unable to give her any guarantees.[6]

'Girls are searching for boys' attention, and MySpace is the ideal platform.' Candice M. Kelsey, The Secret Cyber Lives of Teenagers[7]

MYSPACE . . . EVERYONE'S SPACE

It's now estimated that over half of teens aged 13 to 17 have details on such sites as MySpace, which is thought to attract around 50 million users worldwide. Girls often post their photos. This makes for a massive amount of territory girls have access to beyond the reach of their parents. It's the perfect medium for stalkers, paedophiles and all those who want to prey on young girls. In one survey 45 per cent of teens admitted they had been asked for personal information by strangers. Just under a third had considered meeting someone they'd only talked to online. More than one in ten had actually met a person face-to-face, even though they'd previously only had contact with them over the internet.[8]

Teen girls need to know more about choosing what they post in cyberspace, and how to manage the material they do post. The effects of putting inappropriate photos and information out there are long-term. More often than not this material will hang around, and could very well jeopardise her relationships. It may even come back to haunt her once she's settled down with a family and career, embarrassing her with work-mates and distressing her children. Such material could compromise her ability to take public office, or to get the promotion she's worked hard to achieve. Parents and teachers need to make this clear to girls, so they realise that what is posted is impossible to control. One of the ways to help girls through this phase is to give them more profound, relevant ways to feel acknowledged and belong, other than posting risqué photos on the net. Again we get back to the importance of community and the opportunities to immerse themselves in hobbies and other passions.

'Our research shows that many teen girls are not aware of the potential dangers of communicating with older men online, and they believe that it can lead to genuine relationships.' *Peggy Conlon, CEO, The Advertising Council*[9]

When asked why she thought tween and teen girls are downloading explicit photos of themselves, Anne Collier of NetFamilyNews.org
believes that it's 'partly that "Paris Hilton-wannabe thing" (little girls
dreaming of being supermodels), partly peer pressure ("everybody's
doing it"), partly that sort of spontaneous, slightly risky, "cool" (in the
adolescent sense), approval-seeking behaviour associated with adolescence.' As she rightly points out, 'celebrity news, reality TV, and other
mediums have lowered the threshold of what is considered acceptable.'[10]

WHAT PARENTS CAN DO

So what steps can parents take to better protect their daughters? Once
they become aware of the very real risks their girls may be exposed
to online, it's tempting for parents want to ban them from the net.
Experts warn parents to stay calm and to keep communicating with
their girls, so they don't make a tricky situation worse. 'Teens know
so many workarounds (to rules, filters, etc), there are so many social-
networking and media-sharing sites based in multiple countries, and
the net is so available on so many devices and at proliferating locations
and wireless "hot spots" that they can simply "go underground", where
we have even less influence and they're at greater risk,' warns Anne
Collier. 'It's better, for example, that we know what social networking
site they're using (hopefully one that's showing corporate responsibility
and enforcing terms of use), and can talk with them about how they're
using it.'[11]

Detective Frank Dannahey agrees. He stresses the importance of parents knowing what their child has posted online. He urges them to find
out whether their daughter has a MySpace or Facebook webpage, and
to take a look at that page. 'Being a parent means looking out for your
child's safety interest and reputation in all facets of their lives, including
their online life,' he explained. 'Kids are going to be online, like it or not.
How they behave online is something that a parent has control of if they

approach it with understanding and genuine concern. Kids follow rules when it makes sense to them that it is in their best interest to do so.'[12]

Not all girls are doing silly things on the net. Many are simply enjoying time with friends. According to Anne Collier it's the girls who are already at risk who are most likely to find themselves in trouble on the net. 'They're the runaways, the adventurers, the children living in conflicted or broken homes, the kids who are — as has always been said — "looking for trouble". Technology is giving them more options and expanding their spheres for risk-taking, not really creating new risks.'[13]

As things are moving so quickly with new technologies, the more information we have the better. A recent study reveals that it's not the general personal information girls post on the web that makes them vulnerable, so much as participating in inappropriate behaviour, such as sexy talk.[14] Another study discovered that most online sexual abuse is by people girls know, especially peers, as is often the case with real-life abuse.[15] Girls need to be aware of this. They also need good advice on what to do when they encounter risky behaviour or unpleasant content. When parents are also honest about the fact that everyone makes mistakes, it encourages girls to be more transparent about their own shortcomings. The way forward is not to pretend the net doesn't exist, but to warn girls of its danger and to provide girls with online experiences that will give them resources and expand their visions of themselves.

Girls at work

As the world of work now offers girls plenty of choices, many are eager to embrace them. Work isn't a total mystery for many girls, as they're already working part-time, and enjoy the independence and opportunity to earn their own money. As Peta, 16, informed me, 'Work doesn't scare me at all. I've been working since I was 15. I'm great at working with people. It's been good.' Whether or not they had part-time jobs, all the girls I spoke with were looking forward to having greater spending power. 'Right now I view work as a way I can get money to do the things I want,' said Carly, 16, without hesitation.

When girls look at women already in the workforce, some find the prospect of careers less than enticing. A number of girls saw women's lives as lonely, exhausting, driven. 'They miss out on the joy of life, 'cos it's like they're working nine-to-five jobs, and they're trying to push it up there,' Kiera, 17, told me. Carly, 16, agreed. 'They're going out and a lot of them are like binge-drinking and things, like that's how today's young women cope. I feel like they're missing a kind of more like pure side of life where like happiness comes in,' she reflected.

'I'd love not to work as many hours, that's why I'm choosing to be a teacher. I'd like to be able to juggle family and husband, both together, but separately as well. Like kids and husband, so like they all get my love, and share it around and stuff.' *Kiera, 17*

This is not what they see, however, when they look at celebrities such as Lindsay, Paris or Beyoncé. Here girls see young women not that much older than they are who are successful and popular, and rich enough to afford anything they want and do exactly as they choose. These are the kinds of women they aspire to be – girls who know how to make the system work for them.

CAN I LIVE UP TO EXPECTATIONS?

Although the girls I spoke with were looking forward to a career, almost all were nervous about what was expected of them. 'I don't think much past my immediate future, because it scares you about what's going to happen. I dunno where I'm going to go yet,' Alana, 18, said. As so much is made of women's career opportunities, there's an understandable fear of failure. 'I'm going to have to start working every day of my life and that scares me. I'm not ready for it. It's heaps hard,' said Carly, 16. Ashlee, 15, felt the same way. 'I'm definitely going to be working, but I don't know at what. It is intimidating, because I don't really want to have to think about it now. I don't want to make a mistake and be stuck in it.'

I WANT TO WORK ON *MY* TERMS

What became clear in my interviews with girls was while many wanted a career, they didn't want to be swallowed up by work. 'I think it's a bit sad when work is the centre of a person's life. For me like seeing businesswomen that work twenty-fours hours a day every day, I'm thinking like that they've kind of got it bad for themselves, because there's like so much more you can be doing.' Carly, 16, confessed.

'Work's also exciting because you get to kind of be who you want to be. Not everyone gets that, but I'm going to try.' *Ashlee, 15*

Already girls have given some thought as to how they'll approach work differently. 'We'll slow it down, kind of be a bit more relaxed,' said Kiera, 17. 'Take life as how it comes, and deal with every single step you make, so you don't take like a million steps, then have to deal with the consequences of not dealing with those things. Just deal with everything as it comes, and not let it build up.' Sara, 17, agreed. While she was attracted to a corporate career, there were limits. 'I like the idea, but I don't want to have to bring work home and stuff,' she told me.

None of the girls I spoke with had any sense of committing to a career for life. They have a much more rounded life view; already they were talking of periods out of the workforce to travel, have babies, study. 'It's very important to be balanced at work, and to have time for kids and stuff,' said Whitney, 18. Loving what they did was clearly high on the agenda. 'I wouldn't want to have a job where I'd be working really hard. I would want to do something I really love,' admitted Sandi, 14. This was how Evie, 15, felt also. 'I want to be an interior designer, so I enjoy subjects that are going to help me do that, whereas I hate science because it isn't relevant to me. So I think you make an effort with the things you want to.'

'You look at all the women who are 30 with the big jobs, then think about what it's going to be like when we're 30. It'll be bigger, and it's like women want to push us into it sort of thing. They miss out on travelling, mucking around, not caring about work and school.' *Carly, 16*

DRAWN TO POWERFUL POSITIONS

In spite of their fears, a number of girls were drawn to the power that top jobs bring. They liked the idea of making their own way, and the lifestyle that went with good jobs. 'I would love to see myself like working for a big, well-known production company, or maybe establishing my own, if that's possible. That's what I'm kind of aiming at in the end, just being quite successful. I know money doesn't make you like happy or anything, but in that position I'd like to be doing all right, like to be independent.' Missy, 15, told me.

'I like the idea of a woman in power,' said Sara, 18. 'I like the idea that I can tell people what to do. Being a corporate woman gives women power. It's kinda a sexy outlook on women, because they are so in control. I see all these women in suits in the city, and they're so in control of their lives, in touch with what's happening in the world.' This was also very appealing to Whitney, 18. 'I like the high-flying career woman – it's great. There's something really nice about it. It's inspiring to have so many famous, successful women.'

It's heartening that girls continue to be drawn to challenging roles. To equip them well, parents and teachers need to work with girls to ensure they have a good understanding of success, as genuine success is about much more than talent, the suit and the salary. True success requires good judgement, fairness, leadership by example, flexibility, generosity of spirit, and the ability to formulate and hold a vision. In our rush to equip girls for the workforce, we mustn't neglect these vital life skills that help girls learn emotional intelligence, so they can navigate the ever-changing world of work with greater ease.

DOING THINGS DIFFERENTLY FROM MUM

It was interesting to see how girls' career aspirations were sometimes influenced by their mothers and other significant adults. Sasha, 15, didn't feel that her stay-at-home mum had really done anything with her life as she wasn't in the workforce. 'I really want to be ambitious, and do like all that I can,' said Sasha. 'Like you only live once, and I really want to be independent and make my own money, and I don't want to marry rich or anything. I want to do it myself.' Sara's choice of career is also in part a reaction to her mother's alternative lifestyle. 'My mum's more in touch with the earth and the environment, and kind of off with the fairies,' she told me. 'She and her friends live in a different world. They try to make changes but can't. Corporate women are pretty shallow, but they have the power to make changes.'

Although music is her passion, Danni, 18, is contemplating the security of corporate life. 'I want to play in orchestras, but I have an urge to be a businesswoman, and like work in corporations,' she explained. 'My life has been pretty artistic. With it comes a lot of freedom and instability. I've watched my teacher who's also a performer. His shows aren't regular, so how do you pay your bills and make ends meet? Corporate life will give me the stability of a regular income and it'll give me structure.' Evie, 15, was drawn to the young women in business suits she sees on the way to school. 'They look really smart and cool, that's what I want to be,' she told me.

Regardless of their background and their many challenges as they tread new ground, what impressed me about the girls I spoke with was their determination to get out into the world and make things happen. They are truly courageous and should be respected for their courage. In spite of their fear of failure, they do want to leave their mark. However, they also want more balance. They look forward to embracing work, but not at the expense of leisure, travel and relationships.

As we continue to refine the ways we can support girls, it's important we encourage girls to be the best they can at whatever they do. We have to be more sensitive to what our girls are capable of, what will enable them to be happy and fulfilled, and how we define success.

True liberation comes when we can respect a stay-at-home mother as much an executive, and when we can appreciate the immense contribution teachers and nurses make, as well as those who sit on boards. As individuals we evolve over time, as do our working lives. Not everyone finds their vocation immediately. Most girls will have several or more jobs during their working life. Girls need good life skills and support to move with and handle this change, so they can approach the future with more flexibility and less fear.

Getting married

Weddings are back, bridal magazines are flourishing, and wedding planners are run off their feet helping brides-to-be stage the perfect wedding. This trend has left people wondering whether we are seeing a return to the Fifties. Certainly every teen girl I spoke with wanted to get married, as did younger girls. 'Marriage means there's someone to comfort you and to love,' said Melanie, 10. For teenage girls the attraction of marriage isn't just about romance or their wedding day. 'I know it's not always like happy and stuff, but you have this idea in your head of having a really happy family and stuff, which isn't really like reality,' Joy, 16, told me.

BEATING THE BIOLOGICAL CLOCK

These girls wanted to be married by their mid- to late 20s, or soon afterwards. They were very specific about getting married earlier rather than later, because they have read about the struggles of older women trying to get pregnant and don't want this to happen to them. 'This generation now is getting married really late, very late. They're leaving it very late to have kids as well, until their biological clock is ticking,' Kiera, 17, told me.

For other girls getting married was more about being in sync with their kids. 'I'd like to be successful. By the time I'm 30 I'd like to have kids,' said Whitney, 18. 'I want to be a young mum. I want to be a hip and cool mum.' When pressed she said that having babies early came back to the generation gap. Her mother didn't understand her, and she hated the distance that had grown between them. She was very clear she wanted to do it differently. 'I want to know where my kids are coming from,' she explained.

'I want to be married around 27 sort of, and I want to have been pretty much around the world, that's what I hope.' *Evie, 15*

The generation gap was also an issue for Sara, 18. 'I want to get married and have babies,' she told me. 'My mum had me and my brother late. It makes me want to have them earlier, like at 27. My mum regrets having us later. I think it affects our relationship a bit, because times have changed. She'll be older when like I have kids, so she won't be able to help as much. It's kind of the generation thing.'

ACHING FOR LOVE

Marriage for the girls I spoke with was less about needing a man in their lives than having their personal space warmed by someone who cared. As the girls talked it was clear many were yearning for a nurturing space they could rely on and call their own. They saw marriage in part as a retreat from the harsher realities of everyday life. For many girls marriage was also about commitment. They felt the marriage ceremony was an important way to underline this commitment. 'I like there being a bond between me and my partner – and like a ritual – a celebration of what you have between you,' said Sara, 18.

'I want to be married by the time I'm 25. I don't want to have kids until I'm 30. Just the fact I can say I'm married – it means you're loved, you're doing something right.' *Carly, 16*

It was fascinating to watch the girls' bodies and language soften as they spoke about marriage. When they described the kind of home they wanted to create for themselves and those they loved, frequently their arms would form a circle. This was true both for girls from intact homes, and those in single-parent or blended families. These girls aren't naïve. They know marriage isn't all cupcakes and smiling babies, but they are determined to give it their best shot.

These girls want marriage and families, because they want their adult relationships to be richer and more meaningful than the relationships they see around them. 'My parents are still together, but lots of people I know are divorced,' Carly, 16, told me. 'I want to try not to get in their situation — I really don't want to end up in that situation, so I want to try to start early.' For Sandi, 14, whose parents were no longer together, marriage appealed because 'There's someone you can fall back on.'

'It would be good to come home to someone who needs you, because like other people don't need you.' *Ashlee, 15*

FINDING SOMEONE WHO CARES

As we talked about the future, a number of girls told me that one of the reasons they wanted to create a safe loving space within marriage is because most adults didn't seem to care about them. 'It would be good to come home to someone who needs you, because like other people don't need you.' Ashlee, 15, reflected. Many girls saw adults as too stressed-out and busy, and that their lives were fragmented at best. 'I think people are really more career-oriented — so they don't think about love, and when they find love, it's kind of a rushed thing, instead of being something that you have to work on daily,' Kiera, 17, told me. 'It's like if something doesn't work out they don't work on it, it's over. They're not putting in as much time as it needs.'

'I don't wanna have the perfect partner, I wanna have my perfect partner, but I don't think there's a perfect partner, there's Barbie and Ken, but no-one's Barbie or Ken.' *Sandi, 14*

MORE MARRIAGES, LARGER FAMILIES

Market consultant Liz Nickles predicts a growth in teen marriage and larger families. This doesn't mean girls want to abandon the possibility of careers, but that home is likely to come first. 'For these young women,' she says, 'their heart is in the home.'[1] Relationships do matter for teen girls. Growing up surrounded by broken families makes family that much more precious. For them, a healthy marriage is an indication they are on the right track.[2]

'Marriage isn't what's on a marriage certificate,' Whitney, 18, told me. 'I want to get married and have kids. The appeal is having a strong connection, and being close, having someone around all the time. Physically, if you're with someone, that's far more important than just having the big day. I don't want a big wedding and spending lots of money on one day. I'd like to get married at the beach or something.'

A number of girls from broken homes said they didn't feel their parents tried hard enough to keep the marriage together. Others were able to look back and see their parents' divorce was for the best. The girls I spoke with had few illusions about the way adults behave in relationships. Unprompted, they recounted details of their parents' many and varied liaisons that would spice the pages of any adult novel. Even if girls haven't had to go through parents' divorces, they are well-versed in what life has been like for friends dealing with separated parents and blended families. These girls are very clear they don't want that level of pain.

'Marriage is wanting to be with someone. Not alone and neglected. Having a good friend to talk to, I think talking's really important.

It's about being with someone, around someone who likes you for who you are, and feeling acknowledged and respected.' *Alana, 18*

As she looks back at her parents' separation, Kiera, 17, wants to do things very differently. 'Most parents are divorced, and that's kind of left some kids a bit screwed up,' she reflected. 'A lot of kids are without their dads and their mums, and you kind of need both to raise a child up. I'm not a child with two parents in a household, but I feel like, I dunno, there's different values you'd have yourself if you were raised with both parents. And, um, more of a loving household.'

STABLE HOMES

Stability in the home is fundamental for these girls. 'I'd like to have a stable marriage and a few kids and stuff,' said Joy, 16. 'I just like having family around sort of thing. Just being single doesn't appeal to me that much. I like to have people around – have like a stable life with kids and things – watch them grow up.' Peta, 16, saw marriage as something she could rely on as an adult. 'It's dependable, really,' she said.

While these are material girls living in a high-tech world, it's interesting to see how much they are drawn to the nurturing relationships around them, which they describe as 'really nice', 'kind of lovely' and 'beautiful'. They clearly savour the relationships that do work. 'I have like adopted kind of grandparents, and like they love me. I see how in love they are, and they have grandkids and stuff like that,' Kiera, 17, told me. 'I'd like to be a little bit like them, when I see how in love they are, and how they are still working on their marriage. They still juggle their careers, and they were poor when they were young.'

Instead of seeing this yearning to be married as a retrograde step, surely the answer is to help support girls make good relationship choices, and to give them the tools to help them sustain their relationships through more life education, and greater community and family support. A woman doesn't need a man in her life to be validated, but knowing where to find love, warmth and a genuine sense of belonging does help support girls to be successful in their significant relationships, and in achieving their wider dreams.

Having babies

For all the girls I spoke with, even quite young girls, children were a natural part of getting married. 'I'd like children 'cause of the things they do,' Vanessa, 9, told me. 'They're playful and cute, and like they're yours. I'd like to look after somebody.' Many girls have spent years babysitting, so they felt confident about having their own babies. 'I want kids,' Kiera, 17, told me. 'It's an attractive lifestyle for me.' When I asked her why, she said, 'I want my own little kids I can love, and can help them grow up, help them with things, just 'cos they're mine and a part of me, and like with a husband there is security and love and stuff.'

'There are a lot of mums who leave it too late to have a kid. Then there's distance, not understanding each other.' *Whitney, 18*

'I'm a very big kids person, I love children, I wanna have children,' said Peta, 16. She wasn't quite sure how it would pan out – whether she could take some time out to be with them at home, or whether she'd have to go straight back to work, 'I dunno, maybe I'll be at home, although with interest rates it's not looking too promising,' she reflected.

Having some time with her babies at home was clearly her preference. For Sara, 18, it was, 'Just seeing yourself in something so little. There's that connection and that little you. There's the responsibility, but watching them grow is so rewarding. Every day you're seeing them develop, and like every child is different.'

'I'd like children so I can have someone there to look after me, and have fun with.' *Melanie, 10*

Some of the comments girls made about having children were poignant, hinting that babies might give their lives something they don't presently have. 'Children are never going to leave you,' reflected Sandi, 14. 'And no matter how the child is, you love them regardless, and I reckon they'll be really good to have.' As with a number of girls, Alana, 18, sees having children as a way of recapturing her own childhood. 'I like kids. I do a lot of babysitting. I feel young when I'm with them. It makes me nostalgic. It makes me want to have kids, so I can relive my childhood.'

YUMMY MUMMIES

There are many reasons why having babies is more appealing for this emerging generation of girls. With the growth in lifestyle programs and homewares stores, being a domestic goddess has become an attractive prospect. And now all the celebrities are having children, motherhood is hip. These girls have watched a whole range of stars from Britney to Angelina Jolie embrace motherhood, some more successfully than others. They see how these young mums take motherhood in their stride, how expectant mothers no longer hide their baby bumps, or the fact that they need time with their kids.

These women have taken mothers out of the closet and have made it trendy to have kids. 'You want to be a cool mum. Like my sister has two little kids and she's only 30. You want to be like that and have a good relationship with your kids. Even though you want to be independent and do everything you can before you have kids, this is the kinda age that you want to have them, because then you're not too old.' Missy, 15.

This sudden focus on babies may have some unexpected spin-offs. When speaking with one school counsellor, working in a low-income area, she told me that often girls see teenage pregnancy as a way of giving themselves the nurture they've missed out on. For those few short months of pregnancy, the attention is on them. 'Their expectations about having a baby are so unrealistic,' she said. Other teachers spoke of girls from poor areas as being resigned to having babies. Whether it happened sooner or later was all the same to them.

There's no doubt that the new status given to motherhood is also tied to image and possessions, for some girls at least, which takes us back to where we began – the explosion in baby boutiques full of pricey clothes and accessories for babies, from expensive prams to handmade shoes – that place small babies and young parents on the consumer treadmill within months of a baby's birth.

SEXY MUMS

The sexualised images of women have now extended to motherhood. Mums are now sexier than they've ever been. These young women strive to achieve a fabulous body, baby, partner and career. Just because they have kids doesn't make them any less fashionable or less sexually attractive, hence the expressions 'yummy mummy', and MILFS or 'Mothers I'd like (to) f**ck'.

As with everything around image, being a yummy mummy is no easy feat. As high-profile music video host and founder of the Yummy Mummy Club, Erica Ehm, admits, 'A true Yummy Mummy struggles to find the impossible balance between the single sexpot she used to be, the woman she's become, the professional she works hard to be, the wife she aspires to be and the mother she has to be.' This, she confesses, does tend to leave yummy mummies 'confused and exhausted'.[1]

The girls I spoke with liked the idea of being mums for more down-to-earth reasons. They wanted the opportunity to be loving and nurturing, and have fun with their little ones. They felt that children were extremely important, and deserved their time and attention — even if this meant putting their careers on hold. For them it was the opportunity to create the kind of environment they yearned for as children. Whether or not economic realities will defeat them, only time will tell.

Our children are our tomorrow. When we short-change our children, we diminish their opportunity to build families and communities that benefit their members, young and old, and enable everyone to thrive. The desire for connection is very powerful and deserves our attention. Material comfort does make life easier and give girls more choices, but it isn't sufficient to sustain them. Girls have made huge gains, but there is more to achieve. If we can help our girls enjoy more meaningful relationships, we make it possible for them to build on our successes, and create individual lives, families and communities that are even richer than our own.

Where to now?

In a few short years our girls have become vulnerable – not just teen girls, but young girls and baby girls. Unless we want our little girls to become part of a growing number of children whose first word is a brand name, and whose entertainment is largely product placement, we need to limit the access advertisers and marketers have to them.

First and foremost our girls are children, not consumers. And like all children they have a right to their childhood. To achieve this we need to be clear about the influences we allow into girls' lives. If we don't, we help promote the early sexualisation of girls, their growing concerns about body image, the decline in their imaginations and all the other detrimental influences they now face.

There is so much more to childhood than being cool and sexy, yet the pressure for girls to think and act in this way is real and intense. Childhood is shrinking and fast. Sexualised talk and behaviour is now evident in preschoolers. Long before these children can read or write they are becoming addicted to shopping. The result? A rise in young girls suffering anxiety, depression and eating and other disorders.

As adults it's time we learned to ignore the endless spin that encourages us to appear cool at all costs, and started to focus on giving our girls what they need. Experts tell us that from birth, girls thrive on spontaneous play, good food, regular interaction with adults, and first-hand experience of their world. These precious childhood opportunities are lost when girls spend hours in front of TV or a computer screen.

As our girls grow, so too does the influence of popular culture. Younger and younger girls are striving to be thin, glamorous, and popular, because they think that's what being a girl is all about. In one study of girls aged 5 to 8, over a quarter of 5-year-olds wished they were thinner.[1] By the time girls are now 7 and 8 they are being exposed to influences that were previously the domain of teenagers. All the teenage girls I spoke with were concerned these developments were robbing little girls of their childhood. If parents want to end these influences on their girls, they need to make their voices heard loud and clear.

Our girls may appear confident and have plenty of attitude, but in essence they're still young girls. The choices parents make about TV programs, internet access and their own consumerism will affect how their daughters see themselves and others. What every child wants from a parent is someone who will nourish, protect, engage and guide them. This means parents reclaiming their role as gatekeepers from those whose only interest in their girls begins and ends with the bottom line.

In a number of countries, including Sweden, advertisers cannot market to children under 12. This is something we need to push for. In the mean-time, it is up to parents to minimise the time girls spend in front of TV, on computers and shopping. Restricting the number of catalogues and other sales materials that find their way into the home is another helpful move. We also need more media awareness training in schools and at home to counteract the very real power of advertising. These steps are essential if we are to prevent girls entering a world they're not ready for.

The parties and drug and alcohol consumption our girls are experiencing bears no resemblance to what it was like even a decade ago. Those who think otherwise need to wake up. While the majority of girls aren't doing sex, drugs and alcohol, the number of girls who are is on the rise. It is unacceptable that so many young girls are binge-drinking and involved in drugs and having underage sex, which then makes them prey to a whole range of problems from alcoholism and rape to sexually transmitted diseases. Increasingly these behaviours are seen as normal, which makes our girls more vulnerable.

It is important we appreciate how much of their identity girls are losing to celebrity culture, peer pressure and consumerism. These forces are now shaping almost every aspect of girls' lives, from their friendships and the way they spend their leisure time to their goals and self-image. The more time girls spend on their appearance and trying to be popular, the less time they have to get to know who they are and what they want from life. The continuing emphasis on girls having to look and act sexy isn't helpful. It is driving girls to strip in front of webcams, talk to strangers on the net, drink until they can no longer support their own airways, and take part in a whole range of risky behaviours in an attempt to fit in.

If we want our girls to thrive, we also need to recognise the essential role fathers play in teaching girls about the world of men and boys, and what they have the right to expect from relationships. No-one understands the world of men better. Too many of our girls are growing up without this input, and are more susceptible to inappropriate choices and abuse as a result.

It is vital we recognise that many of our previous reference points no longer apply. While this may be concerning, it offers us new possibilities. The increasing generation gap between parents and girls means we have to work a lot harder to engage girls in ways that are relevant and meaningful to them. It's ironic that in this sex-saturated world parents remain reluctant to talk about 'grown-up' issues with their girls.

Sex education, and a wider education for life, needs to begin earlier, given the material our girls are now exposed to. We need education that not only deals with age-appropriate discussions about sex, but with how a girl's sexual self fits into the wider experience of life – her emotions, the nuances of relationships, how to express desire, what true intimacy means. Sex education by young, grounded professionals needs serious consideration. Girls are more likely to listen to those who are at an age they aspire to be, than teachers their parents' age. Alongside this work we need training in schools on the sexual exploitation of women and girls in the media.

The growth of new technologies has left parents out on a limb. At the same time our girls need to be part of the high-tech, fast-paced world they are to inherit. To help girls achieve this in a productive way, parents must keep abreast of the changes. They need to be technologically savvy, and to check out their daughter's websites. This is no time for parents to be shy about learning new applications on the net and mobile phone. Placing internet access in a communal area in the home is essential. The parents who take a more collaborative approach to technology allow girls to feel good about their technical know-how, and to feel better understood, as these mediums are now second nature to girls.

We cannot underestimate our girls' need to belong. If family and community do not provide the acknowledgement and sense of belonging our girls need, their peers and popular culture will. Their very real need for connection is evident in the hours girls spend texting, socialising and on the net. While it is natural for girls to connect with each other, it isn't helpful if they are only communicating with friends the same age, with the same views and aspirations.

In previous generations a girl's sense of self was more outward-looking. Alongside her own personal development was the opportunity to contribute to family and community, to be part of something larger than herself. This gave her a genuine and ongoing sense of belonging and worth. Our girls shouldn't be growing up feeling as if adults don't care, but sadly, many are. 'It would be good to come home to someone who needs you, because like other people don't need you,' one girl told me.

Parents need greater community support so their girls can be nurtured and encouraged by people they can trust across the generations.

With the growth in opportunities for girls has come an increase in expectations for them to succeed. We must take care not to impose views on girls that are narrowing or inappropriate. As one girl from the suburbs pointed out, 'Now you know you've done well if you are a doctor and marry a doctor, and you have a big house and car, and a couple of kids and a nanny.' Alongside our expectations for girls are the very real pressures to be thin, beautiful and popular. We have fought hard to give girls a wealth of choices, but choice has little value unless girls are able to make good choices, and not those dictated by advertisers.

In our desire to progress we have focused on the material benefits available to women and girls – on job opportunities and spending power. While these gains are significant and to be celebrated, they can never replace the profound need we all have to contribute to the greater good, as well as our own. This surely is one of the central hallmarks of a civilised society. When we deprive girls of this opportunity, we deprive them of an essential part of their humanity. I suspect this is why so many are drawn to early marriages and babies, because it offers them a chance at belonging and human warmth.

Today's girls do want more time for travel and personal relationships. But this does not mean they are blind to the opportunities they have. They appreciate their freedom, and with the right encouragement, will articulate this in wonderful new ways.

While a number of situations canvassed in this book are disturbing, this is no time to feel depressed or helpless. Every new generation has its challenges. Alongside the many issues our girls currently face are a wealth of opportunities. It is our job to help our girls recognise these opportunities, and give them the confidence and resources they need to lead lives that are even richer and fuller than our own, and to find solutions to problems we can but dream of.

For Maggie's talks schedule, reading group notes, or feedback,
please see her website.
www.maggiehamilton.org

Bibliography

Adams, Gerald, ed, *Adolescent Development: The Essential Readings*, Blackwell Publications, Oxford, 2000.

Adler, Patricia A. with Peter Adler, *Peer Power: Preadolescent Culture and Identity*, Rutgers University Press, New Burnswick New Jersey, 1998.

Apter, Terri, *The Myth of Maturity: What Teenagers Need From Parents to Become Adults*, W.W. Norton and Co, New York, 2001.

Carr-Gregg, Michael, *The Princess Bitchface Syndrome: Surviving Adolescent Girls*, Penguin, Melbourne 2006.

Cassidy, Carol, with Joyce George, and Arlene Sandler, *Girls in America: Their Stories, Their Words,* TVBooks, 1999.

Cooke, Kaz, *Girl Stuff: Your Full-on Guide to the Teen Years*, Penguin, Melbourne, 2007.

Cooper, Robbie et al, *Alter Ego: Avatars and Their Creators*, Chris Boot Ltd, London 2007.

Cross, Gary, *Kids' Stuff: Toys and the Changing World of American Childhood*, Harvard University Press, Cambridge, Massachusetts, 1997.

Eckersley, Richard, *Well and Good: Morality, Meaning and Happiness,* Text Publishing, Melbourne, 2004.

BIBLIOGRAPHY

Etcoff, Nancy, *Survival of the Prettiest: The Science of Beauty*, Anchor Books, Random House, New York, 2000.

Kasser, Dr Tim and Kanner, Dr Allen D., *Psychology and Consumer Culture: The Struggle for a Good Life in a Materialistic World*, American Psychological Association, Washington, 2003.

Kelsey, Candice M., *The Secret Cyber Lives of Teenagers: Parenting in the Age of MySpace.com*, Marlowe & Company, New York, 2007.

Levy, Ariel, *Female Chauvinist Pigs: Women and the Rise of Raunch Culture,* Free Press, New York 2005.

Lindstrom, Martin with Seybold, Patricia, B., *BRANDchild: Remarkable Insights into the Minds of Today's Global Kids and Their Relationships with Brands*, Kogan Page, London, 2003.

Louv, Richard, *Last Child in the Woods*, Algonquin Books, New York, 2005.

Pearson, Patricia, *When She Was Bad: Violent Women and the Myth of Innocence*, Viking, New York, 1997.

Ponton, Dr Lynn E., *The Romance of Risk: Why Teenagers Do the Things They Do*, Basic Books, New York, 1998.

Quart, Alissa, *Branded: The Buying and Selling of Teenagers*, Basic Books, New York 2003.

Ritchie, Karen, *Marketing to Generation X*, Lexington Books, New York, 1995.

Simmons, Rachel, *Odd Girl Out: The Hidden Culture of Aggression in Girls*, Harcourt, Orlando, 2002.

Rymaszewski, Michael, et al, *Second Life: The Official Guide*, John Wiley & Sons, New Jersey, 2007.

Sauers, Joan, *Sex Lives of Australian Teenagers,* Random House, Sydney 2007.

Siegel, David L. et al, *The Great Tween Buying Machine: Capturing Your Share of the Multibillion Dollar Tween Market*, Dearborn Trade Publishing, Ithaca NY, 2001.

Simmons, Rachel, *Odd Girl Out: The Hidden Culture of Aggression in Girls*, Harcourt, Orlando, 2002.

Simmons, Rachel, *Odd Girl Speaks Out: Girls Write About Bullies, Cliques, Popularity and Jealousy*, Harcourt, Orlando, 2004.

Snyderman, Dr Nancy, and Streep, Peg, *Girl in the Mirror: Mothers and Daughters in the Years of Adolescence*, Hyperion, New York, 2002.

Thomas, Susan Gregory, *Buy, Buy Baby: The Devastating Impact of Marketing to 0–3s*, Houghton Mifflin, Boston, 2007.

Weiner, Jessica, *Do I Look Fat in This?*, Simon and Schuster, New York, 2006.

Wiseman, Rosalind, *Queen Bees and Wannabes: Helping Your Daughter Survive Cliques, Gossip and Other Realities of Adolescence*, Piatkus, London, 2002.

Notes

STARTING OUT

[1] Ross D. Parke and Armin A. Brott, *Throwaway Dads: The Myths and Barriers That Keep Men from Being the Fathers They Want to Be*, Houghton Mifflin, Boston, 1999.

[2] Ross D. Parke and Armin A. Brott, *Throwaway Dads: The Myths and Barriers That Keep Men from Being the Fathers They Want to Be*, Houghton Mifflin, Boston, 1999.

[3] Ross D. Parke and Armin A. Brott, *Throwaway Dads: The Myths and Barriers That Keep Men from Being the Fathers They Want to Be*, Houghton Mifflin, Boston, 1999.

[4] Robert B. Clyman et al, 'Social Referencing and Social Looking Among Twelve-Month-Old Infants', *Affective Development in Infancy*, edited by T. Berry Brazelton et al, Ablex Publishing, Norwood, New Jersey, 1986.

[5] Douglas Rushkoff, 'Branding Products, Branding People', *Rushkoff.com*, www.rushkoff.com/branding.html

[6] Sarah Schmidt, 'Branded Babies: Marketing Turns Tots into Logo-Conscious Consumers', CanWest News Service, *The Ottawa Citizen*, 6 May 2003,

www.trivision.ca/documents/2003/Branded%20babies%20Marketing%20turns%20Tots%20into%20Consumers.pdf

[7] Sarah Schmidt, 'Branded Babies: Marketing Turns Tots into Logo-Conscious Consumers', CanWest News Service, *The Ottawa Citizen*, 6 May 2003, www.trivision.ca/documents/2003/Branded%20babies%20Marketing%20turns%20Tots%20into%20Consumers.pdf

[8] Douglas Rushkoff, 'Branding Products, Branding People', *Rushkoff.com*, www.rushkoff.com/branding.html

[9] Susan Gregory Thomas, *Buy, Buy Baby: The Devastating Impact of Marketing to 0–3s*, Houghton Mifflin, Boston, 2007, p 2.

[10] Barbara F. Meltz, 'Marketers See Babies' Noses as Pathway to Profits', *The Boston Globe*, 19 May 2005, www.boston.com/yourlife/home/articles/2005/05/19/marketers_see_babies_noses_as_pathway_to_profits?pg=full

[11] Sarah Schmidt, 'Branded Babies: Marketing Turns Tots into Logo-Conscious Consumers', CanWest News Service, *The Ottawa Citizen*, 6 May 2003, www.trivision.ca/documents/2003/Branded%20babies%20Marketing%20turns%20Tots%20into%20Consumers.pdf

[12] 'AAP Discourages Television for Very Young Children', news release, American Academy of Pediatrics, 2 August 1999, www.aap.org/advocacy/archives/augdis.htm

[13] 'AAP Discourages Television for Very Young Children', press release, American Academy of Pediatrics, 2 August 1999, www.aap.org/advocacy/archives/augdis.htm

[14] Susan Gregory Thomas, *Buy, Buy Baby: The Devastating Impact of Marketing to 0–3s*, Houghton Mifflin, Boston, 2007, pp 83–84.

[15] Susan Gregory Thomas, *Buy, Buy Baby: The Devastating Impact of Marketing to 0–3s*, Houghton Mifflin, Boston, 2007, pp 88–91.

[16] Susan Gregory Thomas, *Buy, Buy Baby: The Devastating Impact of Marketing to 0–3s*, Houghton Mifflin, Boston, 2007, p 91.

[17] Janine DeFao, 'TV Channel for Babies? Pediatricians Say Turn It Off',

The San Francisco Chronicle, 11 September 2006, www.sfgate.com/cgi-bin/
article.cgi?file=/c/a/2006/09/11/MNG8KL39DF1.DTL

18   Dr Frederick Hecht and Dr Barbara K. Hecht, 'Attention Problems Due to
     TV Before 3', *MedicineNet*, 5 April 2004, www.medicinenet.com/script/
     main/art.asp?articlekey=31871

19   Email correspondence 10 October 2007.

BABIES WORTH BILLIONS

1   David Futrell, 'Are Your Kids Normal About Money?', CNN, 1 December
     2005, http://money.cnn.com/magazines/money mag/moneymag_archive
     /2005/12/01/8362029/index.htm

2   Martin Lindstrom with Patricia B. Seybold, *BRANDChild: Remarkable Insights
     into the Minds of Today's Global Kids and Their Relationships with Brands*, Kogan
     Page, London, 2003.

3   Rebecca Urban, 'Wiggles Have Whole World in Their Hands', *The Age*,
     13 April 2005, www.theage.com.au/news/Business/Wiggles-have-whole-
     world-in-their-hands/2005/04/12/1113251625530.html

4   Peter Gotting, 'Baby's First Word: Buy', *The Sydney Morning Herald*,
     25 April 2003, www.smh.com.au/articles/2003/04/24/
     1050777358001.html

5   'Advertising and the Industry: Getting the Full Bottle on Alcohol',
     Premier's Drug Prevention Council, Key Stakeholder's Seminar,
     10 December 2004, p 16, www.health.vic.gov.au/pdpc/downloads/
     kirsner_rpt.pdf

6   'Children, Adolescents, and Advertising', *Pediatrics*, vol. 118, no. 6,
     December 2006, pp 2563–2569, Committee on Communications, American
     Academy of Pediatrics, http://pediatrics.aappublications.org/cgi/content/
     full/118/6/2563

7   'Advertising and the Industry: Getting the Full Bottle on Alcohol', Premier's
     Drug Prevention Council, Key Stakeholders' Seminar, 10 December 2004,
     p16, www.health.vic.gov.au/pdpc/downloads/kirsner_rpt.pdf

[8]   P. M. Fischer et al, 'Brand Logo Recognition by Children Aged 3 to 6 Years: Mickey Mouse and Old Joe the Camel', *Journal of the American Medical Association*, vol. 266, no. 22, 11 December 1991, http://jama.ama-assn.org/cgi/content/abstract/266/22/3145

BUT THEY'RE ONLY LITTLE

[1]   Susan Gregory Thomas, *Buy, Buy Baby: The Devastating Impact of Marketing to 0–3s*, Houghton Mifflin, Boston, 2007, p 134–135.

[2]   David Braithwaite, 'Outcry Over Tots' Pole-Dancing Kit', *The Sydney Morning Herald*, 27 October 2006, www.smh.com.au/news/unusual-tales/outcry-over-tots-poledancing-kit/2006/10/27/1161749287304.html

[3]   www.radicagames.com/digi-makeover.php, 12 January 2007.

SURVIVAL OF THE PRETTIEST

[1]   Nancy Etcoff, *Survival of the Prettiest: The Science of Beauty*, Anchor Books, Random House, New York, 2000.

[2]   Tamara Schuit, 'Make-Up Mania: Girls Just Wanna Have Gloss', November 2003, *TD Monthly*, www.toydirectory.com/monthly/Nov2003/PretendPlay_Cosmetic_TS.asp

[3]   'Worldwide Cosmetics introduces the Hotsie Totsie Line – Cosmetics For 7- to 14-Year-Olds', *Drug Store News*, 25 June 2001, http://findarticles.com/p/articles/mi_m3374/is_8_23/ai_76335103

[4]   Paolo Totaro, 'Silk and Lace Turn Little Girls into Eye Candy', *The Sydney Morning Herald*, 18 February 2006, www.smh.com.au/news/national/turning-girls-into-eye-candy/2006/02/17/1140151818732.html?page=2

[5]   'Cosmetic Types and Ingredients', *Indianetzone Cosmetics*, http://cosmetics.indianetzone.com/1/cosmetic_types_ingredients.htm

SHRINKING SELF-ESTEEM AND IMAGINATION

[1]   Sarah Womack, 'Now Girls as Young as This Five-Year-Old Think They Have to Be Slim to Be Popular', *The Telegraph*,

8 March 2005, www.telegraph.co.uk/news/main.jhtml?xml=/
news/2005/03/08/nbody08.xml

2   'Children, Adolescents, and Advertising', *Pediatrics*, vol. 118, no. 6,
December 2006, pp 2563–2569, Committee on Communications, American
Academy of Pediatrics, http://pediatrics.aappublications.org/cgi/content/
full/118/6/2563

3   Sarah Womack, 'Now Girls as Young as This Five-Year-Old Think They Have
to Be Slim to Be Popular', *The Telegraph*, 8 March 2005, www.telegraph.
co.uk/news/main.jhtml?xml=/news/2005/03/08/nbody08.xml

4   Martin Lindstrom with Patricia B. Seybold, *BRANDChild: Remarkable Insights
into the Minds of Today's Global Kids and Their Relationships with Brands*, Kogan
Page, London, 2003, p 12.

5   Paul A. Paterson, 'Pretend Play Heralds the Lost Art of Creative
Playtime', *TD Monthly*, November 2003, www.toydirectory.com/monthly/
Nov2003/PretendPlay_Industry_P.as

6   Charles Fishman, 'Why Can't Lego Click?', *Fast Company Magazine*,
Issue 50 August 2001, p 144.

7   'Is Modern Life Ruining Childhood?', *BBC News*, 12 September 2006,
http://news.bbc.co.uk/1/hi/uk/5338572.stm

8   Gary Cross, *Kids' Stuff: Toys and the Changing World of American Childhood*,
Harvard University Press, Cambridge, Massachusetts, 1997.

9   'Is Modern Life Ruining Childhood?', *BBC News*, 12 September 2006,
http://news.bbc.co.uk/1/hi/uk/5338572.stm

WELCOME TO THE TWEENS

1   David L. Siegel, et al., *The Great Tween Buying Machine: Capturing Your Share
of the Multibillion Dollar Tween Market*, Dearborn Trade Publishing, Ithaca NY,
2001, p 43.

2   David L. Siegel, et al., *The Great Tween Buying Machine: Capturing Your Share
of the Multibillion Dollar Tween Market*, Dearborn Trade Publishing, Ithaca NY,
2001, pp 79–80.

3   Julian Lee, 'Tweens Lap up Bart, Fast Food', 1 July 2004, *The Sydney Morning Herald*, p 10, www.smh.com.au/articles/2004/06/30/1088488024367.html?from=storylhs

4   Julian Lee, 'Tweens Lap Up Bart, Fast Food', *The Sydney Morning Herald*, 1 July 2004, www.smh.com.au/articles/2004/06/30/1088488024367.html?from=storylhs

5   James U. McNeal, PhD, 'The Kids Market: Myths and Realities', cited at Kid Facts, *Kid Stuff*, www.kidstuff.com/info/factspg.html

6   'Simmons Releases Study Measuring Tweens Market', press release, Simmons Market Research, *Directions Magazine*, 29 June 2004, www.directionsmag.com/press.releases/index.php?duty=Show&id=9621&trv=1

7   Transcript of Sherry Turkle interview, *Silicon Valley Radio*, www.transmitmedia.com/svr/vault/turkle/turkle_transcript.html

8   Joan Lowy, 'Kids' Buying Power Lures Advertisers', *Commercial Alert*, 12 December 1999, www.commercialalert.org/news/Archive/1999/12/kids-buying-power-lures-advertisers

9   Martin Lindstrom with Patricia B. Seybold, *BRANDChild: Remarkable Insights into the Minds of Today's Global Kids and Their Relationships with Brands*, Kogan Page, London, 2003, pp 18–19.

10 'Tweens Audience Analysis Profile Data', The Health Communications Unit, Vol 2, 25 June 2004, p 9, www.thcu.ca/infoand resources/publications/tweensaudienceanalysisdataJune.25.pdf

11 David L. Siegel, et al., *The Great Tween Buying Machine: Capturing Your Share of the Multibillion Dollar Tween Market*, Dearborn Trade Publishing, Ithaca NY, 2001, p 31.

12 Lindsay Fadner, 'Market Profile: Tweens', *OMMA*, October 2002, http://publications.mediapost.com/index.cfm?fuseaction= Articles.showArticle&art_aid=4112

PESTER POWER

[1]   Catherine Seipp, 'Marketing the Mouse: The Commercialization of Childhood, from the Left Coast', *The National Review*, 7 July 2004, www.nationalreview.com/seipp/seipp200407070901.asp

[2]   www.limitedtoo.com/wishlist.html

[3]   Jenny Brockie, 'Bratz, Bras and Tweens', *Insight*, 17 April 2007, SBS TV, http://news.sbs.com.au/insight/trans.php?transid=1000

[4]   Daniel Thomas Cook, 'Children of the Brand', *In These Times*, 25 December 2006, www.inthesetimes.com/article/2968/

[5]   Martin Lindstrom with Patricia B. Seybold, *BRANDChild: Remarkable Insights into the Minds of Today's Global Kids and Their Relationships with Brands*, Kogan Page, London, 2003, p 81.

[6]   Stuart Corner, 'Aussie Online Ad Personaliser Targets US Market', *IT Wire*, 1 August 2007, www.itwire.com.au/content/view/13820/53/

[7]   '"Babyish" Barbie Under Attack from Little Girls, Study Shows', press release, University of Bath, 19 December 2005, www.bath.ac.uk/news/articles/archive/barbie161205.html

[8]   Interview, 25 July 2007.

YOUNG GIRLS MATURING EARLIER

[1]   'Girls Speak Out: Teens Before Their Time', Executive Summary, Girl Scouts of the USA, www.girlscouts.org/research/pdf/teens_before_time.pdf

[2]   Andrea Gordon, 'Surprise Developments: New Curves Are a Shock For Young Girls as Puberty Begins to Arrive Earlier', *The Toronto Star*, 30 March 2007, www.thestar.com/article/197527

[3]   Kay S. Hymowitz, 'Cheated Out of Childhood', *Parents*, October 1999, vol.74, no.10, www.manhattan-institute.org/html/_parents-cheated_out_of_childh.htm

[4]   '"Babyish" Barbie Under Attack from Little Girls, Study Shows', press release, University of Bath, 19 December 2005, www.bath.ac.uk/news/articles/archive/barbie161205.html

5   'Girls Admit to Barbie Torture', News, *The Manchester Evening News*, 19 December 2005, www.manchestereveningnews.co.uk/news/ s/191/191999_girls_admit_to_barbie_torture.html

TOO SEXY TOO SOON

1   Interview, 8 August 2007.

2   Jill Parkin, 'Trash the Plastic Slappers', *The Courier Mail*, 20 March 2007, www.commercialexploitation.org/news/plasticslappers.htm

3   Paolo Totaro, 'Silk and Lace Turn Little Girls into Eye Candy', *The Sydney Morning Herald*, 18 February 2006, www.smh.com.au/news/national/ turning-girls-into-eye-candy/2006/02/17/1140151818732.html?page=2

4   Claudia Wallis, 'The Thing About Thongs', *Time Magazine*, 6 October 2003, www.time.com/time/magazine/article/0,9171,1005821,00.html

5   Hal Niedzviecki, 'Can We Save These Kids?', *The Globe*, 5 June 2004, www.thefreeradical.ca/Can_we_save_these_kids.htm

6   Hal Niedzviecki, 'Can We Save These Kids?', *The Globe*, 5 June 2004, www.thefreeradical.ca/Can_we_save_these_kids.htm

7   Claudia Wallis, 'The Thing About Thongs', *Time Magazine*, 6 October 2003, www.time.com/time/magazine/article/0,9171,1005821,00.html

8   'Modern Life Leads to More Depression Among Children', *The Telegraph*, 13 September 2006, www.telegraph.co.uk/news/main. jhtml?xml=/news/2006/09/12/njunk112.xml

9   David Middleton, 'Similarities Found Between Internet Sex Offenders and Contact Offenders', *De Montfort University Alumni Association News*, 7 February 2007, www.dmualumni.org/latest_news.cfm?id=230& start=211&more=1

TWEEN DREAMS

1   Paul Kurnit, 'The New Tween Segmentation', *KidShopBiz.com*, Los Angeles, 18 September 2003, www.kidshopbiz.com/pdf/kid_state- braincamp_lapres.pdf

2   Martin Lindstrom with Patricia B. Seybold, *BRANDchild: Remarkable Insights Into the Minds of Today's Global Kids and Their Relationships with Brands*, Kogan Page, London, 2003, p 25.

3   '"Babyish" Barbie Under Attack From Little Girls, Study Shows', Press Release, University of Bath, 19 December 2005, www.bath.ac.uk/news/articles/archive/barbie161205.html

4   Martin Lindstrom with Patricia B. Seybold, *BRANDchild: Remarkable Insights Into the Minds of Today's Global Kids and Their Relationships with Brands*, Kogan Page, London, 2003, p 25.

5   'Life's First Great Crossroad: Tweens Make Choices That Affect Their Lives Forever', *Youth Campaign*, Center for Disease Control and Prevention, May 2000, p 6, www.cdc.gov/youthcampaign/research/PDF/LifesFirstCrossroads.pdf

6   Martin Lindstrom with Patricia B. Seybold, *BRANDChild: Remarkable Insights into the Minds of Today's Global Kids and Their Relationships with Brands*, Kogan Page, London, 2003, p 12.

7   Martin Lindstrom with Patricia B. Seybold, *BRANDChild: Remarkable Insights into the Minds of Today's Global Kids and Their Relationships with Brands*, Kogan Page, London, 2003, p 196.

8   'Life's First Great Crossroad: Tweens Make Choices That Affect Their Lives Forever', *Youth Campaign*, Center For Disease Control and Prevention, May 2000, p 4, www.cdc.gov/youthcampaign/research/PDF/LifesFirstCrossroads.pdf

9   Martin Lindstrom with Patricia B. Seybold, *BRANDChild: Remarkable Insights into the Minds of Today's Global Kids and Their Relationships with Brands*, Kogan Page, London, 2003, p 196.

10   Farrah Tomazin, 'Depression Worry in Schools', *The Sydney Morning Herald*, 2 February 2007, www.smh.com.au/news/parenting/depression-worry-in-schools/2007/02/01/1169919511957.html

11   'Modern Life Leads to More Depression Among Children', *The Telegraph*, 13 September 2006, www.telegraph.co.uk/news/main.jhtml?xml=/news/2006/09/12/njunk112.xml

12 'Modern Life Leads to More Depression Among Children', *The Telegraph*, 13 September 2006, www.telegraph.co.uk/news/main.jhtml?xml=/news/2006/09/12/njunk112.xml

13 'Is Modern Life Ruining Childhood?', *BBC News*, 12 September 2006, http://news.bbc.co.uk/1/hi/uk/5338572.stm

14 'Life's First Great Crossroad: Tweens Make Choices That Affect Their Lives Forever', *Youth Campaign*, Center for Disease Control and Prevention, May 2000, p 6, www.cdc.gov/youthcampaign/research/PDF/LifesFirst Crossroads.pdf

15 Martin Lindstrom with Patricia B. Seybold, *BRANDChild: Remarkable Insights into the Minds of Today's Global Kids and Their Relationships with Brands*, Kogan Page, London, 2003, p 196.

16 'Eating Disorders', Alpha Phi International Fraternity, www.alphaphi.org/womens_issues/eating_disorders.html

17 Dr Louise Chang, 'Helping Girls with Body Image', *Web M.D.*, 18 October 2006, www.webmd.com/parenting/features/helping-girls-with-body-image?page=2

18 Carma Haley, 'Bikini Babies, Preteens and Summer Body Image', *iParenting Media*, http://preteenagerstoday.com/resources/articles/bodyimg.htm

19 Alissa Quart, *Branded: The Buying and Selling of Teenagers*, Basic Books, New York 2003, p 14.

20 Joan Lowy, 'Kids' Buying Power Lures Advertisers', *Commercial Alert*, 12 December 1999, www.commercialalert.org/news/Archive/1999/12/kids-buying-power-lures-advertisers

21 Hal Niedzviecki, 'Can We Save These Kids?', *The Globe*, 5 June 2004, www.thefreeradical.ca/Can_we_save_these_kids.htm

22 Martin Lindstrom with Patricia B. Seybold, *BRANDChild: Remarkable Insights into the Minds of Today's Global Kids and Their Relationships with Brands*, Kogan Page, London, 2003, p 2.

23 'Tweens Audience Analysis Profile Data', Vol. 2.0, 24 June 2004, p 2, www.thcu.ca/infoandresources/publications/TweensaudienceanalysisdataJune.25.pdf

[24] 'Media & Health', *New Mexico Media Literacy Project*, www.nmmlp.org/store/pdfs/Media_Health.pdf

[25] 'Sexualisation "Harms" Young Girls', *BBC News*, 20 February 2007, http://news.bbc.co.uk/1/hi/health/6376421.stm?ls

[26] 'Tweens Audience Analysis Profile Data', The Health Communications Unit, Vol. 2, 25 June 2004, p 9, www.thcu.ca/infoandresources/publications/TweensaudienceanalysisdataJune.25.pdf

[27] 'Life's First Great Crossroad: Tweens Make Choices That Affect Their Lives Forever', *Youth Campaign*, Center for Disease Control and Prevention, May 2000, p 10, www.cdc.gov/youthcampaign/research/PDF/LifesFirstCrossroads.pdf

TEENS HAVE IT ALL

[1] Mary Carskadon, 'Inside the Teenage Brain', *Frontline*, PBS, www.pbs.org/wgbh/pages/frontline/shows/teenbrain/interviews/carskadon.html

[2] Dr Jim Dollman, 'Sleep Deprived Kids Struggle at School', media release, University of South Australia.

[3] Stephen Corby, 'Our Kids Are Sleep Deprived: Expert Says ADD May Be Wrongly Diagnosed', *The Sunday Telegraph*, 9 December 2007.

[4] Siri Carpenter, 'Sleep Deprivation May Be Undermining Teen Health', *Monitor on Psychology*, vol. 3, no. 9, October 2001, www.apa.org/monitor/oct01/sleepteen.html

[5] 'Sleep Deprivation', *Apollo Health*, www.apollolight.com/new_content/circadian%20rhythms_disorders/sleep/sleep_deprivation.html

LIVING UP TO EXPECTATIONS

[1] Nathan Vass, 'When Sports-mad Parents Go Too Far', *Woman's Day*, 20 December 2004.

[2] Oliver James, 'The Trouble with Girls', *The Observer*, 1 June 2003, http://observer.guardian.co.uk/review/story/0,6903,967699,00.html

[3] 'What's Your Friendship Factor?', *Dolly*, January 2007, p 73.

[4] 'Hairstyles Guys Love Most', *Dolly*, January 2007, pp 88–89.

MATERIAL GIRLS

1   'Teen Spending Estimated to Top $190 Billion by 2006', *Mintel*, 12 April
    2006, www.marketresearchworld.net/index.php?option=content&task=
    view&id=615&Itemid=

2   'Teen Spending and Source of Income: Insights into Money Attitudes,
    Behaviors and Concerns of Teens', Strategy One Research Group, August
    2005, www.aboutschwab.com/teensurvey2006.pdf

3   'Where Teens Shop', *Teen Market Profile*, Magazine Publishers of America,
    Media Market Research Inc, p 3, www.magazine.org/content/files/
    teenprofile04.pdf

4   Jason Clarke, 'Advertising and the Industry: Getting the Full Bottle on
    Alcohol', Premier's Drug Prevention Council, Key Stakeholder's Seminar,
    10 December 2004, p 16, www.health.vic.gov.au/pdpc/downloads/
    kirsner_rpt.pdf

5   'Teen Buying Behaviour', *Teen Market Profile*, Magazine Publishers of America,
    Media Market Research Inc, p 3, www.magazine.org/content/files/
    teenprofile04.pdf

6   'Wanna Be the Next Beauty Reporters?', Clean and Clear ad, *Dolly*,
    January 2007, p 37.

7   'Introducing the Next Modern Day Princess', *Girlfriend*, February 2007, p 16.

8   'Girl Talk' cited in *Media and Girls*, Media Awareness Network,
    www.media-awareness.ca/english/issues/stereotyping/women_
    and_girls/women_girls.cfm

9   Dr Nancy Carlsson-Paige and Dr Diane E. Levin, 'How Commercialism
    Impacts Children in School, Campaign for a Commercial Free Childhood',
    5th Annual Summit, Wheelock College, Boston, Massachusetts, October
    2006, www.commercialfreechildhood.org/
    articles/5thsummit/cp&levin.htm

10 'Summary', *Teen Market Profile*, Magazine Publishers of America,
    Media Market Research Inc, p 3, www.magazine.org/content/files/
    teenprofile04.pdf

[11] 'Teen Magazine Readers Are Active Consumers', *Teen Market Profile*, Magazine Publishers of America, Media Market Research Inc, p 12, www.magazine.org/content/files/teenprofile04.pdf

[12] Karen Kersting, 'Driving Teen Egos – And Buying – Through 'Branding', *Monitor on Psychology*, vol. 35, no. 6 June 2004, www.apa.org/monitor/jun04/driving.html

[13] Jason Clarke, 'Advertising and the Industry: Getting the Full Bottle on Alcohol', Premier's Drug Prevention Council, Key Stakeholder's Seminar, 10 December 2004, p 17, www.health.vic.gov.au/pdpc/downloads/kirsner_rpt.pdf

[14] 'Cool Schools Research Findings', *EdComs*, www.edcoms.com/images_main/Cool_schools.pdf

[15] 'Marketing to Kids Report', Kid Facts, *Kid Stuff*, January 1999, www.kidstuff.com/info/factspg.html

[16] Dr Sharon Beder, 'Influencing Future Decision Makers', *ABC*, www.abc.net.au/science/slab/beder/story/htm

[17] *Caltex Sponsorship Guidelines*, www.caltex.com.au/community_spo.asp

[18] Lindsay Fadner, 'Market Profile: Tweens', *OMMA*, October 2002, http://publications.mediapost.com/index.cfm?fuseaction=Articles.showArticle&art_aid=4112

[19] 'Help Feed Their Minds with Free DK Books for Your School', *BoxTops4Books*, www.boxtops4books.co.uk/home.aspx

[20] 'Soft Drink Ban Inconsequential', Australian Beverages Council, 5 June 2006, www.ferret.com.au/articles/d1/0c040ed1.asp

[21] 'Teenage Girls Prefer Pop: Nutrition Study', *Marketplace Murmurs*, CBC News, 27 February 2006, www.cbc.ca/consumers/ market/murmurs/archives/2006/20060227_pop.html

[22] Lindsay Fadner, 'Market Profile: Tweens', *OMMA*, October 2002, http://publications.mediapost.com/index.cfm?fuseaction=Articles.showArticle&art_aid=4112

[23] 'Cool Schools Research Findings', *EdComs*, www.edcoms.com/images_main/Cool_schools.pdf

24   Alissa Quart, *Branded: The Buying and Selling of Teenagers*, Basic Books, New York 2003, p 16.

25   'Slanted Sex Culture Stoking Deviant Desire in Schoolgirls', *Mainichi Shimbun*, 29 August 2002, www.flatrock.org.nz/topics/men/name_ brand_beauties_on_sale.htm

26   Jennifer Liddy, 'Name Brand Beauties for Sale', *Freezerbox Magazine*, 14 March 2002, www.freezerbox.com/archive/article.php?id=188

27   Jamie Smyth, 'Enjo Kosai: Teen Prostitution, a Reflection of Society's Ills', *The Tokyo Weekender*, 4 September 1998, www.weekender.co.jp/ LatestEdition/980904/oped.html

28   Anderson Cooper, 'Teens Turn to Prostitution to Afford Designer Clothes', *CNN.com*, 11 August 2003, http://transcripts.cnn.com/ TRANSCRIPTS/0308/11/se.03.html

29   Kate Drake, Kyoto, 'She's Only a Little Schoolgirl, Sex in Asia', *Timeasia.com*, 2001, www.time.com/time/asia/features/sex/ sexenjo.html

MAKE-OVER MANIA

1   Alissa Quart, *Branded: The Buying and Selling of Teenagers*, Basic Books, New York, 2003, p 127.

2   www.drbrent.com/press_video.php

3   'Plastic Surgery for Couples Together', *BeautyNova*, 25 December 2006, www.beautynova.com/blog/

4   Dr Lynn E. Ponton, *The Romance of Risk: Why Teenagers Do the Things They Do*, Basic Books, New York, 1997, p 120.

5   Alissa Quart, *Branded: The Buying and Selling of Teenagers*, Basic Books, New York, 2003, p 126.

6   'Mother Defends Teenager's Breast Op', Health, *BBC News*, 4 January 2001 http://news.bbc.co.uk/1/hi/health/1100471.stm

7   'Media and Girls', *Media Awareness Network*, www.media-awareness.ca/ english/issues/stereotyping/women_and_girls/women_girls.cfm

8 'Meet the Patients', *I Want a Famous Face*, www.mtv.com/onair/i_want_a_ famous_face/meet_the_patients/index.jhtml? Patients=Sha

9 'Mother Defends Teenager's Breast Op', *BBC News*, 4 January 2001 http://news.bbc.co.uk/1/hi/health/1100471.stm

10 James Meikle, 'Teen Girls Just Wanna Look Thin', *The Guardian*, 6 January 2004, http://society.guardian.co.uk/publichealth/story/0,,1116982,00.html

11 Afsun Smith, 'Can Bigger Breasts Buy Happiness? No, Say Scientists: Just the Opposite', Focus of the Week, *Talk Surgery Inc*, 21 May 2004, www. talksurgery.com/consumer/new/new00000119_1.html

12 'Dying to Be Thin', Set#1, Share Your Story, *Nova Online*, www.pbs.org/ wgbh/nova/thin/story_001214.html

13 Dr Diana Zuckerman, 'Teenagers and Plastic Surgery', National Research Center for Women and Families, www.breastimplantinfo.org/what_know/ teencosurgery.html

14 Kate Fox, 'Mirror, Mirror: A Summary of Research Findings on Body Image', *SIRC*, 1997, www.sirc.org/publik/mirror.html

15 'Teen Breast Enlargement', *MyBodyPart.com*, www.mybodypart.com/teen-breast-enlargement.html

IT'S IN TO BE THIN

1 'New Editor for Girlfriend Magazine', 7 Corporate Media Release, Channel 7, 24 June 2004, www.sevencorporate.com.au/page.asp?partid=454

2 'New girlfriend.com.au', Girl Trends, *Girlfriend*, February 2007, p 16.

3 *Media and Girls,* Media Awareness Network, www.media-awareness.ca/ english/issues/stereotyping/women_and_girls/women_girls.cfm

4 Kate Fox, 'Mirror, Mirror: A Summary of Research Findings on Body Image', *SIRC*, 1997, www.sirc.org/publik/mirror.html

5 http://forum.ringsworld.com/seeing-the-opposite-t1272.html

6 Aaron Levin, 'Teens' Distorted Body Image May Lead to Unhealthy Behaviours', *EurekAlert*, Center for the Advancement of Health, 16 July 2003, www.eurekalert.org/pub_releases/2003-07/cfta-tdb071603.php

7   'Eating Disorders: Body Image and Advertising', *HealthyPlace.com*,
    25 April 2000, www.healthyplace.com/communities/Eating_Disorders/
    body_image_advertising.asp

8   'Dying to Be Thin', Set#4, Share Your Story, *Nova Online*, www.pbs.org/
    wgbh/nova/thin/story_001214.html

9   James Meikle, 'Teen Girls Just Wanna Look Thin', *The Guardian*,
    6 January 2004, http://society.guardian.co.uk/publichealth/
    story/0,,1116982,00.html

10 'Dove Reveals Results of Second Global Study', *Campaign for Real Beauty*,
    Dove Media Release, April 2007, www.campaignforrealbeauty.co.nz/site/
    pdfs/Dove_Global_Study_2007.pdf

11 Dr Louise Chang, 'Helping Girls With Body Image', *Web M.D.*,
    18 October 2006, www.webmd.com/parenting/features/helping-girls-
    with-body-image?page=2

12 'Models Link to Teenage Anorexia', *BBC News*, 30 May 2000,
    http://news.bbc.co.uk/2/hi/health/769290.stm

13 'Models Link to Teen Anorexia', *BBC News*, 30 May 2000,
    http://news.bbc.co.uk/2/hi/health/769290.stm

STARVING FOR ATTENTION

1   Dr Susan Ice, Medical Director, The Renfrew Center,
    www.eatingdisorderscoalition.org/reports/statistics.html

2   Gwen Morrison, 'Fatal Trend: Pro-anorexia Web Sites', *Preteenagers Today*,
    http://preteenagerstoday.com/resources/articles/fataltrend.htm

3   Karen Springen, 'Study Looks at Pro-anorexia Web Sites', Web Exclusive,
    Newsweek, 10 December, 2006, www.msnbc.msn.com/id/16098915/site/
    newsweek/from/ET/

4   Kat Lewin, 'Eating Disorder Sites Increase Symptoms: School of Medicine
    Study Shows Effects of Pro-anorexia Web Sites', *The Stanford Daily*,
    10 January 2007, http://daily.stanford.edn/article/2007/1/10/
    EatingDisorderSitesIncreaseSymptoms

5   www.xanga.com/TinyxTinks

6   http://gurliegur1614.blogspot.com/

7   www.ringsworld.com/angelicana/77.html

8   www.ringsworld.com/angelicana/77.html

9   www.freewebs.com/pippaspurplepalace/whatisperfection.htm

10   http://gurliegur1614.blogspot.com/

11   www.ringsurf.com/netring?action=info&ring=anorexia

12   'Starving for Perfections Award', *Ana's Underground Grotto*, http://grotto. projectshapeshift.net/

13   www.freewebs.com/pippaspurplepalace/whatisperfection.htm

14   www.xanga.com/pink_sparklygurl

15   www.freewebs.com/pippaspurplepalace/whatisperfection.htm

16   http://forum.ringsworld.com/why-what-another-fast-lol-t7067.html

17   http://forum.ringsworld.com/exercises-u-love-t6521.html

18   'Eating Disorders: Facts About Eating Disorders and the Search for Solutions', National Institute of Mental Health, www.nimh.nih.gov/health/ publications/eating-disorders-facts-about-eating-disorders-and-the-search-for-solutions.shtml

THE FIRST CUT

1   Brad Reed, '"Cutting" On Increase in Teens, Say Experts', *The Wellesley Townsman*, 11 January 2007, www.townonline.com/wellesley/homepage/ 89990106724777995007

2   Karia, 'Scar Fetish', *Everything2*, www.everything2.com/index.pl?node_id=739556&lastnode_id=0

3   Andrew McLaughlin, 'One in 10 Teen Girls Self-Harm: Study', University of Bath, www.euraklert.org/pub_releases/2006-2008/uob-oit082206.php

4   Stand/alone/bitch, *Everything2*, www.everything2.com/index.pl? node_id=838026&lastnode_id=0

5   'Self-Injury Facts 2006', S.A.F.E. (Self-Abuse Finally Ends) Alternatives®Program, www.selfinjury.com/sifacts.htm

[6]   'I Wanna Be Angelina Jolie', Wolfa, 23 February 2005, http://wolfangel. calltherain.net/archives/2005/02/23/i-wanna-be-angelina-jolie/

[7]   Professor Graham Martin, 'On Suicide and Subcultures', *Australian e-Journal for the Advancement of Mental Health*, vol. 5, Issue 3, 2006, www.auseinet. com/journal/vol5iss3/martin.pdf

[8]   Carol Cassidy, *Girls in America: Their Stories, Their Words*, TVBooks, 1999, www.itvs.org/girlsinamerica/speak.html

[9]   'Cutting', *Berkeley Parents' Network*, http://parents.berkeley.edu/advice/ teens/cutting.html

WHY GIRLFRIENDS MATTER

[1]   'Wanting Someone Out of Your Life', *Teen Hut*, www.teenhut.net/friends-family/7798-wanting-someone-out-your-life.html

[2]   Judith Asner, 'Surviving Bulimia', online conference transcript, *Healthy Place*, www.healthyplace.com/communities/Eating_Disorders/Site/transcripts/ surviving_bulimia.htm

[3]   Marlene M. Moretti et al, 'The Dark Side of Girlhood: Recent Trends, Risk Factors and Trajectories to Aggression and Violence', *The Canadian Child and Adolescent Psychiatry Review*, February 2005, (14):1, p 22, www.irm-systems. com/onottaca/doc.nsf/files/A3CA5E72B93BF8D78725712D00527812/ $file/Feb05TheDarkSideofGirlhood.pdf

[4]   *Dolly*, January 2007, pp 26–27.

[5]   *Dolly*, January 2007, pp 115.

THE BULLYING THING

[1]   'Wanting Someone Out of Your Life', *Teen Hut*, www.teenhut.net/friends-family/7798-wanting-someone-out-your-life.html

[2]   Dr Jean B. Healey, 'Peer Abuse as Child Abuse and Indications for Intervention in Schools', Self Concept Enhancement and Learning Facilitation Research Centre, University of Western Sydney, www.aare.edu.au/05pap/hea05418.pdf

[3]   'Girl Talk', La Vida Lonely, http://girlslife.com/g-blog/?p=250

4   'Cyberbullying', www.cyberbullying.us/research.php

5   'Extreme Cyber Bullying: A Mother's Letter to the NZ Health Ministry',
     Net Family News, May 2007, www.netfamilynews.org/karensletter.html

6   Anne Collier, 'The Internet's Underbelly', *NetSmartz*, www.netsmartz.org/
     news/aug02-2.htm

7   'E-Bully's Evil Suicide Plot, Kristian South and Steve Hopkins', *The Sunday
     News*, 27 May 2007, www.stuff.co.nz/sundaynews/4074189a15596.html

SEXY GIRLS IN A SEX-SATURATED WORLD

1   Donna Nebenzahl, 'Are Teens Overexposed?', *The Gazette*, www.canada.
     com/montreal/montrealgazette/news/arts/story.html?id=ed3ad3b6-
     6b31-4fdd-bbe7-59fa1295d3de

2   'Sex Life: Is It Normal?', *Teen Today*, www.teentoday.co.uk/boards/
     ubbthreads.php/ubb/showflat/Number/6112/page/1#Post6112

3   'Sexxxxxxxxxxxxxx f***in', *coolteens.com*, www.cool-teens.com/story.
     php?do=show&sid=45

4   Dr Jane D. Brown, Dr Carolyn Tucker Halpern, and Kelly Ladin
     l'Engle M.P.H., 'Mass Media as a Sexual Super Peer for Early Maturing
     Girls', *Journal of Adolescent Health*, No. 36, 2005, p 421.

5   'Lindsay Lohan's Bruising Workout: Pole Dancing', *Teen People Magazine*,
     18 December 2006.

6   'The Pussycat Dolls Perform with No Panties', www.ninjadude.com/index.
     php/teen-mtv-pussycat-dolls-upskirt-nip-slip-pics

7   Jenna Jameson, 'What We Like About Her', www.askmen.com/women/
     models_250/262_jenna_jameson.html

8   Joan Sauers, *Sex Lives of Australian Teenagers*, Random House, Sydney 2007, p 81.

9   Jenna Jameson, 'What We Like About Her', www.askmen.com/women/
     models_250/262_jenna_jameson.html

10   'America's Most Lovable Pimp', *Rolling Stone*, 28 November 2006,
     www.rollingstone.com/news/coverstory/snoop_dogg_at_home_
     with_americas_most_lovable_pimp

11   Joan Sauers, *Sex Lives of Australian Teenagers*, Random House, Sydney 2007, p 81

SEX LIVES OF TEEN GIRLS

1   Dr Jane D. Brown, Dr Carolyn Tucker Halpern, and Kelly Ladin l'Engle M.P.H., 'Mass Media as a Sexual Super Peer for Early Maturing Girls', *Journal of Adolescent Health*, No. 36l, 2005, pp 420–427, www.unc.edu/depts/jomc/teenmedia/pdf/JAH_1.pdf

2   Dr Lynn E. Ponton, *The Romance of Risk: Why Teenagers Do the Things They Do*, Basic Books, New York 1997, p 2.

3   'Kids and the Media: Media-Saturated Kids Need Parental Involvement', *Media and Society*, Kaiser Network, 19 November 1999, www.kaisernetwork.org/reports/1999/11/kr991119.5.html

4   'Slight', 13 November 2006, www.answerbag.com/q_view/82582

5   'igavehimablowjob!' www.golivewire.com/forums/peer-tesetn-support-a.html

6   AAP, 'STDs on the Rise in Australia: Report', *The Age*, 12 October 2006, www.theage.com.au/news/National/STDs-on-the-rise-in-Australia-report/2006/10/12/1160246203471.html

7   'Shock Report on Teen Sex: Health Fear for Women', *The Mercury*, 4 February 1999, p 7.

8   Rob Stein, 'Increase in Cancer Rates Linked to Oral Sex', *The Sydney Morning Herald*, 11 May 2007, p 9.

9   Dr Gypsyamber d'Souza, et al, 'Oral Sex Increases Risk of Throat Cancer', *Science Daily*, 10 May 2007, www.sciencedaily.com/releases/2007/05/070509210142.htm

10   'Shock Report on Teen Sex: Health Fear For Women', *The Mercury*, 4 February 1999, p 7.

11   Lola, 'Breast Implants', *LiveJournal.com*, http://girldoll.livejournal.com/

12   Dr William D. Mosher, Dr Anjani Chandra, and Dr Jo Jones, 'Sexual Behavior and Selected Health Measures: Men and Women 15–44 Years of Age, United

States, 2002', Division of Vital Statistics, *Advance Data for Vital Health and Statistics*, Number 362, 15 September 2005, p 11, www.cdc.gov/nchs/data/ad/ad362.pdf

[13]   Dr William D. Mosher, Dr Anjani Chandra, and Dr Jo Jones, 'Sexual Behavior and Selected Health Measures: Men and Women 15–44 Years of Age, United States, 2002', Division of Vital Statistics, *Advance Data for Vital Health and Statistics*, Number 362, 15 September 2005, p 11, www.cdc.gov/nchs/data/ad/ad362.pdf

LOSS OF IDENTITY

[1]   Caitlin Flanagan, 'Are You There God? It's Me, Monica: How Nice Girls Got So Casual About Oral Sex', *The Atlantic Online*, January/February 2006, p 3, www.theatlantic.com/doc/200601/oral-sex

[2]   Caitlin Flanagan, 'Are You There God? It's Me, Monica: How Nice Girls Got So Casual About Oral Sex', *The Atlantic Online*, January/February 2006, p 3, www.theatlantic.com/doc/200601/oral-sex

[3]   'APA on Media and Sexualization' *MediaForum.ie*, 19 February 2007, www.mediaforum.ie/

[4]   Mark Colvin, 'Report Claims Sexualisation of Girls Is Pervasive and Damaging', *PM*, ABC Radio, www.abc.net.au/pm/content/2007/s1853636.htm

[5]   Stefan Anitei, 'Girls' Sexual Development Is Negatively Affected by Massive Media Sexualization: Omnipresent Sexual Images Affect the Girls' Mental and Physical Health', *Softpedia News*, 19 February 2007, http://news.softpedia.com/news/Girls-Sexual-Development-is-Negatively-Affectived-by-Massive-Media-Sexualization-47417.shtml

[6]   'Girlfriends Fess Up: The Original Sealed Advice: This Month's Hot Topic: We Explore the Risks, the Consequences and the Long-Term Effects of Being a Promiscuous Girl', *Girlfriend*, February 2007, pp 124–130.

[7]   Roger Horrocks, *Masculinity in Crisis: Myths, Fantasies and Realities*, St Martin's Press, New York, 1994.

8   'Girlfriends Fess Up: The Original Sealed Advice: This Month's Hot Topic: We Explore the Risks, the Consequences and the Long-Term Effects of Being a Promiscuous Girl', *Girlfriend*, February 2007, pp 124–130.

9   Michael Carr-Gregg, *The Princess Bitchface Syndrome: Surviving Adolescent Girls*, Penguin, Melbourne 2006, p 15.

10   'Girls Are More Likely to Drink Because of Peer Pressure', National Institute of Child Health and Human Development, *Parenting of Adolescents*, http://parentingteens.about.com/cs/teendriving/a/impaireddriving_2.htm.

11   Office of Alumni Affairs, 'Absent Fathers Faulted', *Duke Magazine*, vol. 85, no. 9, July–August 2003, www.dukemagazine.duke.edu/dukemag/issues/070803/depgaz6.html

12   Lynn Elber, 'TV Teaches Teenagers About Sex – Media Project Teaches TV', News Update, *CDC HIV/STD/TB Prevention*, 26 December 2002, www.aegis.com/news/ads/2002/ad022489.html

HIGHS AND LOWS

1   Michael Carr-Gregg, *The Princess Bitchface Syndrome*, Penguin, Melbourne, 2006.

2   Miranda Hitti, 'Teen Binge Drinking Common and Risky', reviewed by Dr Louise Chang, *WebMD Medical News*, 2 January 2007, www.webmd.com/content/article/131/117937.htm

3   'Girls and Drugs, a New Analysis: Recent Trends, Risk Factors and Consequences', Office of National Drug Control Policy, 9 February 2006, www.Mediacampaign.Org/Pdf/Girls_And_Drugs.Pdf

4   Dr Jonica Newby, 'Teen Alcohol', *Catalyst*, 9 August 2007, www.abc.net.au/catalyst/stories/s2000936.htm

5   David Braithwaite and Ben Cubby, 'Gang Rape Filmed on Mobile Phone', *The Sydney Morning Herald*, 5 April 2007, www.smh.com.au/articles/2007/04/04/1175366325678.html

6   'Alcopops: Sweet-Tasting, Fizzy Alcoholic Beverages', *e-BasedPrevention.org*, www.ebasedprevention.org/oewn.asp?id=1035

7 'Teenagers and Binge Drinking', *ABC Rural News*, Murdoch Children's Research Institute, 9 November 2005, www.mcri.edu.au/pages/news-events/media/in-the-news.asp?y=2005

8 'Alcopops: Sweet-Tasting, Fizzy Alcoholic Beverages', *e-BasedPrevention.org*, www.ebasedprevention.org/oewn.asp?id=1035

9 J.F.O. McAllister, 'The British Disease', *Time Europe*, 11 December 2005, www.time.com/time/europe/html/051219/story.html

10 Jonathan Owen and Paul Bignell, 'Revealed: Britain's 12-Year-Old Alcoholics: Doctors Want Special Drying-Out Units for Children with Drink Problems', *The Independent*, 18 February 2007, http://news.independent. co.uk/uk/this_britain/article2281379.ece

11 Dr Charles S. Lieber, 'A Stomach Enzyme Deficit May Place Women at More Risk from Drinking Alcohol, Addiction', *Science Research and Education Center*, The University of Texas at Austin, 15 April 2001, www.eurekalert.org/ pub_releases/2001-04/ACER-Ased-1404101.php

12 Andrea Okrentowich, 'Teen Girls and Drug Abuse Addiction in Young Women on the Increase', *Suite 101*, 28 January 2007, http:// substanceabuse.suite101.com/article.cfm/teen_girls_and_drug_abuse

13 Dr Jonica Newby, 'Teen Alcohol', *Catalyst*, 9 August 2007, www.abc.net. au/catalyst/stories/s2000936.htm

14 'Ready to Drink? Alcopops and Youth Binge Drinking', *Australian Divisions of General Practice*, p 4, www.adgp.com.au/client_images/10659.doc

15 www.lion-nathan.com.au/Great-Brands/NZ-Spirits-and-RTDs/ Specialty.aspx

16 T. Buddy, 'Kids Most Influenced by Siblings' Drinking, Smoking', *About.com*, http://alcoholism.about.com/od/teens/a/blajdi060124.htm

17 Arjun Ramachandran, 'Concern at Rise of Alcopops', *The Sydney Morning Herald*, 26 June 2007, www.smh.com.au/news/national/concern-at-rise-of-alcopops/2007/06/25/1182623820488.html

18 'Ready to Drink? Alcopops and Youth Binge Drinking', *Australian Divisions of General Practice*, p 9, www.adgp.com.au/client_images/10659.doc

[19]   Arjun Ramachandran, 'Concern at Rise of Alcopops', *The Sydney Morning Herald*, 26 June 2007, www.smh.com.au/news/national/concern-at-rise-of-alcopops/2007/06/25/1182623820488.html

[20]   'Underage Drinking 2005: Girls Bingeing More', press release, *The Center on Alcohol Marketing and Youth*, Georgetown University, 27 March 2006, http://camy.org/press/release php?ReleaseID=34

WALKING ON THE WILD SIDE

[1]   www.bygirlsforgirls.org/2002/depression.html

[2]   Andrea Okrentowich, 'Teen Girls and Drug Abuse Addiction in Young Women on the Increase ', *Suite 101*, 28 January 2007, http://substanceabuse.suite101.com/article.cfm/teen_girls_and_drug_abuse

[3]   'National Youth Survey 2005: Key and Emerging Issues', *Mission Australia*, p 10.

[4]   'Pediatricians Often Underestimate Substance Abuse Problems in Adolescents', Press Release, *EurekAlert*, 1 November 2004, www.eurekalert.org/pub_releases/2004-11/chb-pou102204.php

[5]   'National Youth Survey 2005: Key and Emerging Issues', *Mission Australia*, p 12.

[6]   'Girls Are More Likely to Drink Because of Peer Pressure', National Institute of Child Health and Human Development, Parenting of Adolescents, *About.com*, http://parentingteens.about.com/cs/teendriving/a/impaireddriving_2.htm

[7]   'Girls and Drugs, a New Analysis: Recent Trends, Risk Factors and Consequences', Office of National Drug Control Policy, 9 February 2006, www.Mediacampaign.Org/Pdf/Girls_And_Drugs.Pdf

[8]   'Girls and Drugs, a New Analysis: Recent Trends, Risk Factors and Consequences', Office of National Drug Control Policy, 9 February 2006, www.Mediacampaign.Org/Pdf/Girls_And_Drugs.Pdf

[9]   'Daughters', March/April 2006, New Moon Publishing, www.newmoon catalog.com/Prodinfo.ASP?NUMBER=DMA06-E

10 'Shoplifting', *TeensHealth*, Nemours Foundation, www.kidshealth.org/teen/
    school_jobs/good_friends/shoplifting.html

11 Peter Berlin, 'Why Do Shoplifters Steal?', National Learning and Resource
    Center, www.shopliftingprevention.org/WhatNASPOffers/NRC.htm

DEPRESSED

1   Clair Weaver, 'The Struggle of Young Women: Six Attempt Suicide Every
    Day', *The Sunday Telegraph*, 17 December 2006, p 11.

2   'Teen Girls Stressed out More Often Than Boys: Mediamark Research Data
    Cite Weight, Physical Appearance as Factors', Press Release, *Mediamark*,
    www.mediamark.com/MRI/docs/pr_12-09-03_Teenmark.htm

3   blondebrat, Girl Talk, La Vida Lonely, http://girlslife.com/
    g-blog/?p=250

4   Girl Talk, La Vida Lonely, http://girlslife.com/g-blog/?p=250

5   Miranda Hitti, 'Prescription Drug Use up in Teen Girls: 5-Year
    Report Shows Sharpest Increase in Type 2 Diabetes Drugs', *MedicineNet.com*,
    www.medicinenet.com/script/main/art.asp?articlekey=81184

6   'Depression Linked with Ultra-sensitivity to Other People's
    Emotions', *Research Digest Blog*, The British Psychological Society,
    22 December 2005, http://bps-research-digest.blogspot.com/
    search?updated-min=2005-01-01T00%3A00%3A00Z&updated-
    max=2006-01-01T00%3A00%3A00Z&max-results=50

7   Riittakerttu Kaltiala-Heino, et al, 'Bullying, Depression, and Suicidal
    Ideation in Finnish Adolescents: School Survey', *British Medical Journal*,
    vol. 319, 7 August 1999, pp 348-351, www.bmj.com/cgi/content/
    full/319/7206/348

8   Jeni Harvie, 'Teens Need Parents to Get a Grip', *The Sydney Morning Herald*,
    11 December 2003, www.smh.com.au/articles/2003/12/11/1071086175
    516.html?from=storyrhs

9   Binge Drinking, 'Gender and Clinical Depression', *Medical News Today*, 2 January
    2007, www.medicalnewstoday.com/medicalnews.php?newsid=60184

[10]   Denise Witmer, 'What Are the Effects of Ecstasy?', *About.com*,
       http://parentingteens.about.com/cs/ecstasy/f/ecstasy1.htm

[11]   www.bygirlsforgirls.org/2002/depression.html

[12]   'The Links Between Depression and Drugs', *GirlsForGirls.org*,
       www.bygirlsforgirls.org/cgi-bin/dcforum/dcboard.cgi

[13]   'Weed a Drug', *LiveWire Teen Forums and College Forums*, www.golivewire.
       com/forums/peer-teesbp-support-a.html

SUICIDAL

[1]   'Girl Talk', La Vida Lonely, http://girlslife.com/g-blog/?p=250

[2]   Elise Whitley et al, 'Ecological Study of Social Fragmentation, Poverty, and
      Suicide', *British Medical Journal*, 319, 16 October 1999, pp1034–1037,
      www.bmj.com/cgi/content/abstract/319/7216/1034

[3]   National Health and Medical Research Council, *National Youth Suicide
      Prevention Strategy: Setting the Evidence-Based Research Agenda for Australia:
      A Literature Review*, March 1999.

[4]   Gail Mason, 'Youth Suicide in Australia: Prevention Strategies', Department
      of Employment, Education, and Training, Youth Bureau, Canberra, 1990.

[5]   'The Social Web's Lifeline', *Net Family News*, 23 March 2007,
      www.netfamilynews.org/nl070323.html#1%3E

VIOLENT GIRLS

[1]   Ursulla Sauter, 'Violent Femmes: Girls Get Ugly', *Time Europe*, 3 August
      2003, www.time.com/time/magazine/article/0,9171,472832,00.html

[2]   Julie Scelfo, 'Bad Girls Go Wild', *Newsweek*, 13 June 2006, www.msnbc.msn.
      com/id/8101517/site/newsweek/

[3]   'Teen Girls "Woke with Murder on Mind"', *News.com.au*, 23 April 2007,
      www.news.com.au/story/0,23599,21606146-2,00.html

[4]   Margo Varadi, 'Schoolyard Violence Not Just for the Boys', *The Toronto Star*,
      26 March 2005, www.thefreeradical.ca/Schoolyard_violence_not_just_
      for_boys.htm

5   Paul Doneman et al, 'Muslim Love Row: Girl Accused of Killing Mum', *The Daily Telegraph*, 7 November 2006, p 9.

6   Late News, 'Girl, 14, Charged', *The Sun-Herald*, 17 December 2006, p 3.

7   Duncan Gardham, '"Happy Slap" Killer Aged 14 Is Jailed', *The Telegraph*, 24 January 2006, www.telegraph.co.uk/news/main.jhtml?xml=/news/2006/01/24/nslap24.xml&sSheet=/news/2006/01/24/ixnewstop.html

8   John Kidman, 'Alcohol Blamed for Teen Crime Rise', *The Sun-Herald*, 29 April 2007, p 35.

9   Linda Silmalis, 'Teens out of Control', *The Sunday Telegraph*, 22 October 2006, p 7.

10   Dr Deborah Prothrow-Stith and Howard Spivak, MDA, 'Troubling Trend: Girls and Bullying', *Stop Bullying Now*, http://stopbullyingnow.hrsa.gov/adult/indexAdult.asp?Area=prothrow

11   Christina Roache, 'Addressing Violence Amongst Girls', *Harvard Public Health Now*, 22 July 2005, www.hsph.harvard.edu/now/jul22/violence.html

12   Georgie Binks, 'Violence by Girls Uncool', *CBC News Viewpoint*, 17 March 2006, www.cbc.ca/news/viewpoint/vp_binks/20060317.html

13   Georgie Binks, 'Violence by Girls Uncool', *CBC News Viewpoint*, 17 March 2006, www.cbc.ca/news/viewpoint/vp_binks/20060317.html

14   Chelsea in Carol Cassidy, *Girls in America: Their Stories, Their Words*, TVBooks, 1999, www.itvs.org/girlsinamerica/speak.html

15   'Are You Generation IM? 10 Great Uses for Immersion's VibeTonz-Enabled Mobile Phones', www.vibetonz.com/docs/Are_You_Gen_IM.pdf

16   'A Growing Problem: Violent Girls', *Tufts e-news*, 2 December 2005, http://enews.tufts.edu/stories/120205AGrowing ProblemViolent Girls.htm

17   Timothy F. Kirn, 'Dangerous Trend: Violent Behavior by Girls', *Family Practice News*, 15 August 2000, www.findarticles.com/p/articles/mi_m0BJI/is_16_30/ai_65349513

18   Georgie Binks, 'Violence by Girls Uncool', *CBC News Viewpoint*, 17 March 2006, www.cbc.ca/news/viewpoint/vp_binks/20060317.html

[19] Olivia Ward, 'Women's Violence', *Harry's News*, 14 October 2004, www.harrysnews.com/tgWomensViolence.htm

[20] Georgie Binks, 'Violence by Girls Uncool', *CBC NewsViewpoint*, 17 March 2006, www.cbc.ca/news/viewpoint/vp_binks/20060317.html

[21] Marlene M. Moretti et al, 'The Dark Side of Girlhood: Recent Trends, Risk Factors and Trajectories to Aggression and Violence', *The Canadian Child and Adolescent Psychiatry Review*, February 2005, vol. 14, no.1, p 22, www.irm-systems.com/onottaca/doc.nsf/files/A3CA5E72B93 BF8D78725712D00527812/$file/Feb05TheDarkSideofGirlhood.pdf

[22] Marlene M. Moretti et al, 'The Dark Side of Girlhood: Recent Trends, Risk Factors and Trajectories to Aggression and Violence', *The Canadian Child and Adolescent Psychiatry Review*, February 2005, vol. 14, no.1, p 23, www.irm-systems.com/onottaca/doc.nsf/files/A3CA5E72B93BF8D7 8725712D00527812/$file/Feb05TheDarkSideofGirlhood.pdf

[23] Marlene M. Moretti et al, 'The Dark Side of Girlhood: Recent Trends, Risk Factors and Trajectories to Aggression and Violence', *The Canadian Child and Adolescent Psychiatry Review*, February 2005, vol. 14, no.1, p 23, www.irm-systems.com/onottaca/doc.nsf/files/A3CA5E72B93BF8D78 725712D00527812/$file/Feb05TheDarkSideofGirlhood.pdf

[24] '2003 NSW Young People in Custody, Health Survey', Key Findings Report, NSW Department of Juvenile Justice, p 9.

[25] 'Marketing Violence to Children', *Campaign for a Commercial-free Childhood*, www.commercialexploitation.org/factsheets/ccfc-facts%20violence.pdf

[26] Ron Powers, 'The Apocalypse of Adolescence', *The Atlantic Monthly*, March 2002, p 74.

[27] Ron Powers, 'The Apocalypse of Adolescence', *The Atlantic Monthly*, March 2002, p 74.

SECRET LIVES

[1] 'Are You Generation IM? 10 Great Uses for Immersion's VibeTonz-Enabled Mobile Phones', www.vibetonz.com/docs/Are_You_Gen_IM.pdf

2   'Are You Generation IM? 10 Great Uses for Immersion's Vibe
    Tonz-Enabled Mobile Phones', www.vibetonz.com/docs/Are_
    You_Gen_IM.pdf

3   'Life's First Great Crossroad: Tweens Make Choices That Affect Their Lives
    Forever', *Youth Campaign*, Center for Disease Control and Prevention,
    May 2000, p 5, www.cdc.gov/youthcampaign/research/PDF/LifesFirst
    Crossroads.pdf

4   'Life's First Great Crossroad: Tweens Make Choices That Affect Their Lives
    Forever', *Youth Campaign*, Center for Disease Control and Prevention,
    May 2000, p 5, www.cdc.gov/youthcampaign/research/PDF/LifesFirst
    Crossroads.pdf

5   Interview, 7 June 2007.

6   Email correspondence, 5 July 2007.

7   'Crimes Against Children, Missing Children and Online Victimization of
    Youth: Five Years Later, 2006', U.S. Department of Justice's Office of
    Juvenile Justice and Delinquency Prevention, Crimes Against Children
    Research Center, National Center for Missing and Exploited Children,
    www.missingkids.com/en_US/publications/NC167.pdf

ALONE IN CYBERSPACE

1   Interview, 8 August 2007.

2   Transcript, Sherry Turkle interview, *Silicon Valley Radio*,
    www.transmitmedia.com/svr/vault/turkle/turkle_transcript.html

3   Tara Bahrampour and Lori Aratani, 'Teens' Bold Blogs Alarm Area Schools',
    The Washington Post, 17 January 2006, www.washingtonpost.com/wp-dyn/
    content/article/2006/01/16/AR2006011601489_2.html

4   Stephen Kline and Jackie Botterill, 'Media Use Audit for BC Teens: Key
    Findings', Simon Fraser University, May 2001, www.sfu.ca/medialab/
    research/mediasat/secondschool.pdf

5   Christine Loftus, '12-year-old Girl Back Home After Ordeal', *NetSmartz*,
    July 2003, www.netsmartz.org/news/jul03-03.htm

6   Cathy Frye, 'Caught in the Web', *The Arkansas Democrat-Gazette*, 15 December 2003, www.ardemgaz.com/ShowStoryPrev.asp?Path=ArDemocrat/2003/12/15&ID=Ar00102

7   Cathy Frye, 'Caught in the Web', *The Arkansas Democrat-Gazette*, 16 December 2003, www.ardemgaz.com/ShowStoryPrev.asp?Path=ArDemocrat/2003/12/16&ID=Ar00103

8   Matt Uffer, 'Pole Vaulting Is Sexy, Barely Legal', *WithLeather.com*, 5 May 2007, www.withleather.com/post.phtml?pk=2811

GETTING INTO PORN

1   Tom Geoghegan, 'Tangled Web', *BBC News Magazine*, 14 June 2007, http://news.bbc.co.uk/1/hi/magazine/6336509.stm

2   'Porn Sites', *LiveWire Teen Forums and College Forums*, www.golivewire.com/forums/peer-teseot-support-a.html

3   Dick Thornburgh and Herbert S Lin, eds, 'Youth, Pornography and the Internet, Executive Summary', Computer Science and Technology Board, National Research Council, http://books.nap.edu/html/youth_internet/es.html

4   Tom Geoghegan, 'Tangled Web', *BBC News Magazine*, 8 February 2007, http://news.bbc.co.uk/1/hi/magazine/6336509.stm

5   Kat Khan, 'EMM, MONSTAR Join Forces Via MySpace.com', *XBiz*, 13 December 2005, www.xbiz.com/news/news_piece.php?id=12069&mi=all&q=monstar

6   Andrew Cantor, '"In-House" Offerings Nab Share of Porn, Modeling Industries', Cyberspeak, *USA Today*, www.usatoday.com/tech/columnist/andrewkantor/2006-01-13-athome-porn-model_x.htm

7   Andrew Cantor, '"In-House" Offerings Nab Share of Porn, Modeling Industries', Cyberspeak, *USA Today*, www.usatoday.com/tech/columnist/andrewkantor/2006-01-13-athome-porn-model_x.htm

8   Email correspondence, 5 July 2007.

9   Rachel Bell, 'Love in the Time of Phone Porn', *The Guardian*, 30 January 2007, http://education.guardian.co.uk/sexeducation/story/0,,2001374,00.html

10   Interview, 7 June 2007.

11   Email correspondence, 5 July 2007.

MAKING IT BIG ON YOUTUBE

1   Emmalina, 'Filthiness and Vulgarity', *YouTube*, http://youtube.com/profile?user=Emmalina

2   Emmalina, 'Profile', *YouTube*, http://youtube.com/profile?user=Emmalina, 20.6.07

3   www.youtube.com/watch?v=6nJPMyGEyuM&mode=related&search=

4   Email correspondence, 5 July 2007.

5   Email correspondence, 5 July 2007.

6   Email correspondence, 5 July 2007.

7   Candice M. Kelsey, *The Secret Cyber Lives of Teenagers: Parenting in the Age of MySpace.com*, Marlowe & Company, New York, 2007.

8   'New Study Reveals 14% of Teens Have Had Face-to-Face Meetings with People They've Met on the Internet', Cox Communications and National Center for Missing and Exploited Children, press release, 11 May 2006, www.netsmartz.org/pdf/cox_teensurvey_may2006.pdf

9   'New Ads Warn Teens . . . "Don't Believe the Type"', *News Detail*, Ad Council, 8 June 2005, www.adcouncil.org/newsDetail.aspx?id=31

10   Email correspondence 14 June 2007.

11   Anne Collier, 'The Internet's Underbelly', *NetSmartz*, www.netsmartz.org/news/aug02-2.htm

12   Email correspondence, 5 July 2007.

13   Anne Collier, 'The Internet's Underbelly', *NetSmartz*, www.netsmartz.org/news/aug02-2.htm

14   Michele L. Ybarra, MPH, PhD., et al, 'Prevention Messages: Targeting the Right Online Behaviors', *Archives of Pediatrics and Online Medicine*, vol. 161, no. 2, February 2007, pp138–145, http://archpedi.ama-assn.org/cgi/content/full/161/2/138

15 'Crimes Against Children, Missing Children and Online Victimization of Youth: Five Years Later, 2006', U.S. Department of Justice's Office of Juvenile Justice and Delinquency Prevention, Crimes Against Children Research Center, National Center for Missing and Exploited Children, www.missingkids.com/en_US/publications/NC167.pdf

GETTING MARRIED

1 'Snapshot of the Teen Market', *Teen Market Profile,* Magazine Publishers of America, Media Market Research Inc, p 3, www.magazine.org/content/files/teenprofile04.pdf

2 'Snapshot of the Teen Market', *Teen Market Profile,* Magazine Publishers of America, Media Market Research Inc, p 3, www.magazine.org/content/files/teenprofile04.pdf

HAVING BABIES

1 Kirsten Andrews, 'What Is a Yummy Mummy?', *West Coast Yummy Mummy Magazine*, 27 December 2006, www.yummymummysite.com/index.cfm?PID=15494&PIDList=15494&PressID=1084&ACT=Display

WHERE TO NOW?

1 Sarah Womack, 'Now Girls as Young as This Five-Year-Old Think They Have to Be Slim to Be Popular', *The Telegraph*, 8 March 2005, www.telegraph.co.uk/news/main.jhtml?xml=/news/2005/03/08/nbody08.xml

ALSO FROM PENGUIN

What Men Don't Talk About

MAGGIE HAMILTON

Every day we read articles about men – men at home, men at work, men in bed – but still the confusion and frustration between the sexes remain. Can we put the differences between men and women down to the influence of Venus and Mars, or are there more intricate dynamics at play? Is it true that men's lives are much easier than women's lives – that they have 'got it made'?

Surprising, illuminating and at times shocking, *What Men Don't Talk About* takes the reader far beyond the many stereotypes of men, and reveals how real men and boys view their world.

A Soft Place to Land

MAGGIE HAMILTON

We all want to find a safe, nurturing place where we can thrive. With her hallmark gentleness and wisdom, Maggie Hamilton shares insights that will help you arrive at your own special place in life.

Discover how to re-awaken the parts of you that have been sleeping, reclaim your passion for living, and nourish yourself in body and spirit. Find new ways to dissolve moments of sadness and despair, and simple touches that will warm your days. Rediscover your faith in yourself and your ability to make good decisions. Savour the gifts of the seasons, and the endless opportunities to celebrate the joy of being alive.

Drawing on a rich mix of everyday experiences, wisdom stories and travels to faraway places, *A Soft Place to Land* offers page after page of beautiful ways to open your heart and make your soul dance.